Academic writing in context

D0300196

...TT ...NIVERSITY

...AR...DED

Academic writing in context

Implications and applications

Papers in honour of Tony Dudley-Evans

Edited by

Martin Hewings

THE UNIVERSITY
OF BIRMINGHAM
UNIVERSITY PRESS

Copyright © University of Birmingham Press 2001

While copyright in the volume as a whole is vested in the University of Birmingham Press, copyright in individual chapters belongs to their respective authors, and no chapter may be reproduced wholly or in part without the express permission in writing of both author and publisher.

First published in the United Kingdom by The University of Birmingham Press, Edgbaston, Birmingham, BI5 2TT, UK.

All rights reserved. Except for the quotation of short passages for the purposes of criticism and review, no part of this publication may be reproduced, stored in a retrieval system, or transmitted, in any form or by any means, electronic, mechanical, photocopying, recording or otherwise, without the prior permission of the publisher.

ISBN 1-902459-26-1

British Library Cataloguing in Publication data
A CIP catalogue record for this book is available from the
British Library

Printed in Great Britain by MPG Books Limited, Bodmin.
Typeset by Book Production Services, London,

LEEDS METROPOLITAN
UNIVERSITY
LIBRARY
1704731207
HY-B
BP-74718
21-8-06
EOE·CC2 HCA

Contents

Contributors

CHARLES BAZERMAN, Department of Education, University of California, Santa Barbara.

DIANE BELCHER, ESL Programs, The Ohio State University.

VIJAY K. BHATIA, Department of English and Communication, City University of Hong Kong.

MERIEL BLOOR, Centre for English Language Teacher Education, University of Warwick.

THOMAS BLOOR, Language Studies Unit, Aston University.

HELEN DRURY, The Learning Centre, University of Sydney.

CHRISTINE B. FEAK, English Language Institute, University of Michigan.

WILLIE HENDERSON, School for Professional and Continuing Education, University of Birmingham.

ANN HEWINGS, Centre for Language and Communication, The Open University.

MARTIN HEWINGS, English for International Students Unit, University of Birmingham.

THOMAS HUCKIN, Department of English, The University of Utah.

ANN M. JOHNS, Department of Rhetoric and Writing, San Diego State University.

TIM JOHNS, English for International Students Unit, University of Birmingham.

ALISON LOVE, Department of Linguistics, University of Zimbabwe.

PETER MASTER, Department of Linguistics and Language Development, San Jose State University.

ANNA MAURANEN, Department of English, University of Tampere.

GREG MYERS, Department of Linguistics and Modern English Language, University of Lancaster.

JOHN M. SWALES, English Language Institute, University of Michigan.

Acknowledgements

The publishers acknowledge with gratitude the support of the English for International Students Unit, the University of Birmingham. in the production of this volume.

The editor would also like to thank Maggie Jo St. John for her help in compiling the list of publications by Tony Dudley-Evans.

Introduction

Martin Hewings

The papers in this volume have been collected as a tribute to Tony Dudley-Evans on his retirement from the University of Birmingham. The authors are all people who know Tony well both professionally and personally, having worked with him in various ways in the world of English language teaching, as colleagues, students, or in connection with his editorship of the journal *English for Specific Purposes*.

The significance of Tony's contribution to English language teaching was already well established before he joined the University of Birmingham, particularly through his work on the pioneering *Nucleus* series of textbooks. However, it has been during his 25-year association with the English for International Students Unit at the university that his work on the teaching of academic literacy has flourished. The university has a sizeable population of international students, and successive groups have presented Tony with both the challenges and opportunities to further his interests in this area. Throughout this period, a number of themes have been recurrent in his work. One is his recognition of the importance of understanding the wider social, institutional and disciplinary context within which academic texts are produced, both those written by students and by professionals. Academic texts have discipline-specific characteristics and conventions, and making students aware of these can ease their progress towards becoming successful communicators within their chosen specialisation. To identify such features, Tony has advocated the importance of close cooperation between English language specialists and subject specialists. His work, together with his long-standing colleague Tim Johns, on the team teaching of lecture comprehension and writing skills for students of highway engineering and plant biology has been particularly influential and widely reported. More recently, his research with colleagues in the field of economics has illustrated the significance of insights from applied linguistics in analysing the relationship between the discipline and its writing.

A second theme is the value of genre analysis, particularly in the form developed by John Swales (see for example Swales 1990) as a foundation for analysing surface features of texts and relating these to their social contexts. Tony was among the first to recognise the contribution that this general approach and its methodologies could make in teaching English for academic purposes. His research has extended Swales' ground-breaking work on the introductions to research articles by exploring other elements of research articles, such as discussion sections, and other genres, in particular student genres such as Master's-level dissertations.

A third theme is the importance of establishing close links between linguistic theory and classroom practice. While the most widely available product of this is his book *Writing Laboratory Reports* (1985), which uses a genre analytical approach to the teaching of this form of writing, it is the 'in-house' material used in writing programmes at the University of Birmingham that has perhaps touched most students and influenced his colleagues most significantly. Through this material, Tony has presented the latest research findings on the nature of academic text, from both published sources, his own work and the work of his research students, in a form that is accessible and relevant to non-native English-speaking students. It is these three themes that are developed in the contributions to this volume.'

There is a growing consensus that the generally held view of academic writing as an information-transmitting, objective and impersonal form of text is a misrepresentation. Research in sociology and applied linguistics suggests that academic writing is more accurately seen as a vehicle through which scholars attempt to persuade other scholars of the validity of their own arguments. In order to do so most effectively, these arguments have to be presented in ways that are acceptable to the members of the academic community within which they work. Academic writing is therefore seen as part of the process of negotiating what is to be taken as accepted knowledge within a discipline and this is best achieved through modes of expression that have become conventionalised through the particular social and cultural contexts in which they arise. Becoming familiar with these modes of expression is part of becoming an established part of the academic community.

The process of initiation of student writers into the academic discourse community is examined in this volume in papers by Charles Bazerman and Ann Johns. In a wide-ranging paper, Charles Bazerman focuses on the means by which the student as apprentice learns the trade of the professional academic communicator. The complex interplay between texts, academic context and personal motivations and aspirations is explored and implications for professional education are highlighted.

Ann Johns discusses the challenges faced by her first-semester university students as they begin the task of becoming effective communicators in tertiary education, and the response to this in the form of an appropriate English language curriculum. Most of these students are the first in their families to go to university, and many are from low-income backgrounds. The principles on which her very successful programme is built are those of respecting the diversity of the student group, encouraging them to build on what they know in order to become innovative and effective learners and exploiting a range of modes of literacy in teaching.

The relationships between academic texts and their cultural contexts is a relatively new area of investigation. Given that English is the predominant language for academic communication, the possibility that within different cultural contexts academic texts have different patterns of rhetorical organisation has great significance. If non-English writers have been socialised into non-English writing cultures, they may have learned rhetorical habits different from those that have become conventional in a largely Anglo-American dominated publishing world. Consequently, their access to publication may be restricted. The paper by Anna Mauranen assesses the state of the art in Contrastive Rhetoric in academic contexts. She argues that now that a considerable amount of empirical evidence exists of rhetorical differences in academic texts from different cultures, it is time to reassess our methods, focusing on understanding how texts are constructed rather than seeking direct causal explanations for differences.

A major part of the process of become a successful writer in academia – either as student or as professional academic – is often seen to be the development of an awareness that there are differences between language used in academic discourse and that used in other, often less 'formal', settings. The papers by Tim Johns and Greg Myers explore such differences. Over a number of years, Tim Johns, Tony Dudley-Evans and their colleagues at the University of Birmingham have researched a computerised corpus of text from the scientific journal *Nature*. An investigation of the function of *that*-clauses in this corpus by Tim Johns is reported in his paper. In it he proposes a semantic/rhetorical classification of reporting verbs followed by *that*-clauses, and compares this with findings from *The Guardian* newspaper. He

LEEDS METROPOLITAN UNIVERSITY LIBRARY

goes on to report his email discussions with some of the *Nature* article authors in his exploration of their use of the verb 'indicate'.

While much of our everyday conversation is concerned with the expression of our own views, the common perception of academic writing is that its objectivity precludes the intrusion of personal opinion. However, as mentioned above, the current view in linguistic and sociological circles is that academic writing has much to do with authors putting forward their views of the world for scrutiny by peers. The linguistic conventions by which this is achieved may be very different from those found in speech or informal contexts for writing. The expression of personal views by students in essays is the focus of the paper by Greg Myers. He argues that we need to reassess the widely stated view that students should avoid expressing their own opinions in their writing, particularly using markers such as 'in my opinion' or 'in my personal view'. This view suggests that there is a clear division between objectivity and opinion, whereas the boundary between them may in practice be hard to draw. He also notes that such markers may in fact serve purposes other than simply marking opinion.

Of all forms of academic writing, it is the research article that has received most attention from both sociologists and applied linguists as the most important channel for conveying claims of new knowledge. Through the research article, published in highly regarded, peer-reviewed journals, authors strive to have their arguments become part of the disciplinary consensus. New findings are contextualised by reference to previous published literature which effectively represents a report of the existing consensus. Analysis of research articles to inform the teaching of English for specific purposes has been greatly influenced by the approach to genre analysis proposed by John Swales (see for example Brett 1994; Holmes 1997; Hopkins and Dudley-Evans 1988; Peng 1987). In his paper in this volume, Vijay Bhatia re-examines some of the key concepts associated with this approach, including the notion of 'move' and the related rhetorical notion of 'strategy', suggesting that, while analysis within this kind of framework provides us with valuable accounts of both academic and non-academic texts for pedagogical purposes, we need more rigorously to define their nature and function in written communication.

One component of the research article which has received considerable attention in recent years is the abstract. Tom Huckin begins by examining the significance of the abstract as a summary – as a 'screening' device through which the reader chooses whether to read the full article or not, as a mechanism for providing an interpretative frame for readers of the article, and as an aid to indexing for database services. The importance of the abstract as an independent entity, detached from the research article to which it relates, is growing as online databases of abstracts are increasingly used as the first point of access to research articles. The vast MEDLINE database, comprising more than 10 million abstracts of medical-related articles, has a keyword system as its primary search mechanism. Tom Huckin explores the relationship between abstracts (produced by the authors themselves) and the associated keywords (provided by professional indexers and based on close reading of the article, not the abstract) and considers the effectiveness of this system for accessing articles.

While the research article in most disciplines is the primary vehicle for presenting new knowledge claims, the textbook is the type of academic text read by the majority of students. It has been argued that textbooks present the disciplinary consensus, providing accepted knowledge rather than the disciplinary conflicts and debate that are the background against which research articles are set (Kuhn 1962; Latour and Woolgar 1979). Thus the limitations of the textbook as a model for the argumentative written discourse that students may be asked to produce have been noted (Hyland 1999a; Myers 1992). However, in this volume Alison Love argues that such a distinction between introductory textbooks presenting accepted knowledge and research articles persuading readers of the validity of new knowledge claims may be a simplification. She demonstrates, through an investigation of two anthropology textbooks aimed at first-year undergraduate students, that there may be considerable variation in the extent to which introductory textbooks introduce disciplinary controversy and complexity. While one of these texts appears to present largely agreed knowledge, downplaying controversy and complexity within anthropology, the other presents the discipline as one which is complex and in which there are conflicting arguments and contested interpretations.

A neglected student genre is that of the 'short answer', which Helen Drury sees as a 'transitional' genre for new tertiary-level students, helping them develop their writing skills as they move from producing descriptive to more expository forms of text. Helen Drury focuses on the 'short answers' written by first-year biology students at the University of Sydney, analysing the genre using a systemic functional linguistics (SFL) approach. She demonstrates the particular value of SFL in making clear the macrostructure of texts for the development of teaching materials.

The impact of electronic forms of text are explored by Diane Belcher. Her paper reviews research on computer-assisted composition and composition instruction, and considers the impact that computer networking and hypertext have had on the efforts by writing teachers to enable their students as authors in the traditional print literacy sense, as creators of rhetorically motivated text. Her conclusions suggest that these new writing technologies offer both serious, and sometimes worrying, challenges and exciting opportunities for teachers and students alike.

In recent years, approaches to the teaching of academic writing have focused increasingly on helping students become aware of the particular features of contrasting genres. Courses have been published on teaching experimental research reports (e.g. Weissberg and Buker 1990), theses and dissertations (e.g. Anderson and Poole 1994), essays (e.g. Roberts 1997) and so on. However, variations in the characteristic patterns of academic writing occur not only from genre to genre, but within genres from discipline to discipline. A number of the papers in this volume examine writing within specific disciplines and some more explicitly compare the frequency and function of particular linguistic features across disciplines. The importance of such work is that it provides insights into the relationship between the subject matter, working practices, values and ideologies characteristic of a discipline and the way it constructs and is constructed by its texts. From a pedagogical perspective, the success of the increasing number of students in inter- or multi-disciplinary academic programmes, may depend on their being aware of disciplinary variation in communication practices and developing sufficient flexibility to produce writing that reflects the predilections of a particular discipline.

Tony Dudley-Evans has collaborated extensively with Willie Henderson, an economist at the University of Birmingham, in researching written text in economics. Willie Henderson's contribution to this volume is an examination of the writing of Adam Smith in his *An Inquiry into the Nature and Causes of the Wealth of Nations*, published in 1776. He uses discourse analytical techniques to investigate Smith's use of exemplification, first producing a categorisation of examples and then identifying recurring rhetorical patterns associated with each category. He suggests that parallels exist between the styles of exemplification used by Smith in his *Wealth of Nations* and those found in modern-day economics textbooks.

The paper by Meriel Bloor and Tom Bloor also researches writing in economics. An area that is generally neglected in the teaching of academic writing is that of predicting future events and future actions. However, in disciplines such as economics in which forecasting and making recommendations about future courses of action are core activities, this is frequently required. In addition to an analysis of the most frequent grammatical realisations of this function, and how these compare with the expression of the future in non-academic genres, they examine the hedging with which it is typically and even necessarily associated. Both the range of expression of future time used in English and the linguistic subtlety of hedging are problematic for non-native speakers, and a sound analysis of this area of language has considerable pedagogic potential for those working in the area of English for academic purposes.

One approach to the study of disciplinary variation is to examine the relative frequency and function of use of certain lexico-grammatical features in comparable writing across disciplines. Peter Master's paper, for example, focuses on active verb forms, particularly those with inanimate subjects. He finds that in research articles taken from five sciences there is considerable variation in the relative frequency of inanimate subjects with active verb forms, ranging from 29 per cent of the total subjects with active verbs in cellular biology down to 0.03 per cent in clinical psychology. The reasons why such variation should occur are related to the subject matter and methodologies of the different disciplines.

Ann Hewings and Martin Hewings see anticipatory *it*-clauses (e.g. *It is assumed* that...) as an important component of the mechanism by which writers negotiate new knowledge claims and establish their standing in their disciplinary community. Variation in use of *it*-clauses is examined in two contexts. First, they compare its use in research articles in the fields of geography, business administration, physics and astronomy, and history. Second, they compare its use in first- and third-year undergraduate student essays in one of these fields, geography, showing how it is indicative of the gradual orientation of the students to the textual conventions of the discipline.

In the final paper in the volume John Swales and Christine Feak offer some personal reflections on Tony Dudley-Evans in their exploration of the process of writing materials for the teaching of academic literacy to non-native English speakers. The starting point for their discussion is Tony's involvement in the Nucleus series of textbooks for the teaching of English for specific purposes. They look back both to this work and to John Swales' collaborations with Tony during the 1970s, before considering their own co-authorship of titles such as Academic Writing for Graduate Students (1994). In this way they trace the evolution of the craft of materials writing over the last 25 years and, in doing so, identify fundamental and contingent assumptions that influence the process.

Publications by Tony Dudley-Evans

1974   with Bates, M. Notes on the introductory English course for students of Science and Technology at the University of Tabriz. *ELT Documents 74*, 4. The British Council.

1975   with Shettlesworth, C. and Philips, M. K. Aspects of the writing and teaching of EST courses. *ELT Documents 75*, 2. The British Council.

1976   with Bates, M. *Nucleus: General Science*. Harlow: Longman.

1976–80 with Bates, M. (series editors) *Nucleus: English for science and technology*. Harlow: Longman.

1978   Report writing. In R. R. Jordan (ed.), *Presessional courses for overseas students. ELT Documents, 75*, 2. ETIC Publications, The British Council.

–   Planning a course for science and engineering students. In A. Holden (ed.), *English for Specific Purposes* (pp.38-41). Modern English Publications.

–   Helping teachers to use *Nucleus. English for Science and Technology, 21*. Oregon.

–   with Smart, T. and Wall, J. *Nucleus: Engineering*. Harlow: Longman.

1980   with Johns, T. An experiment in the team teaching of overseas postgraduate students of Transportation and Plant Biology. In *Team teaching in ESP. ELT Documents 106* (pp.6–23). The British Council.

–   with Swales, J. Study modes and students from the Middle East. In G. M. Greenall and J. E. Price (eds), *Study modes and academic development of overseas students*. ELT Documents Special, 109.

1981   The ELU survey on Ngee Ann College graduates' requirements of English. *RELC Journal, 12*, 1.

–   with Johns, T. A team-teaching approach to lecture comprehension for overseas students. In *The teaching of listening comprehension*. ELT Documents Special.

1982   A model for syllabus design for an English medium technical college in Singapore. Unpublished paper, Ngee Ann College, Singapore.

–   A report on the test taken by incoming Engineering students in April 1980, Ngee Ann Technical College. Unpublished paper, Ngee Ann College, Singapore.

–   Needs analysis for Engineering, Building and Business Studies departments, Ngee Ann Technical College. Unpublished paper, Ngee Ann College, Singapore.

–   Designing a course in listening comprehension at Ngee Ann Technical College. Unpublished paper, Ngee Ann College, Singapore.

1983   *Papers on team teaching and syllabus design.* RLC Occasional Papers No. 27. Regional Language Centre, Singapore.

–   Towards team teaching. A description of co-operation between language and subject teachers at Ngee Ann Technical College. In *Papers on team teaching and syllabus design* (pp.22–34).

–   An experiment in the team teaching of EOP. In *Papers on team teaching and syllabus design* (pp.35–41).

–   with Fish, H. Problems with communicative syllabuses. *RLC Journal, 13,* 2.

–   A communicative approach to the teaching of writing. In D. Richards (ed.). *Concepts and functions in current syllabuses* (pp.65–82). RELC Occasional Papers No. 30, Regional Language Centre, Singapore.

1984   A preliminary investigation of the writing of dissertation titles. In G. James (ed.), *The ESP classroom* (pp.40–46). Exeter Linguistic Studies.

–   A review of the use of an ESP textbook in Egyptian secondary schools. In J. Swales (ed.), *ESP in the Arab World* (pp.292–8). The University of Aston.

–   The team teaching of writing skills. In R. Williams, J. Swales and J. Kirkman (eds), *Common ground: Shared interests in ESP and communication studies* (pp.127–33). ELT Documents117. Pergamon.

1985   *Writing Laboratory Reports.* Melbourne: Nelson Wadsworth.

1986   with Zak, H. Features of word omission and abbreviation in telexes. *English for Specific Purposes, 5,* 59–71.

–   Genre analysis: an investigation of the introduction and discussion sections of MSc dissertations. In M. Coulthard (ed.), *Talking about text* (pp.128–45). University of Birmingham Discourse Analysis Monographs 13.

1987   *Genre analysis and ESP* (ed.). ELR Journal, 1. The University of Birmingham.

–   with Bates, M. The evaluation of an ESP textbook. In L. Sheldon (ed.), *ELT textbooks and materials: Problems in evaluation and development* (pp.99–105). ELT Documents 126. Modern English Publications in association with the British Council.

1988   Practicality. In D. Porter, A. Hughes and C. Weir (eds), *Proceedings of a Conference to Consider the ELTS Validation Project Report*. English Language Testing Report 1.2, ELTS Validation Project. London: University of Cambridge Local Examination Syndicate.

–   Recent developments in ESP. The trend to greater specialisation. In M. L. Tickoo (ed.), *ESP: State of the art* (pp.27–32). RELC Anthology Series 21, Regional Language Centre, Singapore.

–   One-to-one supervision of student writing MSc or PhD theses. In A. Brookes and P. Grundy (eds), *Individualisation and autonomy in language learning* (pp.136–41). ELT Documents 131. Modern English Publications with the British Council.

–   A consideration of the meaning of 'Discuss' in examination questions. In P. Robinson (ed.), *Academic writing: Process and product* (pp.47–52). ELT Documents 129. Modern English Publications with the British Council.

–   with Hopkins, A. A genre-based investigation of the discussion sections in articles and dissertations. *English for Specific Purposes, 7,* 113–21.

–   with Johns, T. Ten years of team teaching. *Teaching News.* The University of Birmingham.

1989   An outline of genre analysis in LSP work. In C. Lauren and M. Nordman (eds), *Special language: From human thinking to thinking machines* (pp.72–9). Clevedon, Philadelphia: Multilingual Matters.

1990   with Henderson, W. The organisation of article introductions: evidence of change in economics articles. In A. Dudley-Evans and W. Henderson (eds), *The language of economics: The analysis of economics discourse (ELT Documents 134)* (pp.67–78). London: Macmillan and the British Council.

–   with Henderson, W. (eds), *The language of economics: The analysis of economics discourse (ELT Documents 134)*. London: Macmillan and the British Council.

–   with Henderson, W. Introduction: the analysis of economics discourse. In A. Dudley-Evans and W. Henderson (eds), *The language of economics: The analysis of economics discourse (ELT Documents 134)* (pp.2–15). London: Macmillan and the British Council.

1991   Socialisation into the academic community: linguistic and stylistic expectations of a PhD thesis as revealed by supervisor comments. In P. Adams, B. Heaton and P. Howarth (eds), *Socio-cultural Issues in English for academic purposes (Review of English Language Teaching 1:2)* (pp.41–51). London: Modern English Teacher in association with the British Council.

–   with Johns, A. English for specific purposes: International in scope, specific in purpose. *TESOL Quarterly 25*, 297–314.

1993   Variation in communication patterns between discourse communities: the case of Highway Engineering and Plant Biology. In G. Blue (ed.), *Language, learning and success: Studying through English* (pp.141–7). London: Macmillan.

–   The debate over Milton Friedman's theoretical framework: an applied linguist's view. In W. Henderson, A. Dudley-Evans and R. Backhouse (eds), *Economics and Language* (pp.132–52). London: Routledge.

–   with R. Backhouse and W. Henderson. Exploring the language and rhetoric of economics. In W. Henderson, A. Dudley-Evans and R. Backhouse (eds), *Economics and Language* (pp.1–20). London: Routledge.

–   with Henderson, W. The development of the economics article: 1891–1980. In S. Ylonen, *Diachrone Fachsprachenforshung: Diachronic LSP Research*. Special edition of *Finlance: A Finnish Journal of Applied Linguistics, XII*: 159–80.

–   with Henderson, W. and Backhouse, R. (eds), *Economics and language*. London: Routledge.

–   with Johns, A. English for specific purposes: international in scope, specific in purpose. In S. Silberstein (ed.), *State of the art TESOL essays: Celebrating 25 years of the discipline* (pp.115–32). Alexandria, Virginia, USA: TESOL Publications. (Reprint of article originally published in *TESOL Quarterly*.)

1994   English for specific purposes: a European perspective. *Les Cahiers de l'APLIUT, 13*, 51–60.

–   Genre analysis: an approach to text analysis for ESP. In M. Coulthard (ed.), *Advances in written analysis* (pp.219–28). London: Routledge.

– Research in English for specific purposes. In R. Khoo (ed.), *LSP: Problems and prospects (RELC Anthology Series 33)* (pp.219–31). Seameo Regional Language Centre: Singapore.

1995 Variation in the discourse patterns favoured by different disciplines and their pedagogical implications. In J. Flowerdew (ed.), *Academic listening: Research perspectives*. Cambridge: Cambridge University Press.

– Genre models for the teaching of writing to second language speakers: advantages and disadvantages. In T. Miller (ed.), *Functional approaches to written text: Classroom applications. The Journal of TESOL France*, 2:181–91. (Reprinted in Miller, T. (ed.) (1997), *Approaches to written text* (pp.150–59). Washington: US Information Agency.)

– BANA v. TESEP: Where does ESP fit in? In R. Budd (ed.), *Appropriate methodology: From classroom methods to classroom processes. The Journal of TESOL France*, 2, 127–32.

– Controversy in economics: an applied linguistics perspective. In F. van Eemeren, R. Grootendorst, J. A. Blair. and C. A. Willard (eds), *Special fields and special cases* (pp.546–53). Amsterdam: Sic Cat.

– Common core and specific approaches to the teaching of academic writing. In D. Belcher and G. Braine (eds), *Academic writing in a second language. Essays on research and pedagogy* (pp.293–312). Norwood, NJ: Ablex.

1996 with St. John, M. J. *Report on Business English: A review of research and published teaching materials (TOEIC Research Report No. 2)*. Princeton, NJ: The Chauncey Group.

1997 Genre: how far can we, should we go? *World Englishes, 16*, 351–8.

– Five questions for LSP teacher training. In R. Howard (ed.), *Teacher education for LSP* (pp.58–67). Clevedon, Avon: Multilingual Matters.

– with Hewings, M. (eds), *Evaluation and course design in EAP*. Hemel Hempstead: Prentice Hall Macmillan.

1998 with St. John, M. J. *Developments in ESP: A multi-disciplinary approach*. Cambridge: Cambridge University Press.

– Developments in ESP. In M. Pavesi and G. Bernini (eds), *L'apprendimento Linguistico All'Universita: Le Lingue Speciali* (pp.193–205). Roma: Bulzoni Editore.

1999 *Annotated bibliography of English for specific purposes*. ABES, University of East Anglia.

– The dissertation: a case of neglect? In P. Thompson (ed.), *Issues in*

EAP writing research and instruction (pp.28–36). CALS, University of Reading.

2001   Foreword. In S. Benesch, *Critical English for academic purposes: Theory, politics, and practice.* (pp.ix–xv). Mahwah, NJ: Lawrence Erlbaum.

–   English for specific purposes. In R. Carter and D. Nunan (eds), *A handbook for applied linguistics* (pp.131–6). Cambridge: Cambridge University Press.

–   Team teaching in ESP: changes and adaptations in the Birmingham approach. In J. Flowerdew and M. Peacock (eds), *English for academic purposes* (pp.225–38). Cambridge: Cambridge University Press.

2002   The teaching of a problematic genre: the academic essay. In A. M. Johns (ed.), *Genre in the classroom: Multiple perspectives.* Mahwah, NJ: Lawrence Erlbaum.

Distanced and refined selves: educational tensions in writing with the power of knowledge

Charles Bazerman

We often look on the rise of disciplines and professions with some suspicion as they are rightfully seen as the site of the aggregation of power – power granted by the importance of knowledge in contemporary society, which is now being regularly designated as an information society (Bazerman forthcoming; Dizard 1982). We now have many historical, sociological and rhetorical accounts of how that power was aggregated and maintained within bounded disciplinary spaces (for example Bazerman 1999; Latour and Woolgar 1979; Shapin 1982, 1994), how institutions of knowledge grew and gained influence (Atkinson 1999; Hall 1984; Jacob 1988; Merton 1973; Morrell and Thackray 1981; Shapin and Schaffer 1985), how decisions became matters for experts (Porter 1995), how authority was constructed for those beyond (Gieryn 1999), how negotiations, cooperations and alliances were created with other powerful disciplines and social actors (Latour 1987; van Nostrand 1997) and how public issues became re-framed to incorporate or exclude various forms of disciplinary and professional knowledge (Myers 1990; Nelkin 1979, 1987; Rudwick 1985). Some of these studies take a highly sceptical view of these powerful formations (Barnes and Shapin 1979; Bijker *et al.* 1987). Others see that the knowledge developed within disciplines warrants the strong influence disciplines and professions maintain over their own conduct and over other domains which depend on their knowledge (Abbott 1988; Gregory and Miller 1998). And many take the middle ground, seeing inappropriately self-interested use of the power of knowledge, and the need for decision making to include interests and knowledge that extend beyond the bounds of the professions. Consider, for example, the history of environmental concern – where different sciences (including chemistry, ecology, biology and demography), government regulators, lawyers, corporations, economists, activists and community groups have all taken complex and shifting roles.

Similarly, some recognise great benefits in the knowledge that disciplines and professions produce and exercise (Heilbron 1979; Holton 1986). Others, while appreciating the knowledge, see it rapidly diffusing throughout society and see the need for all citizens to have a greater share in how the knowledge is used (Commoner 1966; Sclove 1995). And still others remain sceptical about the benefits, and call for Thoreauvian withdrawal (Winner 1977) – although Thoreau himself became a leading naturalist of his time (Thoreau 1980).

But no matter what one may believe about the legitimacy and complexity, openness or closedness of disciplinary and professional power – it is hard to deny that there is power in professions and disciplines. Further, forms of disciplinary expertise have become increasingly elaborate, requiring longer entry times and greater training. By and large, disciplines are not games for beginners, though in new fields sometimes individuals can move very rapidly in non-institutional ways – think of the archetypal teenage computer programmer. Nonetheless, the rise of disciplinary and professional power can be seen as coincident with the growth of university education.

No matter how much we appreciate changes brought about by knowledge/power formations, we are caught in tensions between the democratic distrust of oligarchic authority and the aggregation of power in institutions, even if powerful institutions and elites are formed around something so valued as knowledge. In prior times church and royalty were also taken as the sites of true knowledge and as the sites of institutional power. Nonetheless, democratic revolutions have precisely served to limit the power of each and return degrees of judgement and choice to individuals and voluntary alliances. Are we now to allow institutional power and oligarchy to be reaggregated around disciplinary knowledge and professional expertise? This issue has been at the forefront of the public agenda at least since the introduction of nuclear weapons (Carson 1962; Commoner 1966; Nelkin 1979), and has precursors in earlier debates over technocratic bureaucracy (Layton 1986). The recent development of information technologies has only heightened the tensions, as these technologies provide wider ranges of ever more sophisticated information and communicative means, at the same time as they strengthen some forms of professional and technical authority (Yates and van Maanen 2001). Power and wealth is aggregating within new professions. With these information technologies, our daily choices are both expanding and ever more caught up within organised structures of knowledge and expertise

(Abbate 1999; Berners-Lee 1999, Bowker and Star 1999). We can fly most anywhere in the world we want on short notice – but only through the support and engagement of large professional and corporate information systems relying on such fields as economics, international law, aerospace engineering, flight professionals, air control and marketing.

We are rightly anxious lest sciences and other professions become presbyter or magistrate or police force, and yet some institutional arrangements seem necessary to maintain knowledge production and use. People must be allowed to specialise, to communicate with others of like specialisation, to be supported in their learning and to be recognised as having some authority in their specialisation. Education sits precisely on this tension point: schooling makes knowledge democratically available at the same time as it prepares individuals to pursue careers of specialised authority and knowledge. In higher education, in particular, there is a direct meeting of the knowledge elites with large numbers of people who will carry out powerful roles in the community (Collins 1979). The university provides students with the means and motives to become members of one or another elite. Even the most democratic and egalitarian universities are about access to power.

Learning academic writing sits even more at this tension point between power and democracy, for learning academic writing entails learning to wield tools of symbolic power for immediate rhetorical purposes. What kind of authority, what purposes, what kind of reliance on special knowledge, and what kind of public accountability will be realised in each text we write? Professors in each discipline are evaluating how powerfully their students in their classes are writing within the powerful discourses of their fields (Schwegler and Shamoon 1991). Students are rewarded, and we hope supported and guided, in learning to make statements that are regarded as warrantable and consequential in each area. The professors in these disciplines would not say they are creating arbitrary hoops and distinctions for the general value of discipline, for they believe each of their disciplines provides consequential ways of talking about the world (Walvoord 1997; Walvoord and McCarthy 1990). They believe that the power of their disciplines can only be enacted and harnessed through writing in the ways developed and made accountable in the discipline. If students want the power of their discipline, they have to develop the appropriate ways of expressing and using the knowledge. Students need to learn to speak with voices recognisable as legitimate, warrantable and powerful within the disciplines and professions.

In writing we usually talk about this issue as one of voice, and then treat it as though it were an individual attribute, the way we think of distinctiveness of voice in creative writing (Elbow 1973). We consider it perhaps as something to be found unitarily inside the person needing to be expressed, or perhaps as an external accomplishment of general personality development, or perhaps as even a fragmented response to the multiplicity of the post-modern world (Faigley 1992). In all these ways voice is often perceived as something opposed to disciplines and professions that seem to suppress voice. But when viewed through the lens I offer here, voice can be seen as forming within engagements with the various forums life offers. Voice is developed in learning to speak within ways of being. Powerful voice is gained by learning to speak consequentially within the forums of power. Of course as writers learn to engage with these powerful discourses, their voices change, no matter how much of their old accents they carry with them.

This socio-political tension of developing professional voice also has personal cognitive correlates. The gaining of knowledge transforms the individual's perceptions, choices, affective structure and modes of relationship. As students move into their majors and as they move into the independence of life, their ways of thinking, perceiving and feeling change – even if they become alienated, disengaged or distrustful of the knowledge practices they are learning (Chiseri-Strater 1991; Zamel and Spack 1998). Our students graduate on their ways to becoming chemists, accountants, psychologists, managers, lawyers, novelists or professors – either by entering those lines of work or making decisions to enter further specialised professional training. Seniors already take on the distinctive thought, behaviour and dress of their anticipated professional role, whether engineers or journalists or politicians or actors (Freedman 1993; Freedman *et al.* 1994; Winsor 1996). Many educational theorists and psychologists have talked about the development of the self in relation to modes of engagements with others, the language that mediates those engagements, and the perception of one's own role in that participation – 20th-century social scientists like George Herbert Mead, Ruth Benedict, Edward Sapir, Lev Vygotsky, John Dewey and Harry Stack Sullivan, as well as 18th-century moral philosophers like David Hume, Adam Smith, George Campbell and Hugh Blair.

Yet these transformations that accompany intellectual growth, analytical skill, professionalisation, and the wisdom of learning, also seem to remove us from the most immediate forms of easily recognised human commonality.

Refinement is traditionally a class marker, and much of education historically is associated with producing class distinction (Bourdieu 1984). Some of those class markers we now see as arbitrary, simply reproducing cultural values that reinforce the hold of dominant classes with little value to the rest of society in return (Aronowitz 1988; Foucault 1970, 1980), though medieval clerics and colonial bureaucrats may have given very different accounts of the value of their refined practices and personal development. As long as we hold to some social value for our current set of knowledge practices – as most of us would at least in part – then we set the conditions for classes of people who gain specialised access to these practices. Dedication to the power of learning seems inevitably to create the refined *habitus* of lawyers, mathematicians, litterateurs, engineers (Bourdieu 1990). We suspect these personal refinements may make us forget who we are and our common cause with others. The Richard Rodriguez (1981) story about ambivalence over leaving one's community behind to enter the professional classes is not just one of the struggles of poor Chicano boys. Nor even just the struggles of ethnic identity. Nor even of class loyalty. Even the children of the upper classes become distinguished, culturally and intellectually, from their families as they proceed down particular paths of professionalisation. The pace of professional refinement is now so rapid and so transformed by new technology that professional education is in many fields quite different than it was a generation ago. Even children who follow the professions of their parents may be entering new worlds.

We suspect refinement as elitism. We suspect these refinements may become the vehicles of self-aggrandisement and contempt for others. And again education and particularly learning academic writing sits exactly at the tension point, for it is in our becoming academically articulate that we learn to present our refined selves and commit ourselves to refined perceptions and thought. We learn to use big and unusual words, and we learn to believe them, for we wrote them.

As teachers of academic writing we are caught in the tension between helping students express their thoughts and bringing them into new ways of thinking found within the academy. If we ask them to write from just where they are, we do not ask them to engage the new worlds of powerful knowledge around them. We may even be creating a safe haven for them to reject or deny these new challenging worlds they are coming in contact with. If, on the other hand, we ask them to behave too professionally prematurely, the authority of the disciplinary discourses may wash over and obliterate their ability as individuals to engage with and grow into disciplinary possibilities. We may put them into positions too distant from their current selves for them to make sense of. In both extremes we deny the students the power of the discourses the university offers. It is an important part of our challenge as teachers of academic writing to find the positions of learning and engagement that will allow our students to grow into the power of transforming voices.

For our students, we see these tensions in their struggles to adopt the discourse of their fields, in their sense of discomfort or estrangement or artifice. But if we support the right opportunities and create the space for students to work through the tensions of their discursive transformation, we can witness their integration of knowledges and selves, and their development of complex discursive resources and presentations.

Writing Across the Curriculum and other forms of academic writing draw us into such issues as the emergence of student identities, the meanings and forms of thought students develop and the fractures of power that constantly remake the worlds we live in (Herrington and Curtis 2000). We need to consider where discursive powers come from, what those powers are good for and how they may be used and abused. Teaching academic writing draws us into reflection on the power and ethics of professional being. It is hardly surprising, then, that in the field of the teaching of writing, academic and disciplinary writing is controversial along just these lines.

The root of these tensions is in the ways in which literacy has historically allowed us to gain distance on the world we describe and project, to view the world as more of an object, to free our relationships to an extent of the pressures of face-to-face amity and hostility. These tensions have grown as literacy has facilitated broader communities of inquiry with wider nets of available information, institutions of specialisation, and the reorganisation of daily life on the basis of specialised knowledge. These tensions then have pervaded our very identities – as literacy has helped form communally sharable spaces of personal contemplation and reflection, large publicly available archives that become the basis for cultural knowledge, and social authority and role based on our specialised knowledge. By sorting through our ambivalences about the power of knowledge and academic writing, we can sharpen our sense of social and personal purposes in academic writing. We may also contemplate the consequences of information technologies for proliferating specialised knowledge and its democratic availability. At the very least, we can recognise where our discomfort comes from, as we are caught within the dilemmas of the power of knowledge.

The future is with us: preparing diverse students for the challenges of university texts and cultures

Ann M. Johns

In his thought-provoking volume, *Writing the Future: English and the Making of a Culture of Innovation* (1995), Gunther Kress argues that English educators should be at the forefront of curricular innovation, since the interactions of language, text, and technology are central to our current and future worlds. These are the curricular principles that he urges us to follow:

1 A curriculum should envisage, project, and aim to produce an individual who is at ease with difference and change, whose fundamental being values innovation and is therefore able to question, to challenge, and above all, to propose alternatives constructively.

2 This curriculum should project and aim to take a central role in producing a society which values humans, accords them real dignity, and aims to provide for all its members the possibility of a quality of life which is at least no worse than that enjoyed by my generation. (p.29)

My purpose in this paper is to honor Tony Dudley-Evans, an outstanding English for Specific Purposes practitioner, by using Kress's ambitious goals to outline my own English teaching situation, which is somewhat parallel to Tony's, to discuss some of the challenges that are posed by attempting to achieve the aims that Kress espouses, and to present our local attempts to develop English language curricula which, in our view, honor difference, encourage innovation, and exploit multimodal literacies.

The context

Our public California university, San Diego State (SDSU), has about 27,000 students and is located within a major metropolis with a highly diverse population. At the high schools nearest the campus about 30 different languages are spoken, with Spanish as the predominant tongue. Most of the students in these high schools are low-income; about 85 per cent qualify for a government-sponsored free lunch program. Those few who are fortunate enough to enter my university as freshmen are assigned to a mentoring/advising/financial aid plan (The Educational Opportunity Program (EOP)) and enrolled in a learning communities program called Freshman Success (FSP) (see Johns 1997 for details). For 16 years my colleagues and I have been teaching the FSP cohort of 40 to 44 EOP students. Our cohort currently includes the following classes organized, as an adjunct cluster in which all of the 40+ students enroll:

- a cultural anthropology class, assigned for education 'breadth' (all students are in this class);
- two study groups of 22 students each to support the anthropology class;
- two literacy classes at two levels (22 students in each class); and
- university orientation classes, the University Seminar (11 students per class).

This appears to be the ideal language teaching environment in which to institute Kress's aims: our students are certainly different, culturally and linguistically, from each other and from most students on campus, and they have been encouraged in their high schools to appreciate difference, although perhaps not to fully develop their literacies. Because the class with which our literacy courses are linked is cultural anthropology, we have the tools to investigate, and appreciate, our multicultural worlds, using the available designs of meaning: the methodologies, texts, and concepts of this discipline.

However, there are challenges, and these must be considered as we attempt to provide an appropriate, yet innovative, approach. The first and most important challenge is the students' own perceptions of their needs and goals. These first-year students are considerably different from the international students who enroll in the classes taught by Tony and his colleagues. They are the first in their families to attend university, and many are new immigrants to the United States. When I ask them to complete a needs assessment, essential to any ESP course (see Dudley-Evans and St John 1998), or reflect upon what they want from their education, I find, not surprisingly, that they want what *my* family has – a steady income, middle-class status, etc. – only more. Here are some of the goals for literacy and for their educational experience that they identify year after year. They want:

1. *Rapid progress towards graduation.* In most cases, their large families are making major sacrifices for both boys (as money earners) and girls (as helpers for their mothers) to come to school. The families are, sometimes reluctantly, relinquishing their possibilities for immediate income and for assistance in the home. Thus, rapid and efficient completion of the degree is the students' principal aim.

2. *Majors or academic emphases that assure an excellent income, provide prestige for the family, and do not require much sophistication in English.* Though a few of the young women want to be teachers, the majority of the students have chosen to be in business, preferably majoring in computer science or engineering, '...where I can make a big income and don't have to have good language ability', said one student.

3. *Answers in the literacy classroom about how to most efficiently achieve their textual goals.* Most want *answers*, and they want them quickly, without obfuscation. They believe that because we language teachers have succeeded in university we *know* how to operate in academic contexts and we should be giving them the simplest possible instructions for achieving success. Thus, our students want to know exactly how they can create an effective text, present a talk, or learn a formula – whatever provides the quickest road to their success – and quick graduation.

4. *Few barriers to literacy goal achievement.* Most students come with rather limited views of how English can be exploited for their purposes, particularly the written language, though, of course, they may be highly versatile in their L1 or in their spoken L2. Many have considerable difficulty reading our culture-laden academic English texts, and their theories of writing are limited by their high-school education to the famous 'North American Five Paragraph Essay', characterized by an introduction of a specified length, including a 'thesis', a body of three paragraphs of equal length, and a conclusion that restates the thesis. So they want simple, non-complex answers to how they can write and use the technologies in their new acad-

emic contexts. They do not welcome the complexities of literacy; they have a sufficient number of complexities in their lives. (For useful discussions of this 'Generation 1.5' population and its confrontations with EAP literacy see Harklau *et al.* 1999.)

Though Tony and I would agree that we need to take a more critical stance in the EAP literature (see Tony's foreword in Benesch 2001), I would argue that much of the critical pedagogy literature ignores the central aims articulated by first generation (1.5) university students. Critical pedagogues, most of whom are highly educated, encourage critique of the system before the students can understand and negotiate it; they force immediate acknowledgment of students' oppression by the university and the culture, because they, themselves, are often marginalized and oppressed as teachers (see Johns 1997). Some critical pedagogues call for direct action on the part of the students, action that could, in fact, impede their successful completion of their degrees. Of course, we can call our students to arms, but what they want, at least in their first years of college, is to get ahead - to succeed in the university they have entered with considerable pride, not to tear it down. I am encouraged by Kress's argument, then, that we should evoke critique but move beyond it, for, not incidentally, critique is all too common, and sometimes crippling, to English departments, and their students, everywhere. Kress says:

> Critique is essential in periods of social stability as a means for producing change; by bringing that which is settled into crisis, it is a means for producing a cultural dynamic. In periods of intense change [such as ours], the problem is that the cultural dynamic is too great, so that critique is not the issue; the focus of intervention [and thus curriculum] has to shift to the design of possible alternatives. (1995: 5; my additions)

Thus, I will raise here a number of questions that we have attempted to answer within our own context, often similar to the ones that Tony and his colleagues have attempted to answer within theirs, considering the perceived needs and wants of my students, our own experiences, and Kress's admonitions. The questions are these:

1. How can we respect, and encourage respect of, difference(s) among our multilingual, multicultural students within our classrooms?

2. How can we accept, appreciate, and encourage the generation 1.5 students' need to become comfortable and to succeed within 'foreign' academic cultures and in various professional worlds, thus allowing them to 'participate fully in [the] public, community, and [especially] the economic life' (Cope and Kalantzis 1993: 9; my additions) of their adopted country?

3. How can we destabilize the very limited theories of genre that students bring to our classes (see Johns 2002) yet provide support in learning, using, critiquing and negotiating new genres, especially the genres of power?

4. How can we encourage these students to appreciate the multi-modal nature of literacy: uses of technology, of visuals, and of oral and written discourses, when, in many cases, their economic situations and their underserved schools have not provided them with an array of technological and sophisticated assessment experiences?

5. How can we assist students to 'critically frame' what they have experienced? To come to terms with 'where they stand in relation to the historical, social, cultural, political, ideological, and value-centered relations of particular systems of knowledge and social practice' (Cope and Kalantzis 2000: 34)?

6. And finally, how can students be encouraged to transform and transfer their practices, to negotiate and manipulate the available designs of meaning?

Respect for difference

In the linked classes I have described, the students find it relatively easy to recognize that 'difference is a major resource' (Kress 1995: 95) or to honor the 'salience of cultural and linguistic diversity' (Cope and Kalantzis 2000: 5), for their study of anthropology and their interactions with their peers in the class provides for them ways to examine and appreciate cultural and linguistic difference. In our literacy/anthropology classes in Fall, 2000, for example, were Latino students not only from Mexico but from other countries in Latin America; Asian students from the Philippines, Laos (a Hmong), Cambodia, Guam, Vietnam and China; African-American students who were part American Indian and White; and a number of students who did not claim one dominant ethnic group, e.g. a student whose mother was Japanese and father was Anglo-American.

During the classes, the students read and wrote about difference as constructed by anthropologists: about psychological depression among the Irish and its cultural roots, about first language use and code-switching, about the American Inuit and their relationships with the environment, and about gender roles in African villages. They discussed anthropological concepts: cultural relativism, emic and etic perspectives, and perhaps most importantly, about the ways in which families and individuals choose, or are forced to interact, within a new culture (assimilation and acculturation). To augment their understanding and provide empowering experiences for the students we involved them in a community-based service learning effort during which they visited and interviewed 9th grade (15-year-old) secondary school students from a variety of cultures about cultural and linguistic persistence in their families. These interactions became part of a final paper and multi-modal exposition at the secondary school (see Johns 2000). Thus, we had a number of opportunities to appreciate and discuss the diverse nature of our immediate worlds – and to use academic concepts and texts to write about this diversity.

Comfort and success

A second goal was to acknowledge the students' academic and personal needs and expectations while encouraging them to succeed in our foreign, and sometimes hostile, academic culture.[1] The first major paper the students wrote was about the cultures and traditions of their own families or, as one student (Lailah) put it, about 'the culture I never thought I had'. The secondary school students' cultures, which our students explored through interviews, were different from their own, yet in many cases closer to our students' experiences than were the academic cultures of the university. However, anthropology helped them to understand university cultures too, for they could examine and critically frame the university as a cluster of cultures, with values, texts, and general 'ways of being' as realized in their spoken and written genres.

In their other classes, students also investigated university cultures. They were encouraged by their University Seminar teachers to interview older students from similar socioeconomic backgrounds about the demands and values of their majors, and to question their instructors about what they wrote and read – and about the lives they led as academics. The literature on academic persistence tells us that one of the most important elements in student retention in universities is their ethnic identification with someone within the university culture: a student mentor or an instructor. Encouraging this identification was one of our goals. We urged students to join their ethnic group associations, and we advertised the student mentoring program. We brought a Latina faculty member to the class to discuss her progress through the university system, her parents' efforts to dissuade her, and the problems and successes that she encountered (see also Casanave 1992). From all this, the students learned that taking on a new culture often means surrendering what they value most in their first cultures, that painful decisions must often be made if the they are to continue their education or succeed in mainstream professions.

Destabilizing genres

One of the central goals in our literacy classes is to introduce students to genre theory – at their level, of course – and to help them to draw from their own intertextual knowledge of the 'integration of significant modes of meaning-making, where the textual is also related to the visual, the audio, the spatial, the behavioral, and so on' (Cope and Kalantzis 2000: 5). As noted earlier, these students have limited understanding of written academic texts, views that have been narrowed by the particular instructional and assessment approaches mandated by our state and local governments. Somehow, we instructors must destabilize and complicate these theories in order to prepare students for future experiences with texts. We must assist students to come to terms with both the centrifugal and centripetal forces that influence texts and the perpetuation of genres (see Berkenkotter and Huckin 1995, after Bakhtin 1981). Chapman points out that:

> Although genre is characterized by regular discourse patterns, it is open and flexible rather than fixed or immutable and reflects the interplay of substance, form, context, and intention. (1994: 349)

How do we assist students to adapt, negotiate and revise the genres they know – and to experiment with those they do not know but must process or produce? How do we help students to work with the knowledge that 'text reconstructs ... a world' (Kress 1995: 51), and that rhetorical context causes texts to differ? These are particularly difficult questions as they relate to novice university students in the United States, since many have not yet defi-nitely fixed upon a major where genres may be more well defined and identi-fiable. As Dudley-Evans (2002) points out, most undergraduate papers that students are assigned are 'problematic' in that they are not well defined, or well modeled, by faculty.

What can we do for these first-year students, particularly since they are immediately responsible for textual and intertextual modeling for the secondary school students in their service learning program? After consider-able discussion with the secondary school teachers with whom we were working, we decided to adapt an available, if somewhat ill-defined, 'design of meaning', the Report of Information (RI), from the Genre Studies Curriculum of the San Diego City Schools. Our decision was intended to demonstrate to students at both high-school and university levels how a report of information, frequently called a 'Research Paper'[2] at the university level, might be constructed as a highly intertextual and multi-modal genre in anthropology: how the values, research questions, data collection, and construction of product are influenced by disciplinary practices.

Here, we had considerable assistance from the anthropology instructor who co-constructed the RI assignment in cooperation with the literacy instructors at both sites. One essential element of this construction was a discussion with the anthropologist about what is valued in texts. She immedi-ately responded to our queries by noting how important decisions about, and discussions of, *methodology*, are in her discipline, particularly considering the current debate about current methodological practices (see Clifford 1986). We may have devoted more time to the methodology section of the RI paper than all other sections: asking students to report in detail about how they discovered aspects of their own families' histories and cultures for their first paper; how they approached the interview at the high schools; how they attempted to incorporate their families' discourses with the interviews with the secondary school students and the other texts from which they drew. Since students had had little or no experience with methodology sections outside of the hard sciences, it was rather difficult to convince them of the importance of reporting their procedures.

One of our chief responsibilities, then, was to co-design a report of infor-mation task that took on some of the social practices and values in anthro-pology and provided sufficient academic scaffolding so that our students, and even the 9th graders, could complete a paper in that genre, and could represent that paper visually and orally to others.

These are some of the decisions we made, seemingly simple, but often representing disconcerting moves away from the classic Five Paragraph Essay, the memorized writing template:

1. *Text structure.* The RI would have sections and headings following the IMRD (Introduction, Methodology, Results, Discussion) format common to the sciences and social sciences. This seems like a simple move; however, though our students read textbooks with headings, they had never subsumed their own written text under headings before because even their high school science teachers tended to follow the lead of the language arts instructors, trained in literature.
2. *Writing from varied sources.* Achieving successful intertextuality, especially the use of sources, is probably the most common academic challenge that students face in university environments (see Carson *et al.* 1992). This RI project was multi-modal in that it required drawing from interviews and texts of the students' own families, interviews with student partners in the secondary schools, quotes from anthropology and literacy textbooks, and, in several cases, Websites. One essential aspect of the Web searches was the development of what our university system calls 'information competence': the ability not only to find a relevant site but to evaluate the material from that site in terms of bias, or point of view. Although we were not entirely successful in convincing students that they could accept neither a written nor Web text as truth, with the help of the library, we were able to at least give them pause – and provide tools for discovering the origins of sites from which they drew. Fairclough (1989) refers to chains of texts that contribute to a 'new text'; there was no question that this chaining, this intertextuality, was an important element in the production of a complex final product.
3. *Argumentation.* Because we were using a common research paper format, the 'thesis' was to appear in the discussion section, and it would have to be hedged (see e.g. Hyland 1998a) in ways that would indicate the students' limited data set. Those who operate outside of American English essay contexts may not understand how difficult it is to encourage students to break their belief that they have to 'prove' a thesis stated in the introduction – but it *is* difficult!

Hedging, of course, brought us to the issue of audience, of understanding the ways in which they can 'talk' to instructors and peers about their findings.

4. *Scaffolding*. Because this IMRD paper, with a long methodology section, was so foreign (even the students' research papers had looked like essays in high school!), we designed a scaffolding program within the curriculum, one that required students to prepare a paper plan based upon the IMRD format, complete a thorough methodology section, complete the data analysis and discussion, and finally, write several drafts of the paper.

This was a long, slow process, one that required intensive one-to-one conferencing – and a great deal of convincing on our part that all this effort was worth it. Most of the convincing focused on the 'student as researcher' angle (see Johns 1997): that students would be required to complete different types of research in the university and in their jobs, and we were helping them to develop the types of questions to ask not only about the research but about the texts that reported it. For the untutored student, the most common question for a faculty member about an assigned paper is 'What do you want?' We helped them to ask more pointed, and more acceptable, questions such as: 'What does a successful paper look like?', 'What is important in a paper in your discipline?', 'What referencing style do you want us to use?', 'How will the paper be graded?', 'What kinds of research questions are appropriate?', 'What sources should we use?'.

Multi-modal literacies

Perhaps the most successful aspect of the RI task was the exhibition that our diverse students launched for the students at the secondary school. In groups, they prepared visual representations of their RI papers on trifolds, some of which required 'sampling' from the Web. Then they reported orally on their work to the younger students in an exhibition in the secondary school library.

One of the major problems in our schooling at every level in the United States is the widespread use of inappropriate testing – usually a single measure – to assess students' literacy levels and preparation. The visual and oral components of the RI project, which were also assessed by their instructors, provided for students opportunities to demonstrate abilities that are seldom tested. What we found, not surprisingly, is that many students are much more apt as speakers, presenters, and visual learners, than they are as traditional writers.

Critical framing

One of the major aspects of our RI project was student reflection: upon their reading and writing processes, upon difficulties with gathering data, upon the cultures of their families, upon the attitudes and responses of their high school student interviewees/mentees, and upon the cultures of their classrooms and the university. At every step – after their first 'family' paper, after their visits to·the high school, after certain drafts of the paper, after completing their final RI paper – students were asked to critically frame their experiences with literacies and cultures and to make suggestions for improving the project. A number of students made suggestions for how we might train them to be better ethnographic interviewers, how the secondary school teachers should prepare their students, the timing of the scaffolding sub-tasks, and readings that were either helpful or unhelpful. And, at the end of the semester, we asked for a comment on what they had learned about the discipline of anthropology and the designs of meaning available. Here is a comment from Josh on these topics:

> I learned how anthropologists gather information (their methods). I learned how different cultures have different rules, and in anthropology, one must respect these rules. I learned how cultures may differ, but judging these would be ethnocentric. And cultures change through migration and coming into contact with other cultures.

Or, when commenting on her own culture, Maricela said:

> I never realized that some of the things I 'naturally' do seem very strange to other people ... I have begun to look at the deeper meaning of cultures.

But perhaps the most insightful, and critical comment, was by Jose:

> What I learned is that we can study our families like insects. We can categorize them as 'patrilineal' and stuff. I don't know whether I like studying my family objectively, and I'm sure that my parents wouldn't like it!

Transformed practice

Could our students take what they had learned and negotiate and transform it? Our anecdotal evidence from 18 years of this experience gives us hope. And our students in the Fall 2000 class kept our optimism alive. Sia, a

Cambodian-American student who is devoted to returning to his roots through the Cambodian Buddhist Association, is also determined to become biliterate, to develop a repertoire of abilities that will enable him to be an economic leader in his own community and a spokesperson for that community within this country. About his experience, he said:

> This is the first class that taught me to take academic writing seriously. For now, I am still in the stage of learning to become a fluent academic writer. But I like academic writing because I like seeing the outcome of my work and my improvements ... After this class, I will concentrate hard on understanding ways of writing ... Many students like me, who are bicultural and come from inner-city schools, have disadvantages. I am proud to know that I am improving and can succeed.

And the real optimist, Maricela:

> I enjoyed these classes very much, and I would like to say that I am on my way to learning all I need to know!

Conclusion

How does Tony's work fit into this discussion? I would argue that the particular strengths of his long succession of publications, many written with colleagues, is his ability to grasp and teach the essence of a genre or task, the essential skills and understandings that will enable students to take what they know, write (or read) a text, and apply this knowledge to texts within a discipline or to other textual experiences. Because I am a teacher of novice undergraduates, I am particularly impressed with Tony's ability to create a curriculum for the 'Academic Essay', which, like many genres in undergraduate curricula, is vague and amorphous. Thus, his discussion (2002) of this topic may be most relevant to the 'transformed practice' issue discussed in this paper. This again demonstrates that Tony can reduce complex textual issues to manageable ones for the classroom, yet not fall into the trap of creating templates or oversimplifying. For those of us in ESP, it has been our good fortune to follow the EAP curricular development led by Tony and his colleagues at Birmingham over the years.

A personal note

I first 'met' Tony when we co-wrote a paper electronically for the *TESOL Quarterly* (Johns and Dudley-Evans 1993). We actually met at the TESOL

Conferences – and an ESP conference in Tunisia – that followed. Of course, it was a delight working with him on *English for Specific Purposes*, to which he devoted his editorial skills for several years. Though I am happy that he will be better able to pursue one of his major passions, jazz, when he retires, I will miss our dinners and our shared colloquia at conferences, and I hope that there will be other venues in which to continue our friendship.

Notes

1. Ours is one of the many public universities that uses a single test to assess students' language abilities. Those students from racially-isolated and under-served high schools who do not have direct training for the examination tend to fail in large numbers. This means that if they are accepted into university, they are placed in remedial classes with other low-income students of color. At SDSU, they are given two semesters to complete their remedial requirement through course enrollment and test completion.
2. 'Research paper' is also an ill-defined genre in university. Larsen (1982) argues that Research can inform virtually any writing or speaking if the author wishes it to do so; there is nothing of substance or content that differentiates one paper that draws on data from outside the author's own self from another such paper - nothing that can enable one to say that this paper is a 'research paper' and that paper is not... I would assert therefore that the so-called 'research paper', as a generic, cross-disciplinary term, has no conceptual or substantive identity. (p. 813)

Descriptions or explanations? Some methodological issues in Contrastive Rhetoric

Anna Mauranen

Contrastive Rhetoric (CR) is a typical field in applied linguistics in that it has arisen from practical observation in the context usually taken to be the core of applied linguistics, or even 'linguistics applied': second language teaching. In this way, CR has not had any obvious theoretical foundation, nor has it arisen from a methodological problem to be solved. This origin is present in the field even now that it has become quite established – the theorising that there is has arisen from the need to explain the findings, and the research that has been carried out has made use of a number of methods and methodological emphases, none of which is unique to CR.

In recent years there have been demands, if not downright for more theory in CR, at least for new types of description which also bring cultural and linguistic aspects into a principled relationship. The point has been raised by a number of scholars that we need 'thicker' descriptions of texts in the Geertzian sense (e.g. Huckin 1997; Swales 1998). In the same vein, demands for 'explanation' have been made (e.g. Melander 1996; Scollon 1997) which bear close affinity to the approach to explanation adopted in Critical Discourse Analysis (e.g. Fairclough 1992a, 1995), and also resemble attempts in other disciplines to make sense of cultural comparisons of scientific practice (e.g. Harwood 1995). In what follows, I shall look into some of these demands and criticisms and assess their value for moving CR onwards, particularly in the context of academic writing.

A case study of Contrastive Rhetoric

Let me start by presenting an example of a study in Contrastive Rhetoric for illustration. This is my own research (Mauranen 1993) concerning rhetorical differences in the academic texts written by Finnish and Anglo-American researchers. I analysed the use of text reflexivity, or metadiscourse, and noticed that Finnish writers used considerably less of it than corresponding Anglo-American writers. In addition, I found that in terms of overall text organisation, Finnish writers tended to place their main point towards the end of the text, as opposed to Anglo-Americans who preferred an early expression of the main point. Finns also had a tendency to leave the main point implicit, whereas Anglo-Americans seemed to repeat it rather than leave it unsaid. Finally, Finnish writers made proportionally fewer text references, and used the proximity-inducing deictic 'this' more rarely than their Anglo-American colleagues.

From findings like these, it seemed reasonable to conclude that the two rhetorical styles made very different demands on the reader, thereby also writing a different reader into the texts. Finnish writers seemed to expect a good deal more inferencing on the reader's part, and thus make the reader more responsible for the successful achievement of communication than an Anglo-American writer would appear to do (cf. Hinds's 1987 distinction between 'reader-responsible' and 'writer-responsible' cultures). We might also say that the reader written into a Finnish text is much more patient than the one written into an Anglo-American text, the Finn's reader having to wait for the main import of the text to emerge gradually.

The different reader–writer constructions seemed to derive from different traditions of textual etiquette or politeness. While a Finnish writer wishes to show respect for the reader's intelligence and knowledge, and therefore avoid stating the obvious, the Anglo-American writer respects the reader's time and effort, trying to make the text easily palatable. The general rhetorical styles could then be described as 'implicit' and 'explicit', or, perhaps, from a different perspective, 'poetic' and 'marketing'. The poetic style of Finns would then be understood as a way of leaving things unsaid so as to leave plenty of space for the reader's interpretative skills, and contrasted with the marketing, even didactic, fashion in which Anglo-Americans provide clear guidance for their readers throughout the text.

The above was in some ways a typical CR study. For instance, it dealt with academic texts, looked at whole texts, utilised textlinguistic methods, and compared two cultures, one of which was the broadly defined Anglo-American culture, the dominant culture in today's world. How does such a study fare in terms of description and explanation?

I would first like to relate it to Kaplan's classic study (1966/1972), which set off the whole movement of CR and presented the culture-specific schemata (his 'doodles' as they are fondly known in the profession), representing the paragraph structure in schoolchildren's writing.

Both investigations describe a sample of texts representing a narrowly delimited domain of writing (schoolchildren's compositions and research reports), where the implied causal explanation of textual variation is the writer's cultural origin. In both, systematic differences in textual features can be related to the writer's background culture. In neither is there any serious attempt to explore other elements of the source cultures in order to provide a causal link from text-external conditions to the culture-specific textual observations. In Kaplan's case this was hardly feasible as there were a number of cultures involved and the essential question concerned the connection between cultural background and textual variation. In my case it would have been possible to explore at least the Finnish source culture from non-textual angles as well, but I chose a different path, one of several textual variables in order to strengthen the plausibility of the textual interpretation itself. I shall return to this below, but let me just point out here that apart from making use of several text features, my research diverged from Kaplan's by including data written in the writers' native languages as well as L2 data from the Finns. However, there are ways in which my study is like Kaplan's and I think similar objections can be raised against both.

Widening the horizon

Recently there have been several calls for a more context-sensitive approach to textual analysis of all kinds – including cultural comparisons. In the field of academic writing, Swedish scholars like Gunnarsson (1996) and Melander (1996) have been advocating this, and similarly in the United States, for example Huckin (1997) and Scollon (1997). This is very much in line with the demand for 'thicker' descriptions in genre studies (e.g. Swales 1996,1998), and also to the demands for explanation in Critical Discourse Analysis (e.g. Fairclough 1992a, 1995). What unites these approaches is their emphasis on the social contexts of texts, reflecting the Firthian notion of 'context of situation'. Texts are produced and consumed as part of the text-external social world, which crucially participates in the construction of meaning and values by the texts. From these premises the conclusion is that in order to arrive at an explanation of why texts are the way they are, it is necessary to draw on the social contexts where they occur.

At a general level, this could be taken to imply that texts cannot be used for drawing cultural or social conclusions without independent research into their social determinants. This does not set the investigation of cultural rhetoric apart from any other text research, except for perhaps specifying our explanandum as observations, as descriptions of differences of texts in two cultures, which must find the explanans from the two cultures.

Turning to more specific demands for explaining cultural phenomena, it is useful first to consider a clear and systematic presentation of the problem in a field closely related to academic writing, namely intellectual history.

Harwood (1995) evokes the concept of 'style' in the analysis of cultural patterns of scientific thought. He maintains that in order to define a style, one's analysis must be comparative on two dimensions, the 'vertical' and the 'horizontal' (Harwood 1995: 32). The analysis is vertical if recurring elements (however defined) can be found in various sectors of a given social group's cultural production. So for instance in the field of cultural production we should expect repeated patterns along the different domains of group x, and similarly along the cultural products of group y:

group x   *group y*

POTTERY   pottery
MYTH   myth
MUSIC   music

Harwood maintains that the analysis must at the same time be horizontally comparative in the sense that those recurrent elements must also be 'distinctive'; that is, they must distinguish one group's culture from another's. If we do not perform both comparisons, we can only make statements like 'culture x has similarities in its pottery, mythology and music', or that 'pottery in cultures x and y are different' – but we cannot talk about 'style'. Harwood thus argues that 'The analytical value of "style" as a concept is that it alerts us, not merely to cultural differences, but to cases where such differences are *patterned*' (1995: 33). For him, the most interesting cases are those where the assumptions underlying a given domain, say, science, also recur in other cultural sectors:

group x	*group y*
SCIENCES	sciences
POLITICAL THOUGHT	political thought
POETRY	poetry

In Harwood's view, it is instances of these kinds which make it possible to explore connections between scientists' work and their social or cultural context (Harwood 1995: 33).

Closer to our own field, Scollon (1997) has voiced comparable demands. He appeals to Panofsky's classic essay on Gothic architecture from the early 1950s, and demands of research in CR that it look beyond the writing of students and into structures of architecture, music, advertising, etc.

The vertical dimension

Taking the vertical dimension on board thus requires that we find 'explanation' for text patterns in the rest of the culture; that is, in those domains of culture that are not the one currently investigated. However, the idea is not unproblematic, as it implies a causal type of relationship from culture to text, and in so doing, sets up a dichotomy between text and 'culture'. But if we take up a number of different cultural domains, one at a time, and use the same method with each (this is indeed done or required in other fields too), we notice that whichever we take up, the others are supposed to 'explain' it. So, shifting our attention to art history, text patterns can be an explanans, but looking back at text, they switch roles, and texts constitute an explanandum again. This does not make much sense: if there is a causal relationship, it seems to change places arbitrarily. Clearly, all these various aspects, including texts, constitute culture, and if we can observe systematic differences in the textual practices of different cultural formations, we can say that these constitute cultural differences in a relevant sense. Since it is not possible to postulate causal relations between different cultural products, let alone between some underlying principle, be it a 'national spirit' or whatever, and features observed in the cultural products, the reasonable goal for comparing cultural products is understanding, not explanation in a causal sense. One might perhaps argue that the cultural style thus arrived at enables 'subsumptive' explanations (see, e.g. Chesterman 2000), but this would take us rather far from a causal 'why' question. Moreover, such an interpretation is not explicitly offered by Harwood, nor is this line of thought pursued by any of the scholars demanding explanations in contrastive academic rhetoric.

Another problematic assumption relates to the concept of 'a culture', specifically cultural demarcation lines: what are we to include in 'a culture' if such diverse phenomena as, say, pottery and science are brought together as evidence of some common denominator that we are in search of? Implicitly, such a model requires a priori knowledge of what the culture is – for instance a given national culture. The point is that by combining widely different phenomena and expecting them to support an idea of a particular style or mentality, it becomes difficult to question the cultural formations that have conventionally been constructed for us, such as the European ideology of the nation state for example.

Yet, clearly, cultural units tend to have fluid boundaries, which need not coincide in different domains (say, sports and music) or be co-extensive with nation states. If rhetorical discoveries give rise to hypotheses such as a greater need for explicitness in more spread-out and heterogeneous cultural formations than in more isolated or homogeneous ones, the natural point of comparison would seem to be formations of the predicted types, not necessarily national cultures, let alone their cultural products from non-textual domains.

While text-external social structures undoubtedly participate in setting the terms for producing and consuming texts, there is no necessary connection in a given culture between the conditions for making pottery and the conditions for writing news articles or academic papers. For instance Finnish modernist architects were much influenced by certain Italian traditions in the first half of the 20th century, while influences on academic texts in the same period came from first Germany and after the Second World War from the US. Similarly, many of the features I found in the rhetorical study summarised above are well known in northern Europe – sometimes clearly variants of German intellectual style, or the Humboldtian university ideal. End-weight and fact-based argumentation are familiar in large areas in this part of the world (see for example many studies in Duszak 1997, and Ventola and Mauranen 1996). Yet, implicitness with regard to metatext or personal references does not quite seem to coincide with these two features, so that metatext, for example, is used quite extensively by Germans, and personal references by Swedes (Bäcklund 1998), while Finns remain low on both.

With these caveats in mind, I would like to move on to the more constructive contribution that Harwood's vertical dimension makes to CR research. It seems to me that its real value could be in providing methodological support (and criticism) for culture-related claims about academic writing styles which have very often been based on single genres (typical examples would be studies reported in Purves 1988). Claims based on individual genres or otherwise very limited kinds of writing can be said to remain comparative in the horizontal sense only, which amounts to saying that there are cultural differences, but fails to relate these differences to a definable 'style' displaying significant patterning within its culture.

I would like to suggest, therefore, that academic CR is in need of much more vertical analysis. I am sure that a considerable body of research already exists which could be brought together to deepen our notions of particular writing cultures. For instance, to support my conclusions about the Finnish vs Anglo-American writing culture I can refer to other scholars' results from different textual domains. Thus, the Finnish implicitness in the sense of lack of a clearly identifiable point has been recognised in research grant proposals (Connor and Mauranen 1999), newspaper editorials (Tirkkonen-Condit 1996) and in schoolchildren's compositions (Ingberg 1987; Lindeberg 1988) – that is, mainly argumentative genres. The same implicitness in the sense of indirectness, for example avoiding direct personal reference, has been noticed likewise in grant proposals, in cosmetics brochures (Paasikivi 1995) and self-help literature (Härmä 1994) among other things – that is, in promotional genres. Finally, the tendency to place important points towards the end of the text has been noted in editorials, school essays, and less systematically in other argumentative genres (e.g. Isaksson-Wikberg 1999).

A vertical analysis can also provide a broader understanding of the extension, limits and variability of an observed writing style. As Scollon (1997: 353) points out:

> A very broad range of studies have shown that no language or culture can be reduced to one or two diagrammatic structures that might be applied across the board from internal cognitive schema to paragraph structure, whether these might fly under the flags of *circular, direct, indirect, zigzag, inductive,* or *deductive* .

So although we have indications of intra-cultural coherence over genres, there are counterexamples as well – so to me at least it seems that Anglo-American advertising is a discourse domain which is developing towards increasing implicitness, not explicitness.

The horizontal dimension

Cultural comparisons by definition take place along the horizontal dimension, which would therefore appear to be a much more straightforward case. What complicates matters, however, is that genres or discourses are not unproblematically comparable across cultural boundaries. Scollon (1997), for instance, points out that what is an essay in one culture may be a poem in another. Such an observation is not new – indeed it is a classic problem for translation studies. A systematic and useful conceptualisation of the issues involved is what is known as 'polysystem theory' (Even-Zohar 1990; Toury 1995). Briefly, the idea is that cultures are seen as networks of semiotic and linguistic systems, with literary systems comprising the totality of literary texts in a culture. The systems are complex, consisting of many subsystems, and can thus be regarded as systems of systems, or 'polysystems'. Translations for instance constitute a subsystem of their own, but for a translation to be accepted as an academic translation in a target culture, it needs to be accepted as a translation, as well as an academic text.

Since the polysystems of different cultures are not identical, the status of a given text may change as a result of translation, i.e. the text may enter a different polysystem. An inevitable status change follows from the mere fact of translation itself: a translation is part of the system of translated texts in the target culture, which it was not in the source culture. Other genres than literary can be considered in a similar manner. Texts bearing the same or similar labels in seemingly comparable (sub-)cultures can be part of different genre systems, or textual polysystems – so for instance genres like 'seminar' or even 'lecture' may have different definitions and relative positions in undergraduate studies in different, even if superficially similar, university cultures (Mauranen 1994). Polysystem theory, then, focuses on intertextual relationships at the cultural level, in this way embracing Harwood's vertical dimension, and since it originates in translational considerations, its point of departure is inevitably also horizontal.

Contrastive rhetoric, like many other areas of contrastive or comparative studies, typically investigates a pair of cultures, which leads to an emphasis on their differences at the expense of their similarities. This leads easily (though understandably) to simplifications, which may construct simplified, even stereotypical and static notions of the cultures concerned, even though it is in principle well known that cultures are both internally heterogeneous and constantly exchanging influences. A healthy antidote to such tendencies may from a contemporary perspective perhaps be the study of globalisation, focusing as it does on the convergence of discourses across cultures. Since local features are built into the design of contrastive rhetorical studies, they are not likely to surrender to the most extreme globalisation hypotheses. Contrastive rhetoric may constitute a good test-bed for the concept of 'glocalisation' (Robertson 1995), which in turn can be a fruitful notion for CR (an example from political discourses of the complex relations between global and local tendencies is Fairclough and Mauranen 1997). Both globalisation and glocalisation are notions borrowed from social sciences, which implies a close connection between research into social and economic systems on the one hand and linguistic and textual (poly)systems on the other. Nevertheless, direct causal relations cannot be expected – globalisation in the economic and social spheres may accelerate cultural and linguistic contacts, but will not determine which textual or linguistic features will transfer. By observing the actual influences we can hope to make sense of them in their social contexts – that is, understand them – but this does not amount to causal predictions or explanations.

Glocalisation is based on the realisation that the universal, or the general, and the local are mutually defining, and they receive their meanings and identities from each other. Local identities arise from intercultural encounters, brought about or accelerated by globalisation. And the local is also global: for instance, the originally European notion of a nation state, which is a prototypical example of localised identity, has spread around the world with its associated set of concepts which remain astonishingly similar – thus the discourses of locality have become global.

Glocalisation also reflects the conceptualisation of cultures as hybrid phenomena in themselves. The notion of hybridisation is helpful in capturing phenomena like 'third cultures', such as world music. Hybridness and thirdness in texts has also been recognised in translation theory. Frawley (1984) talks about translation as 'the third code' arising from the interaction of a source language and a target language, Trosborg (1996) about translations as 'hybrid texts'. This notion of thirdness could be usefully introduced in CR research. It is applicable in any domain where cultures, languages and texts come in contact – the knowledge and practices of bilinguals or foreign language learners can be seen in terms of a hybrid 'third', and by the same logic also texts produced at cultural boundaries, as for instance academic texts typically are.

For the actual study of textual representations of thirdness or glocalisation, linguistic methods, specifically text analytical of various kinds, continue to be the most relevant tools. A multidimensional text analytical approach to a set of texts can be fruitfully extended to the vertical dimension of genre polysystems in the cultural formations under study. The relevant demarcation lines that cultures are divided along are less and less likely to be confined to the nation state – ensured by accelerated glocalisation. Text-external cultural divides can be made in different ways, whose relevance is eventually determined by integrating findings from text analyses and socio-economic and cultural studies.

Texts in such an integrative approach are not solely the explanandum, seeking confirmation or explanation from that which is external to them. The characteristics of texts themselves become increasingly important indicators of cultural boundaries and influences as other boundary markers shift or weaken. Similarly, the participation by individuals in certain rhetorical practices plays an increasingly important role in constituting their cultural membership. Capturing this is fundamentally a matter of textual description, whose goal is understanding texts and cultures rather than explaining them.

Conclusion

I have been arguing that CR is in need of methodological development, which has not been a very strong point in its history, given that it has originated in fundamentally applied considerations. Clearly, one of the domains where CR has continued to attract interest has been academic writing at all levels, and there is no obvious end to this in sight, as academic texts continue to be written in a variety of cultural contexts, and at the same time they increasingly interact with texts from other cultural contexts.

I am suggesting that CR explore the vertical as well as the horizontal dimension of culturally situated texts. If we want to make statements concerning given writing cultures, we need to bring together genres which are interrelated in a principled way, and to show that the features we want to highlight as typical of the culture are indeed both recurrent internally and distinctive externally. It is particularly valuable to relate academic texts to other kinds of texts, or textual polysystems, including spoken texts, which in academic settings are only now beginning to attract wider interest.

A fundamental point is to keep in mind that texts are in themselves one of the main keys to understanding a culture. Texts as cultural products act out relevant social relationships within the culture, and in this way provide keys to understanding themselves as well as other aspects of the culture. The explanation derived from analysing different rhetorical aspects of the same texts is immanent, as it were. There is no outside causal force in the same culture that would require the use of rhetorical indirectness, or implicitness, for example. We can of course hypothesise that there is a greater demand for greater explicitness in cultures which are more heterogeneous and cannot expect as much shared knowledge as in more insulated cultures. But the issue is more complex: while, for instance, implicitness characterises Finns in the use of metatext or discourse markers, in terms of providing numerous and detailed facts in text they could more relevantly be deemed over-explicit.

Investigating text systems requires considerations of the social systems they are part of, as many scholars have suggested. Text-external social structures are crucial for understanding why certain kinds of texts do not exist, for example, or why large numbers of legal or religious texts are produced. Micro-level social structures can perhaps be best captured with ethnographic approaches, which have not really reached contrastive studies yet. But this does not imply postulating simple (causal) relationships between text and culture – or even text systems and cultures. One way of avoiding this (at the macro level) is to take on board issues of glocalisation and hybridisation. It is, however, excessively sanguine to believe that in this way, or any other, we should understand texts 'fully'. The possibilities for analysis are in principle infinite. What I want to emphasise is that the social context of a text improves understanding rather than explanation.

For academic texts, globalisation has meant an increasing need for intercultural communication and understanding, even though the academic world has been international for much longer than the current wave of globalisation. It is in the interests of the pursuit of science and scholarship to promote intercultural understanding in order to maintain fairness, as well as in order to make use of the 'hybrid vigour' of text and thinking arising from academic traditions in contact. For both of these reasons it is important that editors of academic journals understand cultural variation in texts, and that those involved in teaching English for academics all over the world have a similar understanding. Moreover, a major challenge ahead for the latter group lies in developing ways of teaching academic writing which are widely accessible but not constrained by any one restricted cultural norm such as the Anglo-American.

From evidence to conclusion: the case of 'indicate that'

Tim Johns

In 1991 Tony Dudley-Evans and I decided that it would be good for the souls of those of us in the English for Overseas Students Unit to undertake some joint research into the English of scientific research papers, since this is one of the main genres where we try to help our students. Tony had already organised the sampling and scanning of a corpus of 434,000 words from the high-prestige research journal *Nature* comprising articles and letters to *Nature*, and we concentrated on examination and analysis of that material. In the event, our weekly Wednesday afternoon meetings were very enjoyable and proved excellent as a way of bonding old and new members of the unit, but somehow we never got round to our original intention of publishing the results of our efforts. As both Tony and I are now taking retirement from the unit (since renamed the English for International Students Unit) this may be an appropriate occasion to rescue, reconsider and expand upon a small piece of work done for one of those Wednesday afternoon sessions ten years ago.

As one of my contributions I offered to look at the main verbs followed by *that*-clauses in the data, with the results presented in Figure 1. (For a more detailed analysis see http://web.bham.ac.uk/johnstf/5_verbs.htm).

The two most striking features of these results both concern the verb **indicate**. Firstly, in these data it is in this syntactic context by far the commonest verb. This contrasts sharply with its frequency in other genres of English: in a comparable corpus of texts from the newspaper the *Guardian*, **indicate** comes in 65th place among the verbs followed by *that*-clauses. This striking difference forms a strong prima facie argument that the verb has a special and privileged communicative role in the *Nature* texts.

The other striking feature of **indicate** is in its selection of subjects. The starting-point here is the observation that of these five verbs, only one – **find** – is in these texts used exclusively with human subjects. Three of the other first five verbs (**show**, **suggest** and **demonstrate**) are in this context more often used with non-human than with human subjects, their essential

	indicate	show	suggest	find	demonstrate	Total
In **finite clause**	**424**	**364**	**182**	**99**	**88**	**1157**
• active	423	343	159	93	82	1100
• passive	1	21	23	6	8	57
In **-ing clause**	**121**	**19**	**25**	**0**	**11**	**176**
Infinitive	**2**	**9**	**3**	**1**	**10**	**25**
Nominalisations (e.g. indication)	10	0	11	22	6	49
Total	*557*	*392*	*221*	*122*	*115*	*1407*
Human subject	1	59	34	93	16	203
Non-human subject	422	284	125	0	66	897
• analysis/analyses	14	27	1	0	2	44
• data	41	30	7	0	3	81
• experiment(s)	15	18	1	0	5	39
• observation(s)	12	3	6	0	2	23
• result(s)	74	30	12	0	11	127
• study/studies	16	24	2	0	16	58
• (other)	257	162	95	0	27	511
Intensifiers	**17**	**7**	**8**	**0**	**2**	**34**
• clearly	4	7	0	0	2	13
• strongly	13	0	8	0	0	21
May/might in *that*-**clause**	**47**	**4**	**27**	**0**	**1**	**79**

Figure 1 Syntactic envirinment of 5 verbs in *Nature*

function being to link experimental or observational evidence (**results, data, analysis**, etc.) to conclusions (in the *that*-clause). For example:

Evidence	*Link*	*Conclusion*
Our results from the Galicia margin	indicate that	the seismic crust beneath may include mantle material transformed into serpentine by syn-rift hydrothermal energy.
These data	show that	most (80-100%) of the neurons that survive retrograde degeneration are GABA-ergic displaced amacrine cells.
There is some evidence, however, that	suggests that	the precursors are in fact biologically refractory.
These results	demonstrate that	the initial visualisation of glomeruli in the living animal is both complete and reliable.

From that point of view **indicate** stands apart, as almost *all* its subjects in the *Nature* texts are non-human; in the *Guardian*, by contrast, 35 per cent of the examples of this verb in this structure have human subjects.

Given that there is immediate evidence for a specialised function of **indicate** in the data, the question remains what that function might be. In particular, does its meaning signal that the conclusion to be drawn from the evidence is certain (cf. **show, demonstrate**) or that it has a degree of uncertainty (cf. **suggest**)? To use a recently popular concept, does it represent a degree of hedging on the part of the writer (see for example Hyland 1998a)? Two pieces of evidence from the extended context in which **indicate** is used are relevant here. The first relates to the co-occurrence of adverbial intensifiers. The verbs **show** and **demonstrate** show nine examples of the intensifier **clearly** but none of the intensifier **strongly**; **suggest** on the other hand shows eight examples of **strongly** but none of **clearly**. With **indicate** there are 13 **strongly**s and four **clearly**s, which seems to place it in the **suggest** camp, though not unambiguously so.

The second feature of the extended context that comes into play is the marking of modality in the *that*-clause. Note that the meaning of **suggest** makes the sense of the following (invented) sentences virtually identical:

These results suggest that X is Y.
These results suggest that X may be Y.

I have been informed by the current executive editor of *Nature* that the style of the journal is to avoid this redundant use of **may** in *that*-causes after **suggest**. Nevertheless, the presence of **may** or **might** acts as a useful diagnostic tool as to the meaning of the link verb. In these data, **may** or **might** gives additional marking of uncertainty in 12 per cent of the *that*-clauses after **suggest**. By contrast, only 1 per cent of *that*-clauses after **show** and **demonstrate**, and none of those after **find**, contain a **may** or a **might**. With 8 per cent of *that*-clauses after **indicate** containing a **may** or a **might,** further evidence is provided that places that verb with **suggest** rather than with **show** or **demonstrate**.

Thus far did we get in 1991. At the time it occurred to me that it would be useful to discover what the writers of papers for *Nature* themselves thought was the meaning of this verb. Since then, it has become the custom for papers in *Nature* to carry an e-mail address for any queries related to the work reported. Clearly the primary intention was not that the authors should be quizzed on their discourse, but this was too good an opportunity to miss to obtain some supplementary evidence as to the meaning of this verb. Accordingly, I contacted by e-mail the authors of some 100 papers published in 1999 and 2000, apologising for the impudence of my enquiry, and asking whether for them, 'indicate' was closer in meaning to 'show/demonstrate' or to 'suggest', and for any other information which might be useful, for example whether they particularly favoured or avoided the use of this word. Expecting to be ignored by the majority of those to whom I wrote, I was surprised and delighted that over 60 per cent took the trouble to reply, many of them with extensive comments, on which I draw below. Quite a few assured me that in their opinion my query was worth making, touching as it does on the central question of how much certainty is to be attached to the writer's conclusions. For example:

This is a reasonable question …

Thankyou for your question – it touches on a critical issue in science.

It is a good question. I am very mindful of the exact phrasing I use when discussing the conclusions or implications of my observations. Not all scientists are so rigorous in choosing their wording.

As to the replies, most respondents placed **indicate** somewhere between **suggest** and **show/demonstrate**. The expected skew towards **suggest** failed, however to materialise, with half of the replies placing **indicate** nearer **suggest** and half placing it nearer **show/demonstrate**. One reply suggested that I might have obtained more interesting results by asking respondents to score the verbs on a point scale. Dovie Wylie at Palo Alto was kind enough to write to me about some unpublished research in which she had adopted such a strategy. She had asked 25 informants to score ten verbs from the point of view of the degree of certainty they implied. While she obtained considerable agreement on ratings for verbs at the top end of the scale (**show, demonstrate** and **reveal**), there was a large degree of spread for verbs such as **suggest** and **indicate**.

The query led some respondents to re-examine their own usage of the word in the paper I had found in *Nature*. One discovered that he had used

indicate six times, each time with the meaning of **show/demonstrate**. Another found seven instances in his paper, of which two were used with the meaning of 'show/demonstrate' and five with the meaning of 'suggest'. He also noted that he had in four instances used adverbial clues to show which meaning was intended: 'clearly' for **show/demonstrate** and 'probably' for **suggest**.

Other respondents claimed that the choice between these verbs is not simply a matter of certainty but (also) involved the nature of the conclusion reached. For example, one said that he used **show/demonstrate** 'with reference to data' (e.g. 'We show that protein X has a certain location in the cell') and **suggest/indicate** for a 'conclusion from data or to propose a model' (e.g. 'These data indicate that protein X is required for function Y'). Re-examination of the data failed, however, to show evidence for this distinction. Others linked the choice to particular subject areas. One suggested that the term **indicate** is used more frequently in experimental physics than in theoretical physics, while another said that for structural biologists **indicate** is close to **demonstrate** since they have a picture at atomic level to help support their conclusions. Again, it was difficult to support these claims from the data.

In some of the most interesting replies to my query their authors took the time and trouble to outline a view of the nature of science against which it must be considered. Many respondents, for example, emphasised the conditionality of all science; that:

> ... to a working scientist – the good ones at least – everything is conditional i.e. always at least partly wrong.

while one linked that conditionality to the preference for verbs such as **indicate**:

> ... uncertainty is at the heart of all scientific endeavour, and it is the consciousness of this uncertainty that leads many scientists to favour words like 'indicate' or 'suggest' rather than 'show', 'demonstrate', or 'prove'. These word choices represent the thoughtful scientist's awareness that he or she may be reaching conclusions that will later prove to be flawed, because the starting assumptions were flawed ... (they) reflect a scientist's fundamental approach to experimental elucidation of the workings of the world. Scientists must be prepared to disregard accepted 'truths' if they obtain data that invalidate these truths ...

Others emphasised the high level of conditionality and uncertainty inherent in their own subjects – for example in what may be termed the 'Human Survival Sciences'. The reply of one respondent developed this theme in such an interesting way that it is worth quoting *in extenso*:

> When I discuss global climate change and responses of the earth system to those changes, I try to keep in mind that I am dealing with high levels of uncertainty that will not be bounded any time soon. In a bigger view, paradigms are constantly being broken and new ones created. What was 'demonstrated' last year was recently shown to be incorrect. For these reasons, I lean to the 'indicate' side of the confidence scale, especially when discussing ecological systems where many variables are operating, some of which are unknown or interact in ways that cannot be understood, and evidence exists for several possible outcomes. I have a feeling that 'indicate' is frequently used in *Nature* for this reason.

Another respondent made a similar point in relation to ecology:

> In Ecology uncertainty is a constant issue and we are constantly trying to define the level of our uncertainty. In other fields where uncertainty may not be such an issue, words that can imply subtle gradations in the level of certainty may not be as necessary.

It may be noticed at this point that all respondents in the Human Survival Sciences classified 'indicate' as closest to 'suggest'.

Against this background, some of the respondents wrote of the political and commercial pressures on them to make fine adjustments to the certainty with which they expressed their conclusions. One medical researcher, for example, had research results which tended towards the conclusion that much time and money had been spent on eliminating a bacterium which was considered harmful but which might also have beneficial effects. As a result, his paper was 'as welcome as a skunk at a tea party', and he described the complex history of conflicting referees' reports and rewriting at the invitation of the editors that led to the published version:

> ... the MS submitted to *Nature* was originally 3–4 times longer than the printed version. One of *Nature*'s referees said 'this is the most ridiculous speculation and the MS should be rejected' while the other said 'this is quite a new aspect, the data seems convincing as far as the technique makes it possible and I think the paper deserves to be published in *Nature*.' After many a letter, a third referee was consulted and he recommended

acceptance after some minor changes. Then the Editors returned our original MS with certain paragraphs marked in color which we should stick together to shorten the MS.

Another respondent claimed, a touch cynically perhaps, to have noticed a tendency on the part of subeditors to 'reduce expressions of uncertainty' in order to make it more likely that the findings will be picked up in the general press, and the reputation of *Nature* as a journal of groundbreaking research thereby reinforced.

A rather different view of the importance of fine gradations of certainty was given by a physicist. He pointed out that theoretical physicists typically write prose that is 'densely populated' with mathematical equations, and that their papers are unlikely to be published outside specialist journals for other theoretical physicists. If and when they write for *Nature*, they tend to produce strongly opinionated pieces that can be understood by a more general readership. In any case, he claimed, 'theoretical physics texts are never truly serious' since their purpose is to play with ideas and see how far they can be taken; in that context it 'counts as good taste ... to exaggerate the [ironical] use of understatements, stressing the transient nature of the pursuit'. That view was mirrored by a respondent in the field of biology who particularly commended English as 'there are many synonyms and there can be both ambiguity and understatement and sometimes hidden irony that seems so innocent'. For that reason, he suggested, fine distinctions between 'suggesting' and 'indicating' are not as important as knowing the intellectual and research background against which the paper is written.

In conclusion, **indicate** may be chosen precisely because its meaning is not entirely clear; that is to say, it incorporates a measure of deliberate vagueness (Channell 1994), avoiding the clearer specifications of **suggest** or **demonstrate**. For example, another respondent, a physicist, noted that a sentence containing **indicate** had been skilfully added to his paper by a scientific editor of *Nature* to deal with the comments of a referee, who was 'slightly more doubtful' about its conclusions. In this situation, the respondent noted, both sides could be happy with **indicate**, as the editor of *Nature* could interpret it as being close in meaning to **suggest** and the authors as being close in meaning to **show/demonstrate**.

If the view is taken that a precise meaning is not to be found for **indicate**, no matter how much one may be sought by scientists or by linguistic analyst, that may help to explain the dominant position of this verb as a link between evidence and conclusion, a link which needs to be evaluated anew every time it is encountered since it covers all meanings between **show** and **suggest**. A couple of respondents referred to the etymology of the word as an *index*, a finger or a signpost pointing towards the conclusion. If we **show** or **demonstrate** a place, it must be clearly within sight: this is a destination that cannot be missed. A pointing finger gives no information as to how far away the destination is, but simply states that it is there for the traveller who wishes to go along that path.

Acknowledgements

I am grateful to colleagues who took part in the *Nature* research group; to Maxine Clarke, executive editor of *Nature* for her comments on the paper; to Tony Dudley-Evans who not only instigated that research, but has also provided the occasion for reconsidering it after an interval of ten years; and above all to·my respondents, who put so much work and thought into answering my 'impudent enquiry'.

'In my opinion': the place of personal views in undergraduate essays

Greg Myers

Twenty years ago, Jack Rawlins summed up a common attitude among teachers of writing in an essay entitled 'What's so wrong with "In my opinion"?' He began:

> For years, I have methodically crossed out phrases like 'I think', 'I feel', 'I believe' or 'in my opinion' when I encountered them in my students' writing on literature. Whenever I did, my students' faces would go blank with wonder and they would ask me why. 'But it is my opinion,' they would purr. (1980: 670)

Here is an example of what Rawlins is talking about from a linguistics essay in which a student was asked to say why texts should be studied in relation to social practices:

> In my personal opinion, I find it very difficult to imagine a social practice without language.

Why is this odd? Rawlins and others would say that the student's opinion hardly matters here; what is at issue in this exam is the ability to provide evidence to support one view or the other, thus showing one understands the concepts. How could a student get to the end of the first year without understanding this distinction between what is a matter of opinion and what is not?

My argument in this paper is that the effect of declaring a statement to be an opinion is not that simple. First, the boundary between what is a matter of opinion and what is not, which seems so clear to us when we are marking exam scripts or drawing up course descriptions, is complex and open to negotiation in any particular case. Second, a marker such as 'in my opinion' or 'in my personal view' is no guide to this boundary; these markers are used for many purposes besides labelling opinions. Third, the boundaries of allowable opinion are problematic in other genres as well, in public opinion as well as in academic writing.

The use of a phrase like 'in my opinion' has two aspects: one is marking that this is *just* an opinion, therefore apparently weakening the statement, but one is also saying it is *my* opinion, personalising it and thus potentially either inviting or fending off a challenge. An opinion applies, by one definition, to one that which is not demonstrable:

> **Opinion** ... **1.** What one opines; judgement resting on grounds insufficient for complete demonstration; belief of something as probable or as seeming to one's own mind to be true (Dist. from *knowledge*, *conviction*, or *certainty*; occas. = *belief*). (OED)

That is why it seems odd to academics to mark as opinions statements about demonstrable facts or definitions of concepts:

> In my opinion, limestone is a sedimentary rock.
> In my opinion, culture is a set of shared, tacit beliefs.

On the other hand, it is equally odd to challenge the basis of personal opinions:

> I don't like Frasier.
> Yes you do.

In academic discourse, to declare a statement to be one's own opinion has implications for the positions of the reader and the writer and for how they are to interact (Hyland 2000). Expressions of opinion play an acknowledged role in various forms in law (experts), journalism (leaders and op-ed pages), and social research (surveys and focus groups), but they have an uneasy place in academic discourse. Ivanic *et al.* (2000) discuss a comment by a university tutor who says 'avoid personal pronouns and expressions like 'in my view' in all academic work' (2000: 51). As they point out, this is hardly a universal rule, even in the department of this tutor. It could be argued that students (at least in the humanities and social sciences in British universities) are required to have an opinion, on exams as well as in essays and seminar discussions. Students who simply repeat the lectures and reading get low marks in many subjects; students who want 2:1 class marks are expected to do something of their own with this knowledge, something that will make their script at least slightly different from the hundred or so others. But clearly there are constraints on how they express this 'something of their own'. To violate these constraints seems to signal not just a stylistic gaffe, but a misunderstanding of the whole academic project and their place in it. I would like to reflect on some markers of opinions statements, not to criticise the students but to investigate that project.

To provide a starting point for this reflection I asked my students to contribute copies of their essays on disk. I got 40 essays from 19 students, about half from my first-year course Culture Media and Communication, and half from other first-year courses in business and social sciences. This collection of essays is neither very big nor particularly representative, but it provides enough illustrations of the ways students can mark their own opinions. I wasn't concerned whether the essays had good marks or bad, or were by native speakers of English or not; issues of opinion in academic writing seem to pose problems for all sorts of students.

I searched these essays for explicit markers of opinions (*my, opinion, view, personal*) and for a set of words that seemed to be alternative ways or expressing academic views (*analysis, think, argue* and *argument*). Of course writers can express opinions without drawing attention to them in this way; the whole essay could be treated as a personal view. But it is a significant pragmatic move to mark a statement explicitly as an opinion, just as it is significant to mark explicitly the illocutionary force of an utterance, as in 'I'm asking...' (Thomas 1983). Harvey Sacks (1992: 344) notes that when a speaker says 'I still say...', it marks the current interaction as an argument. 'In fact' is not just used to mark facts, 'arguably' doesn't invite an argument and 'literally' almost never means a statement is to be taken literally, so we wouldn't expect 'in my opinion' just to mark opinions.

One way to look at the uses of 'in my opinion' is to see them as signalling problematic aspects of responding to questions like these. We can see them as what Gumperz called 'contextualisation cues':

> constellations of surface features of message form ... by which speakers [and writers] signal and listeners [and readers] interpret what the activity is, how semantic content is to be understood and how each sentence relates to what precedes or follows. (1982: 131)

'In my opinion' doesn't just indicate that what follows is an opinion; it may indicate their relation to the topic, the text, the readers' role, and their own role as academics.

I will consider how students use opinion statements in the essays I collected, without trying to say whether these uses are legitimate or not. I will argue that they use such markers for a variety of shifts in the kind of activity they are performing as writers, particularly activities that may be new to them. I will then look briefly at how similar phrases are used in other contexts to show that these tensions about the function and value of opinions are not confined to academic discourse.

Functions of opinion statements in students' essays

If opinion statements were foreign to academic writing, one might expect some hints or guidance in the essay questions, but they do little to clarify where or why a personal element would be excluded. The questions to which the essays I am studying are responding include the following:

> 3. In what ways have electronic media made the world what McLuhan called a 'Global Village'? Is this change limited to some cultures, or is it truly global? Discuss specific examples.

> 7. 'A raw historical event cannot, in that form, be transmitted by, say, a television news-cast' (Hall, p. 42). Choose one recent 'historical event', and one radio or television news item related to it, and discuss the ways it has been transformed from any 'raw' form by selection, framing, editing, commentary, and other processes of news production.

These questions (I have quoted only those from my own course) each include a big vague statement from the reading, and then ask the students to do some analysis. The implication is often that this will involve agreeing or disagreeing with the statement, so each of these questions requires a personal view, but each also suggests a kind of evidence – specific examples, one news item – that will be needed to support it. It is a complex task, and students have various ways of signalling their stance towards it.

Arguability of the claim

Any signal of personal involvement in a statement can work as a hedge (Conrad and Biber 2001; Hyland 2000). One function of the phrase 'in my opinion' and its equivalents seems to be to mark views as the writer's own, on matters that might be open to alternative views:

> 1. The characters are divided often with very different nature and personality. ... When these characters appear to the story line, it can always be more or less predicted how the story continues or what will happen next. The women in the soaps *in my opinion* do have some reflection to women in reality. The way that culture and societies are changing, I think the changes of soap opera characters and their representation can be noticed.

> 2. I *personally* do not fully agree with Golding and Elliott. As I have illustrated, the news' aim, if one is to be mentioned, is to convey a 'news' that will attract as many viewers as possible. We live in a competitive world, so why would any institute compromise their popularity ratings, and hence their annual income? The news has become, *in my opinion*, a source that tells society what (and how!) to decode this selected form of reality we 'see'. News cannot claim to present a news service, which is impartial, objective or even accurate. They are all illusions that are just not possible.

In these two examples, the writer takes any academic statement as something with which one can agree or disagree (even if not asked to do so by the question). The statement of disagreement is followed immediately by a reference to evidence. This is just the kind of opinion permitted within the constraints of undergraduate essays.

The same sort of marker can be used to signal what the student is offering as their own interpretation. First-year students may be hesitant about claiming an interpretation, even when they offer what would seem to be good academic evidence:

> 3. With an advert whose visual image is as ambiguous as this, questions are posed, and depending on who is looking at the advert, different answers may arise. For example, the woman has suffered a loss of concentration, but why? What context is the advert set in, where are they? Do the two people know each other? The evidence seems to point to a woman applying lipstick, who smells the scent of Addiction on a man she sees in her mirror, and in turning to look at him, smears the lipstick on her cheek. However, *this is only a personal opinion*, but I have no real way of knowing if it is correct or not, and can only go on my own interpretation of the advertisers' references.

Tutors may find it odd to insist on this being *only* a personal opinion, because the statement is the kind of allowable interpretation that need not be so hedged. The difficulty for the student here is in figuring out just what is an allowable interpretation, and how such an interpretation is to be signalled. In these essays, all the uses involve interpretations of popular culture, and students usually haven't developed a sense of how one makes serious arguments on what may seem to them to be trivial topics. The 'in my opinion' marks where they step into this still-uncomfortable role.

Truisms and common knowledge

While the examples so far signal the legitimate arguability of a claim or interpretation, another use of such statements is to hedge claims so broad that no one could disagree with them. These are not the writer's own opinions, but truisms. Their function seems more to provide a basis for other statements that are the main business of the essay.

> 4. Product or brand loyalty has a great deal to do with consumer behaviour, as *in my opinion* that would be useful knowledge to all marketers to know exactly what make the consumer to purchase the particular product or brand.

> 5. Especially today, when the globalisation is very strong, the importance of language has become more important, but the culture and understanding different cultures is *in my opinion* is coming more important as well.

> 6. *In my opinion*, the language is still the most important element that enables us to continue with learning and discovering the changing organisations and changing environment.

I would imagine that no reader denies that marketers want to know why consumers buy their product, or that understanding cultures is important, or that language enables us to learn about the changing organisations and environment. The marker sets aside the claim as something serious, as likely to be agreed with, in the same way as would using the adverbial 'indeed'. Tutors may despair at having to read such big vague claims, but students seem to feel they offer necessary support. We need to look not just at what these individual statements are doing, but also at how they function in the structure of the essay. These signals do not so much say what kind of claim it is as mark out the upper, most abstract level of the argument. They provide a ceiling from which to hang more specific statements, a general sense of topic area that will hold the whole thing together.

Register

Writers may also use marked opinion statements when they are dealing with a new register, the technical terms of a field they are still mastering, such as 'diegetic', 'connotation,' and 'decoding'.

> 7. I imagine a milkman as a tranquil and peaceful person; instead Pat Mustard is, *in my opinion*, a living metaphor – in the diegetic world – for sex, seen as a threat to the peace of the organic unity formed by the four usual characters.

> 8. Although I would conclude from my television viewing as a culture, media, and communication student, that I was aware of the presence of a potential preferred meaning and so was reluctant to 'decode' any of the information. It is important to note that *in my opinion*, decoding is not a conscious process, therefore, even though I was aware that a preferred meaning might be present, I cannot say that I did not adopt it as the deciding of such an adoption is not conscious.

Pompous as such awkward use of the specialist register ('diegetic', 'decoding') may sound, it is a stage in figuring out how to write these essays. 'In my opinion' here seems to have less to do with the content of the statements than with their style; it acts as a kind of defence, as it does when prefacing an interpretation.

Structure

For some writers, the place of opinion is simple – it comes at the end, after one has done the required review. In this view, opinion is something added on, earned by the work of discussing other people's ideas. But it still sounds a bit odd to academics, because it does not emerge out of that discussion of other people's ideas, and the evaluations made and arguments presented, but comes as a sort of coda.

> 9. To conclude *I would say that* although it is the aim of public service broadcasters to be as objective, impartial and accurate as they can, this is not always possible. The news *in my opinion* will always have a certain amount of unobjectivity and a lack of impartiality and accuracy, as there will always be a bias towards a story no matter what topic area that it covers. This is because the complete information and facts about most stories can not be gathered and sometimes are not completely told.

Here the expression of opinion is something quite separate from, and after, the regular work of doing an essay. In example 9, the personal judgement is stated, and then a reason is given ('this is because ...'). In this last stage, the writer gets to step outside their student voice, and present something as their own. Or to put it another way, they say something of their own in order to bring the essay to a stop.

Arguing and showing

Phrases like 'in my opinion' might be seen on a scale of ways students could use to present their own speech acts, running from the very objective ('the data show') to the very subjective ('I'm just guessing but ...'). One might expect them to use such phrases as 'I will argue' or 'I will show', to emphasise that they are presenting evidence, as published articles in linguistics do (Myers 1991). These verbs are used occasionally, but only occasionally, by the first-year students for their own papers:

> 10. *One can argue* that such interaction through the Internet is limited tending to reinforce the distance and time barriers that actually exist. This is chiefly demonstrated in the manner in which we can now shop via this medium implying that we would not have to leave our homes.

> 11. In order to fulfil the given task I intend to use recent examples taken from BBC news broadcasts. Through doing this *I aim to show* the difficulties in presenting a completely impartial, accurate and objective news broadcast.

This choice of verbs varies discipline to discipline – more than half my examples of 'argue' and 'show' are from the four essays for history and two for women's studies, while psychologists and business researchers don't seem to refer to themselves as arguing or presenting opinions. And they use such verbs much more to describe what others – usually textbook authors – do. They, as students, just have opinions.

In this brief exploration of functions, we see that 'in my opinion' does not just mark opinions, but proposes a relation between self, reader, and topic. It marks a topic as a matter of opinion – not of argument and evidence – in which the student's statement can be juxtaposed to the printed comments of others, and in which the writer's own interpretation can be allowed without evaluation. It marks very general statements that the writers expects readers to grant as a linking or introductory material. It can mark the sometimes awkward entry into a new register. And it can mark the stepping back from argument and evidence in the conclusion of an essay.

This complexity of function should not be too surprising, because there are tensions about the uses of opinions in other genres as well. If we compare some of these other genres, we can get some sense of the contradictions that students may bring with them to these tasks.

Genres of opinion

Opinions are often treated as if they were objective entities out there, already in people and groups, to be elicited by more and more sophisticated instruments. There are criticisms from time to time of how these opinions are elicited, and whether they should be elicited, but it is seldom questioned that they are there, waiting. But all opinions emerge in specific interactions – the respondent says something to someone at a particular point, in response to something, in a particular setting (Houtkoop-Steenstra 2000; Suchman and Jordan 1990). This is certainly true of many essays; the students may have had no opinion at all of the Global Village, the centrality of language to management, or products becoming services, before they were asked to produce an opinion as part of their display of learning. But they do know a lot about the expression of opinion, from other genres, because opinion is an important part of our political, cultural and economic lives. There are industries of surveys, market research, political polling, talk shows and columnists devoted to gathering and packaging opinions for other uses. Here I will consider just a few of these other genres in relation to the academic essay.

We can get an idea of the range of uses by looking at a few of the 644 occurrences of the phrase 'in my opinion' in the British National Corpus. (BNC code and line numbers are given after the examples below.) One of the pleasures of running a concordance in a large corpus is that one turns up all sorts of fascinating fragments, like phrases overheard on the bus or train that one can't quite believe someone actually said. For my purposes, the fragments are enough to tell the discourse in which the phrase is used. First, there are uses of the phrase to give a professional or expert opinion.

I examined the body again, a few minutes ago. In my opinion, the onset of rigor is now complete. (ANL (433))

Dear Patient: In my opinion you are unfit to work/ join the army / propagate ... (CAT (1262))

The words 'cause or matter' are, in my opinion, apt to include any form of proceeding ... (FCE (220))

'Every band is a risk,' he said, 'but in my opinion the Sex Pistols are less of a risk than most.' (FNX (112))

In these examples, admittedly out of context, we seem to be hearing a pathologist, doctor (in a joke I hope), a judge or lawyer, and an agent giving opinions they are paid to give. This is one sense of *opinion*, as expert opinion, within institutions (courts, hospitals, A & R ('Artists and Repertoire': music business agents)) that validate their authority. To declare an opinion in this context is to make the statement stronger, not weaker. This usage does not seem to be open to students.

Usually, though, the phrase does not mark the writer's authority, but some orientation to the reader's response. It can, as one might expect, be used to weaken a statement, along with other hedges or signs of hesitation.

He was the greatest bowler I ever faced or saw, and in my opinion certainly the best bowler Australia ever produced. (CH3 (7624))

Erm eh in my opinion they are a very good tenant. (F7A (829))

In the first of these examples, the speaker distinguishes what he knows by experience from what he extrapolates; in the second, the speaker allows for other possible opinions by those with different experiences. This is like the hedging done by students.

The phrase is sometimes used in the middle of what is clearly intended to be a statement with which some readers would disagree, one that is provocatively overstated or unexpected.

Wholewheat pasta is, in my opinion, more suited as building material than sustenance. (A8B (41))

Rupert Sutcliffe declared. 'A waste of time and money, in my opinion, those conferences'. (ANY (924))

'It's due for demolition. About time, too, in my opinion.' (CD1 (1071))

Clinton's sex appeal shot up, in my opinion, when he became President. (CEK (2287))

The placement of the 'in my opinion' here serves to increase these sense of witty opposition to the anticipated beliefs of those who, for instance, like wholewheat pasta or doubt the sex appeal of the President.

While the phrase can be used to mark statements with which disagreement is expected, it can also be used, as we have seen in the student essays, to mark statements that are not opinions at all, but are truths or truisms that must have the consent of all readers.

Beatitude is, in my opinion, a possession of all things we believe to be good. (ARG (902))

The secret of success, in my opinion, is to make pars when you aren't playing well. (ASA (2159))

Principles, in my opinion, are more important than cash. (CBG (215))

I may be wrong in my interpretation here, but the first of these seems to be a matter of definition, the second to be one of those thumping obvious statements that sports heroes make when interviewed after an event, and the last is a statement of moral principles that the writer is assuming must be shared by all right-thinking people. So it is not the case that we can assume 'in my opinion' is always some sort of hedging device. As with the student essays, all we can say for certain is that it calls upon the reader to make a shift in how this statement is to be evaluated, relative to previous statements.

These examples of the use of the phrase raise some issues of structure that would need to be explored in a more systematic concordance (on the position of adverbials of stance, see Conrad and Biber 2001). The phrase has a different effect in a sentence initial position, where it seems to make some claim for what follows. It is by far more common inserted parenthetically, just before or after the verb. When it comes at the end of the statement, as it does only once in my sample, it seems to orient to the possibility of disagreement. It is also worth noting that my quick concordance turned up several examples in reported speech but only one spoken example, though 10 per cent of the BNC is spoken material. I think that may reflect actual usage; it sounds like a formal phrase, and indeed in half the examples

I've given, it could mark a mock formality that would go with the joking statements. That means it comes to student writers not just with a range of functions, but associations of formality and authority that could be either off-putting or tempting.

Allowable opinions

There are many forums in which one is specifically asked to give an opinion, including market research interviews, polls and the focus group sessions that are the main material for my current research (Myers 1998). But the boundary between public and private remains; there is always an issue then of delimiting appropriate areas for opinions. Here, for instance, is what happens to a moderator of a focus group who ventures into a touchy topic. He uses hypothetical reported speech to suggest a view they might have had of the Louise Woodward case:

Mod I mean there's a lot of er . public concern for Louise Woodward . er . you know
      . when the trial was going on and everything but . you're not talking that way now
      . you kind of think well she's kind of
F1   well it's a very personal opinionated view
F2   it is
Mod sorry
F3   it's a very personal opinion

The moderator has projected or modelled an opinion for them, suggesting, by contrast, that sympathy with her may have ebbed after the trial. He offers this as something they might share and take for granted. But instead of agreeing or disagreeing, they reject it as 'a very personal opinion', not meaning it is too private for discussion, but that it is too idiosyncratic. Focus groups can take on highly controversial topics. But they do so always ruling out some topics as beyond public discussion, even as they circle around these topics. For instance, there is little discussion in these groups of religion or party politics, and a great deal of discussion of national and regional differences, changes in society in recent years, and local land use. There is a strong sense of what is appropriate to talk about, even if some participants sometimes violate it. The word F1 uses sums up this sense – to express opinions beyond the bounds of possible group discussion is to be 'opinionated'.

Participants in focus groups may sound out the boundaries of what is possible in this group. In the following example, the participants are not discussing a particularly controversial topic (they are sorting pictures of public figures), but Dave offers an opinion very cautiously, in a jokingly colloquial form.

BS	I get you, I get you. And why is Bob Geldof there?
Dave	Well, *if I could put my two pennorth in*, I wouldn't have those 2 in. I'd have that person in because I don't know her and she's obviously passionate about something. I'm always a little bit mistrust in these 2 in terms of using the cause for manipulative.
Mod	Swampy and Geldof.
Dave	I saw some pictures of Swampy this weekend, now he's got himself this job and he looks absolutely the banker type.
Mod	He's got a job in a bank?
Dave	Well, it's in that sort of area.
Lynne	He's been smartened up, I didn't read the article but he was being smartened up.
Dave	But that marks a *personal opinion*.
Mod	OK.

When the moderator and Lynne challenge Dave's assertion about how Swampy (a famous roads protester) had changed, Dave backs off and marks it as a 'personal opinion'.

There are other forums in which opinions are expressed to a wider public, but here too participants draw boundaries of what is allowable. 'Opinion' columns in newspapers or broadcast news are set aside, supposedly in contrast to the factual reporting of the rest of the paper or programme. The pleasure of reading someone like Julie Burchill is in the wild flow of totally unsupported and overstated opinions. There must be similar pleasure in talk radio (Hutchby 1996). But we still recognise that such self-assertion can be taken as threatening. On email discussions, in which overstated and under-supported opinions seem to be the norm, there is an abbreviation IMHO for 'in my humble opinion', to defuse possible offence. As with the student essays, this is not so much the marker of an opinion as a signal that calls attention to the fact that something is in dispute. One assumption of such forums is that no opinion is better than any other. Thus the academic mechanisms of argument, persuasion and evidence are unnecessary – anyone can keep holding their opinion. Brodkey (1996: 160) comments on the difficulty of penetrating the wall of 'everybody has a right to their own opinion', to make students take responsibility for the implications of what they argue. Their expression of it is not so much to change the world as to say something about themselves.

There is another kind of genre that might influence students, if only indirectly: published academic articles. Here too there is a tension. Academics avoid presenting their claims as opinions; that is why we are so touchy about students using this phrase. But every article must make some claim to say something that is novel, beyond or against the claims of other researchers (Myers 1991). In the sciences, this is typically presented as the passing on of objective information:

> In this paper we report...

In linguistics it is more typically presented as an argument or analysis:

> I will argue that...

The aim is to show that it is indeed personal, but not an opinion. To say 'I think' is a hedge, weakening one's claim by presenting it as personal rather than objective. But an eminent figure in the field can present an opinion as would a doctor or a lawyer, as an expert judgement, backed by personal expertise. For instance, Francis Crick, the Nobel Prize-winning biologist, marks some of his statements in a review article as personal:

> I have been so rash as to say, more than once, that we might expect between 10 and 100 different enzymes, but that was pure guesswork. The number could be as low as two. (Crick 1979, quoted in Myers 1991)

This is an extreme form, in which he presents his claim as 'pure guesswork'. There is a rhetorical strategy in presenting one's claims in such ostentatiously weakened form (see examples in Hyland 2000).

I started with a quotation from Jack Rawlins about the place of opinion in student essays about literature. Similar issues apply to the courses in academic writing taught in most American universities. These courses, typically taught in English literature departments, have a long tradition of encouraging 'expressive writing', partly as an antidote to the kind of conventional and jargon-filled writing students will have in other courses. Essays in these courses might be about the expression of personal opinions on public issues, or may draw on personal experience. But some critical composition theorists have argued that such writing is not, in fact, a good preparation for the writing needed in the university. In a classic essay, 'Inventing the University', David Bartholomae (1984) compared different first-year placement essays with lower and higher scores, and suggested that what was needed was not just a facility at stating one's views, but a sense that one was entering an ongoing discussion, in which people had said things before that needed to be taken into account. Similarly, Patricia Bizzell, discussing possible conflicts between the culture of a student's home and that of the university, comments, 'The student is asked to take a certain distance on all of his or her Commitments, and to give allegiance only as a result of a careful deliberative process' (1992: 171). Both suggest that students feel the kind of tension we see here: on one hand constraints on statement of anything as an opinion, on the other a demand that one have a view in the ongoing discussion.

Conclusion: my personal opinion

No wonder students are confused. The problem is not, as one might think, that they haven't learned to separate knowledge, supported by evidence, from opinions. These were never far apart, and there is clearly a personal element in professional academic writing. Nor is the problem simply that they have misunderstood the phrasing and give the wrong signals by using everyday phrasing ('in my opinion') that jars academic readers. Nor is it a matter of having to reach a certain academic status to be entitled to opinions; even the most eminent academics (such as Francis Crick) deliver opinions under complex constraints.

There are two main problems for students trying to figure out how to present personal views:

- expressions of opinion can have different functions in the text;
- expressions of opinion have different constraints in different genres.

Thus one cannot read off epistemic effects from the surface features of the texts in a concordance. More fundamentally, I would argue (and I mean argue) that there are tensions inherent within the uses of opinions in society: they are public and private, personal and shared, consistent and contradictory. To assert an opinion is not just to say something about a topic – it is to say something about oneself, and the person one is saying it to, and the forum in which one is saying it. That is why these tiny stylistic slips can seem so very odd. We are as much caught up in the paradoxes of opinion as our students are.

Analysing genre: some conceptual issues

Vijay K. Bhatia

Overview

Genre analysis continues to provide an attractive framework for the analysis of language use for a variety of applied linguistic purposes, particularly for the teaching and learning of English for academic and professional purposes. Although recent research (see Bargiela-Chiappini and Nickerson 1999; Bhatia 1998, 1999a, 1999b, 2000, 2001; Candlin and Hyland 1999; Candlin and Plum 1999; Fairclough 1993, 1995; Hyland 2000; Sarangi and Candlin 2001; Swales 1998, to name only a few) provides a significant and desirable extension of interest in the direction of multifaceted, multidimensional and ethnographically grounded *thicker* descriptions of genres, rhetorical move analysis continues to provide insightful information for pedagogic practice. However, it is becoming increasingly clear that, for a consistent and systematic analysis of cognitive and rhetorical structuring in genres, it is necessary to refine and adequately specify the nature, function and distribution of a number of methodological concepts like the rhetorical *move* and *strategy*, which often illuminate our understanding of 'levels of generic specification' (i.e. genres and sub-genres), mixing and embedding of genres, and some aspects of *generic appropriation* across related genres. In this chapter, I would like to revisit some of these crucial methodological concepts, such as *moves, strategies, stages, communicative purposes, cognitive structuring* and *generic integrity* in an attempt to demystify some of the fuzziness and uncertainties surrounding the use of these terms for analytical investigations of genre, especially for EAP applications.

However, before I begin with any detailed discussion of some of these important analytical concepts, it is necessary to emphasise that discourse and genre analysis is an area of enquiry that is and will always be fuzzy to some extent, even though we often find it based on highly conventionalised and standardised social actions (Miller 1984; Swales 1990). In analysing language use, we are invariably investigating human behaviour, which is not entirely predictable, for the simple reason that most of us, even in highly predictable settings, like to exploit conventions to express 'private intentions' within the framework of socially constructed discourse forms (Bhatia 1995). Analysing discourse with any expectation of a high degree of predictability or certainty is like analysing the stock market in a highly complex and volatile economic environment, where it is almost impossible to take into account all the variables contributing to the process. In fact, analysing genre within any framework is essentially an attempt to explain and account for the realities of the world, which are often complex, dynamic and unpredictable. There are, and will always be, a number of contributing factors in the construction, interpretation, exploitation and use of academic and professional genres which it will not always be possible to take fully into account even in the most rigorous forms of analysis. It is precisely for this reason that generic integrity in academic and professional discourses is often viewed as dynamic, flexible and sometimes contested. Let me now begin with the notion of *communicative purpose*, which has been used as a privileged criterion (Bhatia 1993; Swales 1990) for the identification of genres.

2 Communicative purpose

The status of communicative purpose has rarely been questioned in existing literature, though the process of specifying communicative purposes has often been found somewhat difficult. Swales (1990: 46) finds considerable heuristic value in this difficulty because it 'may require the analyst to undertake a fair amount of independent and open-minded investigation', which is viewed as the essence of analysing discourse. In a way, the difficulty in establishing a communicative purpose for a specific genre or a 'set of communicative purposes', as Swales (1990: 46) rightly points out, is very much part of the design rather than a handicap, as some might see it. If one were looking for clear-cut, definite and objective criteria to define and identify communicative purpose for each genre, one would necessarily be frustrated not simply by the complex realities of the world of discourse, which obviously must be reflected in the discourse, but also by the static and formulaic nature of language use that such a view would give to the emergent forms of discourse. Fortunately, we live in a world that is still largely unpredictable and hence interesting. An additional factor in this difficulty specifying communicative purposes, especially in EAP contexts, is the lack of knowledge of the disciplinary cultures that we, as genre analysts, are often concerned with. Although we can claim to have expertise in the text-internal aspects of language use, including some areas of lexico-grammar, which reflect communicative purposes, they often need to be interpreted in the context of text-external aspects of genres, i.e. the goals of the specialist communities and the contexts in which these genres are constructed, interpreted and used in real-life situations, sometimes referred to as 'critical sites of engagement' (Scollon 1995).

Although text-internal factors are important for the identification of communicative purposes, they can give misleading insights when used on their own. Textual factors typically depend on their form-function correlation, and it is not always possible to have one-to-one correlation in this area. There are linguistic forms that can attract several discoursal values; on the other hand, a particular discourse value can be realised through several syntactic forms. However, it would be somewhat naive to assume it to be as chaotic a situation as it may sound. Linguistic forms do carry specific generic values, but the only way one can assign the right generic value to any linguistic feature of the genre is by reference to text-external factors. Similarly, any conclusion based on text-external factors needs to be confirmed by reference to text-internal factors. Bhatia (1992) discusses this issue by considering the case of complex nominals in three different genres – academic scientific genre, advertising, and legislation – on the basis of which he concludes that although one may find an above average use of complex nominals in all the three genres, their form, distribution and generic values are very different in the three cases. Generic values in these genres can only be assigned by references to the communicative purposes these different genres tend to realise in the context of specific disciplinary concerns and a number of other text-external factors. In this context, it is interesting to note that Askehave and Swales (2001) suggest a more 'context-driven' procedure for genre analysis, in which communicative purpose takes into account a number of factors other than textual or intertextual.

Another interesting aspect of communicative purposes is that they can be specified at various levels based on an increasingly delicate degree of specificity, which makes it possible for genres to be identified either narrowly or more broadly, depending upon the objectives of the investigation. This kind of flexibility allows genre theory a degree of versatility that otherwise would be impossible. Let me give more substance to this aspect of genre analysis.

3 Versatility in genre

The concept of genre necessarily needs to be versatile enough to be able to account for the complex realities of the real world of discourse, not simply in the context of a particular disciplinary field, but also across disciplinary boundaries. One of the important issues related to genre identification therefore is the status of super-genres, genres and sub-genres. It is difficult to arrive at a classification of professional genres in a clear-cut and objective manner, and the generic boundaries between and across genres are even more difficult to draw. In fact, in whatever manner one may define genre, the boundaries between different genres will always be fluid to some extent. It has very little to do with the framework one uses, but more to do with the complex and dynamic variation and constant development of generic forms used within and across disciplinary cultures. Conventionally we have been using a number of broadly defined terms to identify genres, such as *Introductions, Reports, Promotional genres*, etc. which can be posited at various levels of generalisation. *Introduction*, for example, can be treated as a form of primary genre, or more appropriately, a generic function, which can realise a number of related genres. Introducing a friend, introducing a speaker in a symposium or a political meeting, introducing a business proposition, introducing a new product in the market, introducing a new book, a new research finding in a research article, a point of view in a student essay are some examples. All these are closely related genres, and they all appear to form a colony, with members restricted not necessarily from the same domain or discipline. To take a specific case let us look at *academic introductions* more closely. Under this category of genres, we again find a number of variations, some easily distinguishable, other more difficult to identify. The picture that emerges will look something like this.

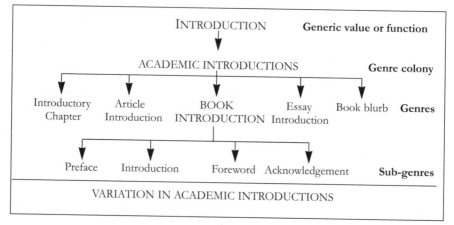

One may notice several interesting aspects of this view of genre classification. First, it allows genres to be viewed at various levels of delicacy, vertically as well as horizontally. Vertically, *academic introductions* can be seen as a member of a genre colony, with several individual genres to be identified at the next level. Then at the next lower level of delicacy, one could identify sub-genres of various kinds. The other interesting aspect of this view is that all these genres and sub-genres display linguistic as well as other discoursal features which may appear to be common to most disciplines, whereas others may be realised differently in different disciplines (see Bhatia 1998, 1999a; M. Hewings 1999; Hyland 2000). This kind of analysis also helps one to see disciplinary variation as part of generic variation.

Reporting as a function or generic value is another interesting case. At the top level, one could consider *academic reports, business reports, law reports,* as typical of disciplines in academic settings, and *accident reports, first information reports* (FIR), *inquiry reports,* etc. as typical instances of macro-genres in professional settings forming a colony of reporting genres. However, one could go further down the level of delicacy to identify variations within *business reports,* for example, *company report, financial report, feasibility report, investigation report, annual report,* etc. which cross academic boundaries and are often used in both academic as well as professional contexts. The same will be true of a number of other genre colonies, such as those incorporating promotional genres of various kinds. One could even establish interesting relationships across genre colonies, as in the case of genres like *reviews* of books, films, events (social, academic, business, etc.), on the one hand, and more specific *promotional genres,* on the other. The emerging picture is rather complex and mixed, crossing disciplinary, professional and often institutional boundaries.

The above discussion shows that although genres are products of specific (combinations of) rhetorical values that linguistic forms attract in discourse, they are primarily identified in terms of the communicative purposes these forms of discourse serve in specific disciplinary and professional contexts. At the super-genre level, these may be called genre colonies, at the next lower level of delicacy they may have a range of closely related genres which may not appear to be similar in terms of a number of other contextual parameters such as the medium, participant relationships, style, etc. but will have considerable overlap in terms of communicative purposes. Although some of them will have their own specific lexico-grammatical and stylistic realisations, they will also have a lot in common to justify their inclusion within the same colony of genres. One of the interesting aspects of this view is that there are several levels of generalisations and it is possible to analyse these levels in different ways. However, one needs to be rather careful about reading too much into such classifications, as the nature of genre analysis is rather fuzzy and fluid, rather than clear cut and precise. It is more clarificatory than classificatory (see Swales 1990; Bhatia 1993, 1995).

This kind of complex and yet very subtle variation at different levels of generalisation makes it almost impossible for any specific framework to devise objective criteria to account for their identification. Although a number of factors – linguistic, contextual, socio-cognitive as well as discipline specific – will help the analyst to explain this kind of variation (which may include genre mixing and embedding, and also what Fairclough (1992b) includes under 'hybridization'), none of these alone can satisfactorily account for the integrity of these realisations. It will also be impossible to devise a hierarchy of genres, except in a very general sense. Let me now proceed to more delicate levels of genre specification.

4 Moves and strategies

Before getting into the complexities of move analysis, I would like to mention a general point about move analysis as part of genre theory. As referred to in the earlier sections, *moves* are rhetorical instruments that realise a sub-set of specific communicative purposes associated with a genre, and as such they are interpreted in the context of the communicative purposes of the genre in question. They may not have an independent existence outside the framework of a genre, except in the case of hybrid or mixed genres. The unity and integrity of a typical genre therefore crucially depends on the nature and function of moves employed in the textualisation process. Although it is difficult to offer an objective and detailed specification of the exact relationship between communicative purpose of the genre and the set of moves employed to give effect to it, it is often the case that expert genre writers, and EAP teachers, effortlessly notice any attempt to undermine the generic integrity of a specific document. Although in the case of novices or new members of the discourse community the boundaries are often preserved, it is not uncommon to find that expert members of the community take liberties with some of these generic constraints to express their own 'private intentions'. Within the context of the 'socially recognised communicative purposes' of genres, they may mix two genres, or 'embed' one within another, or even 'bend' genres to exploit convention to extend generic boundaries (Bhatia 1995). However, the integrity of each specific genre is still noticeable in most of these creatively constructed artefacts.

Since generic integrity plays a significant role in the construction of academic and professional discourse, it is important to recognise that it plays a similar role in the analysis of genres. Some of the important consequences of this recognition are not only to reduce any unnecessary proliferation of the number of moves assigned to a specific genre, but also to assist in the identification and explanation of such moves. It is important to remember that although moves have surface-level lexico-grammatical realisations, they are essentially functional in character and are closely associated with the realisations of the communicative purpose(s) of the genre. Moves are recognised in terms of the functional values that are assigned to linguistic forms. Therefore, in analysing genres we do not target lexico-grammatical forms, but the communicative values that these linguistic forms carry, although these lexico-grammatical forms signal and often realise relevant aspects of such communicative values. By analysing communicative values, rather than linguistic forms, one can better focus on the integrity of the genre in question, and hence avoid a tendency to assign values to every linguistic form leading to a rather misleading proliferation of moves.

Move-analysis is the most popular aspect of applied genre analysis, and has been found very insightful for everyday genre analysis in EAP contexts (see Bhatia 1993; Dudley-Evans 1987, 1994; Swales 1981, 1990). Although it has become increasingly popular as a useful analytical tool to assign rhetorical values to features of lexico-grammar in EAP genres, it has not been adequately developed, discussed or specified in existing literature. *Moves* are well established, but the status of *rhetorical strategies* has so far been neglected. Although both of them have linguistic correlates, they are different and perform different functions in genre analysis.

Moves are essentially elements of rhetorical structure, whereas *strategies* are motivated by variations in the way these elements of rhetorical structure are realised. Moves are functional in character and often have some correlation, though not always one to one, with linguistic forms that are used; however, in the case of strategies, it is more difficult to establish any direct correlation with linguistic realisations. Although there has been some discussion of *strategies* in Bhatia (1993), it does merit a more elaborate illustration here. Let me take an example from the 'CARS' model put forward by Swales (1990: 141), in which he proposes three moves in 'Creating A Research Space' in research article introductions. It is interesting to note that these can be realised in various ways, depending upon the nature of the discipline, intended audience, the relationship between the writer and the reader, the status of published work in that area. Swales (1990) introduces a separate category of what he calls *steps* to realise moves, however in his example (Figure 10, p. 141) he seems to have two very different kinds of rhetorical items under steps. Some of the steps seem to have optional status, which he indicates as step (1)A, (1)B, etc., whereas others are more like parts of the same rhetorical structure, and are indicated as step 1, 2 or 3. To me they seem to have very different status. Step 1A *Counter-claiming* or Step 1B *Indicating a gap*, or Step 1C *Question-raising*, or Step 1D *Continuing a tradition* are all different rhetorical strategies, which are simply different ways of realising the value of Move 2 *Establishing a niche*. The choice of an appropriate strategy will depend on factors like the nature of the disciplinary research available, the nature of the work reported and the kind of positioning the writer would like to take. Compare this with steps included in Move 3 *Occupying the niche*. Here we have two different kinds of steps. Step 1A *Outlining purposes* or Step 1B *Announcing present research* are rhetorical strategies, whereas Step 2 *Announcing principal findings* and Step 3 *Indicating RA structure* are steps or stages realising part of the rhetorical *move*. These could be seen as sub-moves as well.

Another illustration of steps, stages, or what I have termed *sub-moves* can be taken from the analysis of sales letters. In Bhatia (1993: 48), the move *introducing the offer* is realised in three stages, i.e. *offering product/service, essential detailing of the offer* and *indicating value of the offer*. The status of these *stages* is different from that of *strategies*, in that there is no element of choice. The move, in this case, is realised in three stages, all of which are more or less steps to the fulfilment of the function of the move, and hence are often used together as sub-moves. To avoid this confusion between Swales' notion of *steps*, and that of *stages* suggested here, I find it useful to distinguish *steps* or *stages* from strategies to refer to various ways of realising *moves*. The important thing is that one may use any of the strategies; the move will still fulfil the same aspect of the communicative purpose. The strategies therefore are non-discriminatory, whereas moves can make a significant difference in the status and identification of genres.

It is necessary to posit these two different kinds of elements here because they can be useful in the analysis of genre complexes involving mixing, embedding and generic appropriation. Often such a subtle variation is also useful in analysing genres across cultural boundaries. This kind of information is also extremely helpful in pedagogical contexts in explaining why a particular rhetorical choice is made the way it is. Bhatia and Tay (1987) give a good indication of this in their materials for written business English.

At this point, it is also necessary to clarify one further aspect of cognitive structuring in genre analysis. Genre theory attempts to account for the intricacies of socially constructed human linguistic behaviour. Although this kind of behaviour appears to be manifested, though superficially, in linguistic realisations, the real nature of this behaviour is essentially socio-cognitive, especially when grounded in disciplinary and institutionalised settings. The relationship between linguistic form and the ultimate social meaning it acquires is interpreted not simply through semantics, but more importantly through socio-pragmatics. In the light of recent developments in the field of discourse and communication, such a relationship is taken for granted. However, one may legitimately raise the question of the relationship between text-structures and cognition, where the notion of schematic structure is important. Although schema theory has provided interesting answers to several questions raised in this context, they are essentially relevant to purely cognitive aspects of text-structures. There is also a strong link between schematic structures and individual variation in text construction and comprehension. In genre theory, however, the nature of discourse structure is essentially socio-cognitive (see Berkenkotter and Huckin 1995), where individual variation is underplayed and disciplinary community consensus is given foremost importance. The two approaches to text-structures are therefore fundamentally different.

5 Generic integrity

Let me now take up the most important aspect of applied genre analysis; that is, the notion of *generic integrity*. It is important because it has the potential to enhance our understanding of the role and function of genres in everyday activities that we are all engaged in not only through language, but also through other semiotic means. Although I have discussed this notion in general terms elsewhere (see Bhatia 1993, 1994, 1997, 1998, and 1999b), its detailed discussion and elaboration is necessary, especially in the light of recent analyses of academic and professional genres. The explication of this notion will also, I hope, offer a much broader understanding of genre as a complex and increasingly dynamic, and at the same time a multifaceted construct, which in turn will need a much more multi-dimensional approach to the identification, function and role of genres in academic and professional contexts (Bhatia 2001).

The most important aspect of a genre is that it is recognisable, sufficiently standardised and is based on a set of mutually accessible conventions, which most members of professional, academic or institutional organisations mutually share. In general terms, a typical instance of a specific genre looks like the one intended, in the sense that the members of the discourse or professional community with which it is often associated, tend to recognise it as a typical or valid instance of the genre in question. Most successful constructions of professional textual artefacts have recognisable generic integrity (Bhatia 1993). It may be complex, in that it may reflect a specific form of mixing and/or embedding of two or more generic forms, or even dynamic, in the sense that it may reflect a gradual development over a period of time in response to subtle changes in the rhetorical contexts that it responds to; but it will certainly continue to have a recognisable generic character, which might undergo slow and subtle changes over a long period of time. This generic character is more easily accessible to the established members of the professional community rather than to those who have a peripheral involvement in the affairs of the professional community in question (Swales 1990).

Generic integrity thus may be understood in terms of a socially constructed typical constellation of form-function correlations representing a specific professional, academic, or institutional communicative construct realising a specific communicative purpose of the genre in question. It is possible to characterise it in terms of text-internal and/or text-external or a combination of such features. It is not static, fixed or prescribed, but is often flexible, negotiated or sometimes contested.

The important question is: 'How do we as members of various professional communities recognise these generic artefacts?' The answer could be that each of these artefacts has a generic integrity of its own, which most of us as members of a specific professional community share and use to recognise, construct, interpret and use these generic artefacts to achieve the goals of our own specific professional and disciplinary community, and often extend their use to our advantage, which leads to innovations in otherwise conventionalised generic forms.

There may be three major indicators of generic integrity: the rhetorical context in which the genre is situated, the communicative purpose(s) it tends to serve and the cognitive structure that it tends to display in the structuring of professional practice. If, on the one hand, the communicative purpose of a generic construct is embedded in the rhetorical context in which the genre is often used, on the other hand, it is also transparently reflected in the cognitive patterning of the genre. Some of the main perspectives on generic integrity in major genre-based frameworks are the following:

Contextual perspective

This includes both the communicative purpose, and the communicative context, including both the immediate context with which a genre is often associated, and the more general context in which the genre takes shape. Some of the main indicators may include, among other things, the historical, socio-cultural and professional nature of the discipline that the genre is embedded in, the social structure, interactions, beliefs and goals of the relevant professional, academic or workplace discourse community, the complexities of the medium in use, etc.

Textual, intertextual and interdiscursive perspective

There are text-internal indicators associated with genres, which are easily accessible to good professionals and discourse and genre analysts. These indicators are generally of three types: textual, intertextual and interdiscursive. Textual indicators are typical features of lexico-grammar, textualisation and cognitive patterning. Intertextual indicators are those patterns of semantic relationships which make a particular instance of textual genre cohesive, such as texts providing immediate context, texts surrounding a particular text in question, texts explicitly referred to within the text, texts embedded or quoted within texts in question, etc. In addition, there often are interdiscursive patterns significantly reflected in specific genres. The mixing of legislation and judgements in law textbooks is a very typical example, where typical conventions from three genres are interdiscursively exploited to achieve a specific disciplinary output. Similarly, one may find a typical blend of promotional and informative genres within the same context (see Bhatia 1995, 1997; Fairclough 1992b), and it is not uncommon to find patterns typical of corporate advertising finding a place in fund-raising genres. Even in research article introductions one often notices efforts to promote the author's own work. All these hybridisations and embeddings of one genre in the context of another are typical instances of interdiscursivity, where one often needs to resort to the conventions of one genre to understand the other.

In addition to these indicators of generic integrity, i.e. rhetorical context, communicative purpose, and lexico-grammar, cognitive structuring, intertextuality and interdiscursivity, there are a number of text-external indicators of generic integrity. Most often experienced professionals and expert practitioners of specific genres use these text-external features to identify, construct, interpret, use and exploit these genres to achieve their professional objectives. Some of these include the professional or institutional context in which the genre is used, typical sites of engagement that invoke the use of the genre in question, the disciplinary practices of which the genre is an important instrument used to achieve disciplinary or institutional goals, typical processes and procedures employed to represent institutional, organisational or professional identities through and within the genre, and systems or colonies of genres, of which this particular genre is seen as an important member. Let me summarise some of these extra-textual perspectives:

Institutional and disciplinary perspective

The most significant contributor to institutional perspective is the role played by disciplinary cultures, in providing answers to questions such as, 'How do professionals participate in the disciplinary activities specific to their profession, especially to achieve their disciplinary goals, to express private intentions within the context of disciplinary practices, and to exploit generic conventions to respond to recurring and novel rhetorical contexts as part of their professional activities?' Similarly, the role of disciplinary practices is equally important in providing answers to the questions related to the choice of genres or systems of genres to meet disciplinary goals. The role of discursive processes is also significant in providing answers to several types of issues related to the construction, interpretation, use and exploitation of textual genres, such as who contributes what in the collaborative construction of professional practices. This leads us to think of the nature of discursive processes in specific disciplinary contexts.

Ethnographic perspective

In addition, grounded ethnographic procedures contribute significantly to our understanding of the functioning of professional discourses at typical sites of engagement by focusing on the physical circumstances that influence the nature and construction of genre, the critical moments of engagement or interaction, and on modes of genre construction or communication available at the critical moments or sites.

Socio-cognitive perspective

Finally, in establishing the role of socio-cognitive aspects of genre analysis, we often find it useful to focus on textual knowledge, which underpins the importance of lexico-grammar, text construction, text interpretation and text exploitation to suit changing demands. In a similar manner, the role of pragmatic or tactical knowledge is helpful in providing input based on our knowledge of the world, socio-cultural knowledge in the construction of social identities, and analysis of social structures.

6 Genres in applied linguistics

One of the major problems with genre analysis is that it has often been constrained by applied concerns, in that most of the analyses and investigations have been carried out with a specific application in mind, in particular the teaching and learning of EAP. In order to come up with useful, and often convenient insights for such applications, the investigators have often underplayed the role of the complex and dynamic realities of the real world of discourse, often focusing on standardised and idealised instances of generic constructs. In principle, there is nothing wrong with adopting this perspective; after all, the discourses to be used as input to language teaching and learning materials must have some similarities to or correspondence with what is being learnt and taught in the classroom. However, in doing so, one often forgets that there is yet another perspective which connects the classroom to the real world. So we have three rather distinct worlds, as it were, not just two. First and foremost, we have the real world of discourse, where language is used, interpreted and exploited by real people in the conduct of social affairs. We then have the world of the classroom, where pedagogical action takes place for the teaching and learning of linguistic and communicative skills, often in contrived circumstances, sometimes far removed from the realities of the world of discourse. Somewhere between these two worlds, and yet distinct from them, is the world of the discourse analyst, who, within the constraints of the paradigms, frameworks, tools and the nature of the data available to him or her, somehow tries to connect the other two worlds, making the world of pedagogy, which is restricted and given, relevant to the real world, which is complex, dynamic and unpredictable. In this context, one may legitimately raise one of the most fundamental questions about analysing genre:

Is genre description a reflection of reality, or a useful fiction for pedagogic application?

Abstracting from abstracts

Thomas Huckin

Journal article abstracts have become an increasingly important genre, especially in science and technology. Faced with an 'information explosion', members of the worldwide scientific and technical research community have become more and more dependent on abstracts to keep them up to date in their respective fields. Abstracts have at least four distinct uses. First, they serve as stand-alone *mini-texts*, giving readers a quick summary of a study's topic, methodology, and findings. Second, they serve as *screening devices*, enabling the reader to decide whether to read the article as a whole. Third, for those readers who do opt to read the article as a whole, abstracts serve as *previews*, creating an interpretive frame that can guide reading. Finally, abstracts serve as *aids to indexing* by professional indexers for large database services.

Because of their multivalent importance, abstracts have drawn the attention of a number of genre researchers. In Berkenkotter and Huckin (1995), for example, I studied the evolution of the scientific journal article abstract during the period 1944–89. Examining a random sample of 277 abstracts published in 12 top journals (including *Nature*, *Science*, and *Physical Review*) during this 45-year period, I found that abstracts steadily increased both in length and informativeness. Graetz (1985) studied 87 abstracts from a variety of disciplines, noting that abstracts avoid repetition, examples, preliminaries, descriptive details, and other matters not essential to the main points conveyed. A number of researchers have compared traditional abstracts to formulaic (or 'structured') abstracts, claiming that the latter are generally more effective. Taddio *et al.* (1994), for example, found that structured abstracts can be of higher quality and usually contain more information than traditional abstracts, although they also take up more space and sometimes omit important information. Hartley *et al.* (1996) found that structured abstracts are easier to search.

In scientists' effort to stay abreast of new developments in our Information Age, probably their single most useful tool has been the online computerized database, particularly that which permits users to retrieve not only titles of articles but abstracts as well. Such abstracts can be used both for keyword searches to generate lists of candidate articles and for close perusal to narrow down those lists. Keyword searches alone (that is, searches without abstracts) have been shown to be unreliable. For example, in their evaluation of a full-text document retrieval system using keyword searches, Blair and Maron (1985) found that the system had a false-negative rate of over 80 per cent. That is, less than 20 per cent of the relevant documents in a large database were retrieved using keywords. Keyword searches *with* abstracts are likely to be far more reliable, provided that the abstracts themselves reliably encode appropriate keywords.

According to the American National Standards Institute, 'An abstract is an abbreviated, accurate representation of the contents of a document, preferably prepared by its author(s) for publication with it' (ANSI 1979: 1). Until now, however, no one has tested how accurate abstracts actually are in indicating the content of their accompanying articles. The situation is especially significant in a field such as biomedicine, where rapid retrieval of information may actually save lives. The main purpose of the present study was to see how accurately biomedical abstracts indicate the actual content of articles. (A secondary purpose emerged in the course of the study, namely, to see what sort of 'rhetorical moves' (Swales 1990) characterized the abstracts analyzed.)

The study was carried out for the US National Library of Medicine (NLM). As the world's largest research library in the life sciences, the NLM maintains a computerized database, called MEDLINE (Medical Literature, Analysis, and Retrieval System Online), which is accessible online at over 4,000 institutions around the world. MEDLINE contains more than 11 million citations of biomedical research articles from 4,300 international journals going back to 1966, and approximately 400,000 new ones are added each year. Although these citations can be in any of 30 languages, nearly 86 per cent are published in English and about 76 per cent have English abstracts written by authors of the articles. Citations typically include a title, an author-generated abstract, and a number of keyword descriptors (or 'MeSH headings') provided by the NLM's staff of professional indexers. These keyword descriptions are based on a careful reading of the entire article, not just on a reading of the abstract. In fact, the standard indexing procedure at NLM requires indexers to look at the abstract only as a final, optional step. Thus, the keyword descriptions in a particular citation record have two characteristics which are crucial for the research reported on here: first, they reflect the key information in the article as a whole and, second, they are created independently of the abstract. By having an independent measure of the key concepts in these articles, we can analyze the abstracts and see how well they capture – linguistically and rhetorically – these same concepts.

In effect, I am using a system of triangulation represented below:

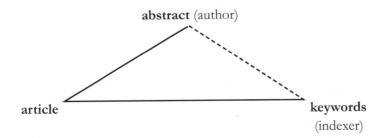

Both the keywords generated by the indexer and the abstract generated by the author are based on the same linguistic object, the article. The keywords are specifically and deliberately selected to capture the most important concepts in the article. The question is, does the abstract also capture these keywords/concepts? If not, then we are either confronted with very different perceptions of the article (which is unlikely, given the professional expertise of the indexers) or with a badly written abstract, one which will not serve very well for information retrieval. But if there is close congruence (represented by the broken line), then we can claim that the abstract does capture the most important content in the article and we can then turn our attention to seeing exactly how it captures it. It turns out that in the random sample of biomedical abstracts I studied, the abstracts not only captured the most important content but presented it in prominent and well-patterned ways. This finding has implications for indexing, for information retrieval, and for the teaching of writing.

Method

The study corpus consisted of a stratified random sample of 90 abstracts from approximately 60 international biomedical journals. They were divided equally among three broad domains: basic science, clinical medicine, and health care delivery. All were written in English, though not all by native speakers of English. All were published in 1986. They ranged in length from 64 to 277 words, with a mean of 121.3 words. An example is given in Figure 1:

Figure 1 'Carbamazepine' abstract.

TITLE: Carbamazepine lowering effect on CSF somatostatin-like immunoreactivity in temporal lobe epileptics.

AUTHORS: Steardo L; Barone P; Hunnicutt E

SOURCE: Acta Neurol Scand 1986 Aug;74(2):140-4.

CITATION IDS: PMID: 2877537 UI: 87044958

ABSTRACT: The effect of carbamazepine treatment on CSF-somatostatin-like immunoreactivity (SLI) in patients suffering from temporal lobe epilepsy was investigated. A baseline lumbar puncture was performed on 12 patients and 10 normal volunteers. A second tap was repeated only in patients when they were on peak of carbamazepine concentration for 10 days. Levels of CSF-SLI were measured by RIA. No significant differences were found in CSF-SLI basal concentrations between epileptics and controls, whereas a significant decrease (p less than .0002 Duncan's multiple range test) of CSF peptide levels occurred in 9 of 12 patients under medication. Although the neural mechanism through which carbamazepine lowers CSF-SLI is still unknown, the results of the present study suggest that the reported effect might be part of the apparatus by which carbamazepine exerts its anticonvulsant action.

MAIN MeSH
HEADINGS: Carbamazepine/*therapeutic use
Epilepsy, Temporal Lobe/*drug therapy
Somatostatin/*cerebrospinal fluid

ADDITIONAL
MeSH HEADINGS: Adolescence
Adult
Epilepsy, Temporal Lobe/cerebrospinal fluid
Female
Human
Male
1986/08
1986/01

PUBLICATION
TYPES: Journal Article

CAS REGISTRY
NUMBERS: 298-46-4(Carbamazepine)
51110-01-1 (Somatostatin)

LANGUAGES: eng

As can be seen, the complete citation record includes the title, the authors' names, the name of the journal, the abstract, and various keyword descriptors. All of this information is available to users online.

Not all of the keyword descriptors are equally important. The starred terms represent concepts that are of major importance in the article, the other terms do not. I focused only on the starred terms.

My basic approach was to inspect each abstract for either explicit or implicit reference to these starred terms. I did this by mimicking the reading process and, in particular, by adhering to what psycholinguists have called the 'levels effect' (Kintsch and Van Dijk 1978). That is, I looked first at the most prominent and general discourse constituent (in this case the title), before I looked at any others. I considered the title to be part of the abstract, on the grounds that the title and abstract always occur together. And since the title is the most prominent and most general discourse constituent in an abstract, it was the logical starting point of my analysis. My specific procedure is described below.

1. For each abstract, list the starred keyword descriptors. In cases where the starred heading is actually a subheading, assume that the star applies to its header as well and list both heading and subheading as a single relational concept.
2. For each of these concepts, search the title for the same (identical or nearly identical) term. If there is one, write 'same in title'.
3. For each remaining starred concept, search the title for a synonymous, near-synonymous, or derivational variant. If there is one, write 'variant in title'.
4. For each remaining starred concept, search the title for words that imply the concept. If there are such words, write 'implied in title'. (Steps 3–4 often required specialized medical knowledge; I used three medical consultants, one from each domain, for assistance.)
5. All remaining concepts are 'not in title'. For each of these, search the rest of the abstract.

Results

My findings are shown in Table 1.

Table 1 Main-concept MeSH headings and their textual correlates in 90 abstracts.

Same in title	74
Variant in title	107
Implied in title	103
Not in title	19
Total	303

There were 303 main concepts in the 90 abstracts I studied. Almost 94 per cent of them were represented either directly or indirectly in the title. Seventy-four were represented with a similar or nearly similar term. One hundred and seven were represented with a variant term. And 103 were implied. Only 19 of these concepts were not reflected in the title at all.

For example, in Figure 1, the key concept 'Somatostatin/*cerebrospinal fluid' appears in the title with virtually the same wording. The key concept 'Carbamazepine/*therapeutic use' does not appear as such in the title but is implied by the expression 'carbamazepine lowering effect'. The key concept 'Epilepsy, Temporal Lobe/*drug therapy' is likewise implied.

Of the 19 cases where key concepts were not reflected in the title, all but two were accounted for at the next level down; that is, at the level of major rhetorical moves. For example, consider Figure 2.

Figure 2 'Intraoperative' abstract.

TITLE:	Intraoperative probe-directed immunodetection using a monoclonal antibody.
AUTHORS:	O'Dwyer PJ; Mojzisik CM; Hinkle GH; Rousseau M; Olsen J; Tuttle SE; Barth RF; Thurston MO; McCabe DP; Farrar WB; et al.
SOURCE:	Arch Surg 1986 Dec;121(12):1391-4.
CITATION IDS:	PMID: 3789910 UI: 87075254
ABSTRACT:	To assess monoclonal antibody (MAb) 17-1A and its F(ab')2 fragment in intraoperative radioimmunodetection and to evaluate further the clinical usefulness of a hand-held gamma-detecting probe (GDP), we injected radiolabeled monoclonal antibody 17-1A three to six days preoperatively or its F(ab')2 fragment two to three days preoperatively into 18 patients with colorectal cancer. Intraoperative GDP counts with tumor-tissue ratios of 1.5:1 or greater were obtained from 15 (75%) of 20 tumor sites, with ratios averaging 2.3:1 for fragments and 3.4:1 for whole antibody. The GDP counts contributed to intraoperative decision making in three patients, either by localization of tumor not identified by inspection or palpation or by mapping margins of resection with histologic confirmation of a local/regional recurrence. These preliminary data demonstrate that probe-directed, intraoperative radioimmunodetection can assist the surgeon in detecting subclinical tumor deposits and thus better evaluate the extent of primary or recurrent colorectal cancers intraoperatively.
MAIN MeSH HEADINGS:	Antibodies, Monoclonal/*diagnostic use Colonic Neoplasms/*diagnosis Immunoglobulins, Fab/*diagnostic use Iodine Radioisotopes/*diagnostic use Rectal Neoplasms/*diagnosis Scintillation Counting/*instrumentation

ADDITIONAL
MeSH HEADINGS:Adult
                Animal
                Case Report
                Colonic Neoplasms/surgery
                Evaluation Studies
                Female
                Human
                Intraoperative Care
                Male
                Mice
                Mice, Nude
                Middle Age
                Rectal Neoplasms/surgery
                1986/12
                1986/01
PUBLICATION
TYPES: Journal Article
CAS REGISTRY
NUMBERS: 0 (Antibodies, Monoclonal)
                0 (Immunoglobulins, Fab)
                0 (Iodine Radioisotopes)
LANGUAGES: eng

There are three key concepts that, according to my specialist consultant, are not even implied in the title: 'Colonic Neoplasms/*diagnosis', 'Iodine Radioisotopes/*diagnostic use', and 'Rectal Neoplasms/*diagnosis'. However, all three are referred to quite clearly in the main clause of the first sentence of the abstract. This first sentence is rhetorically prominent, combining as it does a statement of Purpose and the description of Methodology. Most of the 19 non-title cases were represented like this, as can be seen in Table 2.

Table 2 Textual correlates of the main-concept MeSH headings not represented in titles.

Good rhetorical clues in abstract	11
Fairly good rhetorical/linguistic clues in abstract	6
Weak rhetorical/linguistic clues in abstract	2
Total	19

In all, 99.3 per cent of the key concepts in this corpus, as determined by independent experts, were referred to in these abstracts. Thus, it is fair to say that the writers of these abstracts did a competent job of covering the material in their respective articles.

Rhetorical moves

Previous research on scientific and technical abstracts by Maeda (1981), Graetz (1985) and others has either assumed or claimed that they contain four major parts, or 'rhetorical moves' (Swales 1990): a statement of Purpose, a description of Methods, a listing of Results, and a discussion of Conclusions. Indeed, this four-move template has been canonized in many technical and science writing textbooks. In my research, however, I found that only three of these moves (Methods, Results, and Conclusions) appeared consistently.

Table 3. Percentage of biomedical abstracts (n=90) containing explicit rhetorical moves

Purpose	22%
Methodology	63%
Results	88%
Conclusions	78%

Methodology statements appeared in 63 per cent of these 90 abstracts, Results statements appeared in 88 per cent, and Conclusions appeared in 78 per cent. The major exceptions to this pattern were abstracts from review-type articles. Meanwhile, only 22 per cent of the abstracts contained an explicit statement of Purpose, and in most of these cases, the Purpose statement was not a full sentence but only a subordinate clause attached to the Methods statement, as in the following example:

> To assess monoclonal antibody (MAb) 17-1A and its F(ab')2 fragment in intraoperative radioimmunodetection and to evaluate further the clinical usefulness of a hand-held gamma-detecting probe (GDP), we injected radiolabeled monoclonal antibody 17-1A three to six days preoperatively or its F(ab')2 fragment two to three days preoperatively into 18 patients with colorectal cancer. (O'Dwyer *et al.*)

In general, it seems that Purpose statements are often unnecessary in biomedical abstracts. The 'problem spaces' in biomedical research are so well-defined that mere mention of certain diseases, certain chemical substances, certain research tools, and so on makes the purpose of the research immediately obvious, at least to a specialist. There may be an opening background statement, or a statement of the topic (what Swales (1990: 181) calls 'establishing a territory'), but for many specialized readers of these specialized journals, the purpose of the research does not need stating. Instead of wasting precious space on an explicit Purpose statement, the abstract writer can simply begin his or her abstract with a general statement of Methodology and let the reader *infer* the purpose. Figure 3 provides an example:

Figure 3 'Brain Dopamine' abstract.

TITLE:	Brain dopamine metabolism in patients with Parkinson's disease measured with positron emission tomography.
AUTHORS:	Leenders KL; Palmer AJ; Quinn N; Clark JC; Firnau G; Garnett ES; Nahmias C; Jones T; Marsden CD
SOURCE:	J Neurol Neurosurg Psychiatry 1986 Aug;49(8):853-60.
...	
ABSTRACT:	L-[18F] fluorodopa was administered in trace amounts intravenously to healthy control subjects and to patients with Parkinson's disease. Striatal uptake of radioactivity was measured using positron emission tomography. The capacity of the striatum to retain tracer was severely impaired in patients compared to controls. This may reflect a reduction of striatal dopamine storage in Parkinson's disease. Patients showing the 'on/off' phenomenon had an even greater decrease of striatal storage capacity.

Notice how the first two sentences of the abstract describe the general methodology in such a way that the primary purpose of the research is transparent: simply, to see how these two groups differ in brain dopamine metabolism. But the purpose of the research is not just exploratory. It is also to test a pre-existing hypothesis that Parkinson's patients have a reduced capacity to store striatal dopamine. Notice how this more focused purpose can be referred to in the Conclusion statement, without having been mentioned in a Purpose statement.

I therefore conclude that while there *is* a text-schema for biomedical abstracts, it consists not of four moves but of only three: Method, Results, and Conclusions. Further analysis reveals that there are clear linguistic markings for these three rhetorical moves. For example, *Methods* statements were marked by verbs like *used* (three times), *measured* (12 times), *evaluated* (nine times), and *performed* (eight times); the past tense was used 90 per cent of the time. *Results* statements were most often marked by the verb *showed*, which appeared 27 times; other commonly occurring verbs were *demonstrated*, *found*, and *was observed*. In every case except review-type abstracts and case studies, the past tense was used in these Results statements. Other lexical items were associated with Results statements as well; for example, *significant* occurred 18 times and *significantly* 19 times. *Conclusions* were almost always marked by a shift to the present tense (93 per cent of the time), and they often began with an explicit signal phrase such as *This study shows* or *I conclude that*. Half of the Conclusions contained single-word hedges like *suggests*, *appears*, and *may*, and many others contained more elaborate hedges. Statements of Conclusions typically restated and added information to the topic given in the title.

A good example of these text features working together appears in Figure 3. This abstract opens with a sentence establishing the topic and the basic Method; the Purpose of the study can be inferred and is therefore left unstated. Sentence two continues the description of Method, featuring the common expression *was measured*. The Results section starts with sentence three and concludes in delayed fashion with sentence five. All of these sentences (1–3, 5) are in the past tense, describing what happened. The Conclusion is presented in sentence four. Notice how the shift to present tense, hedged by the modal *may*, creates a statement at the appropriate level of generality.

Conclusion

In conclusion, this analysis of 90 randomly chosen abstracts from international journals suggests that the typical author-generated abstract in biomedicine not only refers to the main concepts of the article but refers to them *prominently*, and also that the typical author-generated abstract in biomedicine has a three-move text schema consisting of Method, Results, and Conclusions.

These findings have implications, I feel, for indexing, for information retrieval, and for pedagogy. First, to the extent that abstracts conform to such a text schema, indexers should find it easier to locate key information for indexing. If frame-based knowledge representations and parsers are used, even semi-automated indexing becomes a possibility. Using linguistic features like those described here, a text-analyzing program could identify first the conclusion and/or title. An indexing program could then analyze these parts for disease names or other major frame headings and call up the appropriate knowledge frames. Next, the text-analyzing program would identify the results statements, and the indexing program would analyze it according to appropriate slots in the knowledge frames. Names for major frame headings and key related terms could then be converted into their equivalents in the controlled language being used for indexing. A weighting scheme giving priority to titles and conclusions might account for those headings marked as major ones. Headings related to methodology could be handled in the same way or, perhaps better, could be determined in a totally different, non-computational way, by having authors simply fill out a checklist before submitting their articles for publication.

If frame-based knowledge representations and parsers are used, information retrieval could also take advantage of my findings. After using an indexing system to narrow the search, users could employ the sort of text-analyzing program just described to zero in on only those abstracts where the target information appears, say, in titles, conclusions, or results statements.

Finally, my findings could easily be converted into guidelines for authors and for students. Among the guidelines would be these:

1. Create a title that includes the major concepts in your article and, if possible, the most important point.
2. Try to describe your methodology in such a way that the reader can infer the purpose of your work. This will save you the necessity of stating your purpose explicitly.
3. Write the rest of the abstract so that results and conclusions are emphasized.
4. Make sure the statement of conclusions emphasizes the most significant points of the article.
5. Use past-tense verbs to describe the specific results of the study. Use present-tense verbs to state general conclusions.

Short answers in first-year undergraduate science writing. What kind of genres are they?

Helen Drury

Introduction

The study of science genres has tended to focus on those produced in professional settings, such as the research article, rather than those produced within a pedagogical context. For example, studies have investigated the ethnographic context of the research article (Gilbert and Mulkay 1984; Myers 1990), its evolution (Bazerman 1989), and its linguistic characteristics (see Swales 1990 for a summary of these studies). This body of research has supported the development of teaching/learning materials, although these interventions have largely occurred within the field of English as a second or foreign language (ESL/EFL) at the postgraduate level (see for example Johns and Dudley-Evans 1988, on team teaching in plant biology, or Weissberg and Buker 1990). At the undergraduate level, the focus has been on investigating the laboratory report in different discipline areas and providing teaching materials, once again primarily in the ESL/EFL area (Drury 1997; Dudley-Evans 1985; and the Singapore University Technical Writing Project developed by Bhatia (Bhatia 1994; Bhatia and Tay 1987)).

Within the Systemic Functional Linguistic (SFL) tradition, professional and school-based scientific discourse has been described and analyzed (Halliday and Martin 1993; Martin and Veel 1998). The genres of science writing in the Australian secondary school setting have also been researched (Veel 1997, 1998) and compared with those required in industry (Rose 1997). Teaching/learning materials for writing school science have also been developed (Christie *et al.* 1990, 1992) based on this research. However, the different disciplinary demands of written communication placed on students during their transition to university in the first year of an undergraduate program in the sciences have not been investigated, apart from the genre of the laboratory report, as mentioned earlier. In particular, the genres of the short answer in this setting remain to be described and analyzed.

The 'short answer' is taken here to mean an extended text, usually one to two paragraphs in length, written in response to a question or instruction. Such short answers or 'elemental genres' as they have been termed (Martin 1994) have been shown to make up the different parts of larger texts or macro-genres (Martin 1994) and as such are important building blocks for apprentice writers in the discipline. It could be argued that unless students have control over these elemental genres, they will not be able to move on to the more demanding macro-genres they will be required to write in the later years of their degree program. In addition, the short answer tends to be the dominant form of extended writing used for assessment purposes in the first year of an undergraduate science degree.

This paper will begin by identifying and describing the range of short-answer genres which students are typically required to produce during their first year of study in the biological sciences at Sydney University. One particular text type, the comparative short answer, considered to be a key 'transitional genre' for first-year Biology, will be focused on with an analysis of the genre based on an SFL approach. It has been termed a transitional genre as its classification as a type of genre, either a factual report or an exposition, is problematic. In addition, it appears to play a developmental or transitional role in first-year Biology, moving students from writing factual, descriptive reports at the beginning of the academic year to expositions at the end. In the paper, brief reference will also be made to some of the teaching approaches and materials used for helping students write these short answers.

Short answers in first-year Biology

The content of the short-answer writing tasks and their sequencing is determined by the first-year curriculum. The curriculum document itself specifies the biological knowledge students need to understand on graduating from their first year of study. However, it does not specify, and nor were subject specialists able to clarify, what was expected of students in terms of communicating this knowledge in writing. A clear articulation of the kinds of short-answer writing tasks, together with their purposes, which students would be expected to have mastered by the end of their first year of study would be a useful addition to the traditional curriculum document. This is one of the goals of the ongoing joint project between the School of Biological Sciences and the Learning Centre at Sydney University which aims to integrate the teaching of writing into the first-year curriculum.

The range of short-answer writing tasks produced in the first year of under-graduate study are shown in Table 1. Half of these tasks are used for teaching/learning purposes. Texts 1 and 4 in the table are used as model texts in laboratory sessions where they are accompanied by exercises which focus attention on their structure and lexicogrammar. Text 2, set early in first semester, is used for a practice writing exercise. The other texts listed in the table are used for assessment of student writing. Texts 3 and 7 consist of a number of short-answer texts which together form field reports. Only Texts 5 and 6 consist of a single short-answer writing task. The generic labels given in the table follow the terminology developed by Martin and other SF linguists who have been investigating the written genres of the primary and secondary school in the Australian context (Disadvantaged Schools Program 1988; Martin 1985, 1993a/b; Martin and Peters 1985). The descriptions of the texts in the first column follow those used commonly in educational settings.

Table 1 Short-answer writing tasks in chronological order in first-year Biology at Sydney University.

TEXT TYPE	QUESTION/TOPIC/ PURPOSE	GENRE (SUB-GENRE)
Semester 1		
1 *factual description* model text	To describe the characteristics of a beetle	report (descriptive)
2 *factual description* practice writing exer-cise	To describe the characteristics of a seedling	report (composition)
3 *field report* visit to Australian Museum's 'Fossils and Dinosaurs' exhibit: assessed assignment	i Describe the features of the group of organisms ii Describe the typical habitat of the group of organisms iii What events may have led to the extinction of this group of organisms?	macro genre: report (descriptive) and explanation (explo-ration)

4 *Factual comparative description and explanation model text*	How are the structure and function of stems and roots similar and why? How do they differ and why?	exposition (comparative/ contrastive)
5 *factual comparative description and explanation* assessed assignment	The digestive systems of the cat and rat have been modified from the same basic mammalian plan to suit their respective diets. Compare and contrast the structure and function of the two systems and explain why there are differences	exposition (comparative/ contrastive)
Semester 2		
6 *factual contrastive description* assessed assignment	Contrast the process of mitosis and the process of meiosis.	exposition (contrastive)
7 *field report* visit to the Botanic Gardens: assessed assignment	i Write a brief description of the field characteristics which you would use to distinguish the Cactaceae from species of *Euphorbia*. ii Write a brief description of the difference between convergent, parallel and divergent evolution. Then use these definitions and the information you have collected from the gardens to describe which evolutionary trend(s) may have accounted for the morphological similarities between the two plant groups. Give justifications for your answer.	macro genre: discussion or exposition, report (superordination), discussion

On looking at Table 1, there are a number of generalisations that can be made about how short-answer writing is developed in first-year Biology. In general, underlying most, if not all, of the short-answer tasks is the necessity to describe accurately the biological features or characteristics, functions, etc. of a phenomenon or phenomena. This is in fact the sole purpose of the model text, the descriptive report, which is used to introduce students to writing in the discipline at the beginning of the year. However, the majority of texts do not merely describe but also classify, either by organizing information about the phenomenon/a in terms of a taxonomy, either predominantly a composition taxonomy (part/whole) or a superordination taxonomy (class/sub-class). A significant feature of the texts written later in the year is that they require descriptive and classifying information about two phenomena to be organized around the similarities and/or differences between them and, in some texts, reasons given for these patterns of similarity and difference. The final field report of the year represents the end point in the sequence where students are expected to evaluate descriptive and classifying information to develop arguments about the validity of a biological taxonomy and the evolution of its members. Thus the writing tasks are sequenced in increasing order of complexity and this, to some extent, mirrors the increase in complexity of the subject matter itself. As students proceed from first semester to second they are being moved from descriptive and classifying report writing towards exposition and discussion. In order to achieve this transition, however, they will need to be able to manipulate the descriptive and classifying information they used for writing a report to write an exposition or discussion. As will be shown later, some students are able to make this shift, while others are not.

The activity of comparing and/or contrasting seems to play a dominant role in these short-answer texts and to be a key activity for first-year Biology writing. This appears to be in contrast to the science genres of the secondary school (Martin 1993a; Veel 1997). Whereas the activity of reading reports and writing explanations seems to be of major importance in the final years of secondary school science (Martin 1993a: 187/191), in first-year Biology, report and explanation writing appears to be subsumed within other genres. In order to be able to create valid taxonomies, and challenge invalid ones, an important task of a biologist, students need to be able to distinguish phenomena on the basis of their similarities and differences and give reasons for common characteristics and variations. The comparative/contrastive short-answer writing task is the beginning of this activity. To examine in more detail the linguistic characteristics of such a text, the model text written to compare and contrast stems and roots (number 4 in Table 1) will be analyzed in the next section. The status of this text as an example of an exposition genre will also be discussed.

What kind of genre is a comparative short answer?

Figure 1 represents a generic analysis (using the framework developed by Halliday 1984, and Martin 1992) of the model comparative/contrastive short answer. The text, written by a first-year Biology lecturer, is used to introduce students to how Biology lecturers assess student writing. Students work in groups to compare the model with a second, poorly written text on the same topic in order to develop their own criteria for assessing writing in Biology. The model text is divided up into numbered 'messages' or 'conjunctively related units'; that is, clauses or clause complexes which extend or develop the main message of the text (Martin 1992: 235). Themes are shown in bold and thematic elements which develop cohesion through the reference system are shown in bold italics.

Figure 1 Generic structure of model short-answer text number 4, a response to the following questions.
How are the structure and function of stems and roots similar and why?
How do they differ and why?

SCHEMATIC STRUCTURE	TEXT: Exposition genre
(paragraph 1) THESIS 1 and Argument 1.1	(1) **The main similarity between the stem and root** is the fact that they both contain the vascular tissues.
EMBEDDED REPORT	(2) **The main components of the vascular tissue** are the phloem and xylem. (3) **Phloem** is composed of sieve tubes, in which the products of photosynthesis are transported bi-directionally around the plant, and companion cells whose function is not clear. (4) **The main components of the xylem** are the vessels, a series of dead, open ended, thick walled cylindrical cells forming a tube through which water is transported. (5) **The movement of water in the xylem** is uni-directional from the roots to the leaves.

(paragraph 2) ARGUMENT 1.2	(6) *Other* **similarities** include the presence of parenchyma cells, which function as storage areas, (7) **and** make up a large proportion of both the stem and root.
ARGUMENT 1.3	(8) *Both* **stems and roots** also have a single outer layer of protective epidermal cells.
(paragraph 3) THESIS 2 and ARGUMENT 2.1	(9) **Differences** are apparent in the arrangement of the vascular tissues. (10) **In many stems** they are present in discrete vascular bundles which are situated in a peripheral ring, (11) **whereas in roots** they are arranged in a central core.
ARGUMENT 2.2	(12) *Other* **differences** include the fact that only the stem is covered with an outer layer of waxy waterproof cuticle. (13) *Its* **presence in a root** would hinder water uptake. (14) **Roots**, however, have root hairs on the outer surface, which aid in water uptake.
ARGUMENT 2.3	(15) **Also roots** have a unique ring of cells, called the endodermis, which surrounds the vascular tissues. (16) *These* **cells** are differentially suberised, (17) **and** are responsible for the control of water movement, from the surrounding root tissues into the xylem in the vascular core.

The schematic structure is shown as a number of repeated stages, primarily two 'thesis' stages which respond to the questions posed, followed by a number of arguments to support each thesis. This structure is that of an expository genre, although the reiteration stage which typically closes this kind of genre is not found in this text. Expository genres are used to present arguments in favor of a position, and to do this they need to use language in an abstract way which will construct the text as an argument. The activities of comparing and contrasting require reorganization of the information about the phenomena in question so that the relationships of similarity and difference in the content are made clear. This activity of analyzing the information means that writers must 'distance' themselves from the content more than the activities of observation, description and classification which result in a typical factual, report genre. Such distancing develops a more abstract genre which is removed from its real-world experiential content. This can be seen in the foregrounding of the purpose of the text (to compare and contrast stems and roots) in Theme position at the beginning of the text,

(1) The main similarity between the stem and root ...

and at key stages in the text's development. For example:

(6) Other similarities ...
(9) Differences ...

The abstract, nominalized forms of the conjunctions of similarity and difference 'scaffold' the text (Applebee and Larger 1983, cited in Martin 1999: 126), in other words, create and emphasize its purpose as a text that compares and contrasts stems and roots rather than describes them.

Themes operate at different hierarchical levels in the text and once again the upper levels of the hierarchy are dominated by the comparative purpose of the text. The Macro-Theme or Theme for the whole text,

(1) The main similarity between the stem and root is the fact that they both contain the vascular tissues.

helps the reader predict that since similarities are identified, differences will also be identified and these will, most likely, also focus on the vascular tissues.

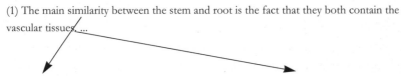

(1) The main similarity between the stem and root is the fact that they both contain the vascular tissues. ...

(9) Differences are apparent in the arrangement of the vascular tissues.

At the paragraph level, Hyper-Themes (Martin 1992) perform a similar role. For example:

(9) Differences are apparent in the arrangement of the vascular tissues.

(12) Other differences.

At the level of the clause, stems and roots and other experiential content begin to dominate in Theme position, although reference (in bold italics in clause 8) and conjunction (in bold in clause 11)

(8) **Both** stems and roots also have a single outer layer of protective epidermal cells.

(11) **whereas** in roots they are arranged in a central core.

remind the reader that the purpose of the text continues to be one of comparison. These, however, are congruent or non-metaphorical language structures unlike the nominalized forms found in the upper levels of the text's thematic hierarchy.

However, seen from the perspective of the social sciences and humanities, and indeed later forms of science writing, the status of this text as an exposition can be questioned. Stating a comparison, although an abstract, analytical activity, is not presenting a position to be argued about. The 'arguments' themselves are merely other kinds of similarities and differences rather than evidence to support a thesis position. On the other hand, the thesis statements do present the writer's interpretation and, to some extent, evaluation of the biological information.

(1) The main similarity between the stem and root is the fact that they both contain the vascular tissues.

(9) Differences are apparent in the arrangement of the vascular tissues.

However, these statements are not seen to be contentious since biologists would generally agree on the facts about the similarities and the differences between roots and stems. If this is the case, then the text could be seen as a kind of report genre whose purpose is to present scientific facts and the thesis and argument stages in the schematic structure could be interpreted as general statements followed by descriptions as in a report genre. Furthermore, a report genre, unlike an expository genre, would typically have no need of a concluding stage or a reiterative stage in the schematic structure and, as has been said earlier, there are no paragraph or text conclusions in this text. The New information or the 'point' of the text consists of the similarities and differences themselves, and once stated there is no need to repetitively summarize these.

The division of the factual, descriptive information about stems and roots into similarities and differences can also be seen as a more elaborate form of a superordinate taxonomy and in this way more like a classifying report genre where various characteristics of stems and roots are identifed as either kinds of similarities or differences. This taxonomy is illustrated in Figure 2.

Figure 2 Superordinate taxonomy of similarities and differences between stems and roots in model short-answer text number 4

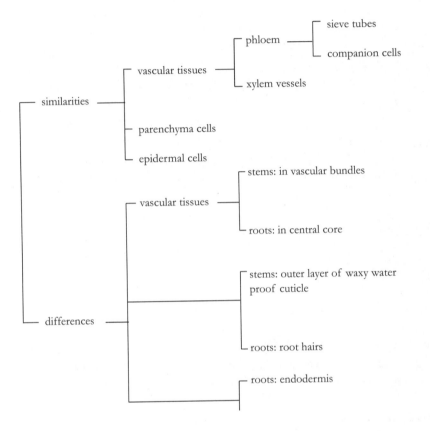

However, although the taxonomy in Figure 2 uses the technical language of the discipline to foreground the things roots and stems have and do not have in common, this is not the case in the text itself where the basis for the analysis of the content into similarities and differences is given priority in the logical unfolding of the text. This occurs largely within the nominal group structures found in the clause endings or News. The 'Thing' or 'semantic core' (Halliday 1984: 167) of these nominal groups consists of abstract nominalizations of the criteria used for identifying similarities and differences. For example:

(6) the **presence** of parenchyma cells
    Thing

(9) the **arrangement** of the vascular tissues
    Thing

This foregrounding of the analytical rather than the descriptive would suggest an expository genre rather than a report genre.

On the other hand, at the micro or local level, other structures associated with a report genre can be identified. The dependent clauses at this level all further describe or elaborate on the information in the main clause in the complex. These elaborating clause complexes have generic participants (in italics in the example below) and predominantly relational processes (in bold) which either reflect the compositional purpose of the report at this level or give reasons for the similarities and differences between stems and roots. For example:

Text extract	Purpose of extract
(14) *Roots*, however, **have** *root hairs* on the outer surface,	State the composition of roots
which aid in *water uptake*.	Give a reason why roots have this composition

It should be noted that the reason why roots have root hairs is expressed incongruently in an elaborating clause which involves the nominalisation of the verb 'take up' rather than in a congruent, enhancing clause of purpose:

Roots, however, have *root hairs* on the outer surface, **so that they can take up water.**

If the congruent version had been used, this clause would have become a 'message' in the macro-level development of the text and would also have given this status to the purpose of explaining.

However, as has been said, the text characteristics described above operate at the local level and this suggests that the activities of reporting and explaining are certainly present in the text but are subsumed by the more macro-level activities of comparison. Thus, reporting is a lower level purpose of the text and exposition can be considered as its main purpose. When the above example is placed in the context of its stage in the schematic structure of the text as a whole, the additional structures which are necessary for the purpose of contrast can be seen (in bold).

(12) **Other differences** include the fact that **only** the stem is covered with an outer layer of waxy waterproof cuticle.

(13) Its presence in a root would hinder water uptake.

(14) Roots, **however**, have root hairs on the outer surface, which aid in water uptake.

The use of 'only' in clause 12 to intensify the meaning of contrast points towards an expository text. In addition, if the implicit conjunction of cause between clauses 12 and 13 and the condition that is implied within clause 13 are revealed, the writer can be seen to be developing an argument rather than merely providing biological information. If clause 13 is rewritten to show these relationships, it would be as follows:

(12) Other differences include the fact that only the stem is covered with an outer layer of waxy waterproof cuticle.

This is because, if it were present in a root, it would hinder water uptake.

On the other hand, the lexical cohesion in the above extract can be considered as real-world or field contrasts – stem contrasted with root, waxy waterproof cuticle with root hair and hinder with aid – and such contrasts would support the classification of this text as a kind of report genre.

There are other instances in the text of lexicogrammatical resources being used for the purposes of writing a report, in particular, what has been labeled the 'embedded report' which decomposes the vascular tissues into two main parts and describes the composition and function of each part. However, this activity is clearly a sub-purpose of the text, although it is appropriate at the stage where it occurs and cannot be omitted. In general, the biological knowledge and accompanying technical terminology of this text is taken as already known. The main purpose of comparing and contrasting requires other lexicogrammatical structures, as we have seen, which reflect the more analytical and abstract nature of this task. An example of such resources can be found in the first clause of the text:

(1) **The main similarity between the stem and root is the fact [[that they both contain the vascular tissues]]**

This clause is characterized by complex nominal groups in both Theme and New (both in bold) which are linked by an identifying relational process. The Theme contains a nominalised conjunction of similarity which in turn is valued as the main similarity between the stem and root and this is identified as an abstraction, a 'fact' noun qualified by an embedded clause which attributes the common characteristic of stems and roots as containing the vascular tissues. These meanings, if written in a report genre, would probably appear as follows:

Stems contain vascular tissues. ... Roots contain vascular tissues...

An analysis of conjunction in this text also tends to support its classification as an exposition rather than a report. This analysis is set out in Figure 3. The reticulum in Figure 3 displays internal conjunctions, those which organize rhetorical meanings, on the left-hand side, and external conjunctions, those which organize real-world experiential meanings, on the right hand side. Explicit external relations of addition are placed in the middle. The numbers refer to the 'messages' in the text shown in Figure 1. The conjunctions themselves, both explicit and implicit (in brackets), are given on the far right-hand side of the figure. Arrows and lines show the direction and extent of each conjunctive relation (Martin 1992).

The text displays a predominance of internal conjunction, which is indicative of an exposition genre. The resources of internal conjunction are needed to shape biological knowledge to the rhetorical purpose of a certain text type, in this case comparison. External conjunctions tend to predominate if the biological knowledge itself is to be described or explained as in a report genre. Internal conjunction develops the rhetorical structure of the text according to the writer's ordering of the similarities and differences, whereas external conjunctions of contrast are used in the last paragraph to develop the text in terms of real-world or field contrasts. The external status of the latter conjunctions is, however, debatable. It can be argued that the writer is

Figure 3 Analysis of conjunction in model short-answer text number 4

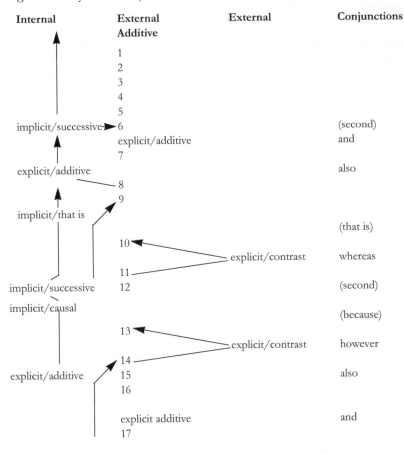

| Internal | External Additive | External | Conjunctions |

responsible for organizing these oppositions to develop the text, and is using linguistic rather than biological knowledge to do so. If this is the case, these conjunctions would be considered to be internal and all conjunctions in the text would be of this kind (see Figure 4).

Although this analysis of internal conjunction lends support to identifying this text as exposition, once again this is not clear cut because of the real world, field-based similarities and differences between stems and roots which are described in the text.

On the basis of the analysis of one sample text, it is impossible to come to a firm conclusion as to what kind of genre a comparative text is and more data from a number of disciplines, not only science, need to be examined.

Figure 4 Alternative analysis of conjunction in the last part of short-answer text number 4

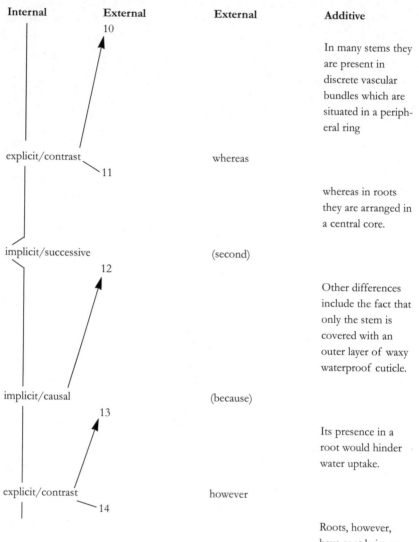

Internal	External	External	Additive
	10		In many stems they are present in discrete vascular bundles which are situated in a peripheral ring
explicit/contrast		whereas	
	11		whereas in roots they are arranged in a central core.
implicit/successive		(second)	
	12		Other differences include the fact that only the stem is covered with an outer layer of waxy waterproof cuticle.
implicit/causal		(because)	
	13		Its presence in a root would hinder water uptake.
explicit/contrast		however	
	14		Roots, however, have root hairs on the outer surface, which aid in water uptake.

In addition, more information on the context of situation and culture is needed to identify what counts as expository writing at first-year university level in the Biological Sciences. It may also be more helpful to see this kind of comparative text as part of a genre continuum between a report and an exposition, rather than attempting to allocate it to a specific type of genre, report or exposition. Indeed, on the basis of further research, it could be given generic status in its own right, although most likely as a kind of exposition genre. A genre continuum, such as that in Figure 5, may also be useful from a pedagogical perspective especially as this type of text appears as a kind of 'transition' genre within the first year curriculum in the Biological Sciences

Figure 5 Genre continuum in first-year short-answer writing in the biological sciences

Students can recycle their knowledge about writing reports as they move through the first-year curriculum and use it to move on to writing comparative texts, and knowledge about these texts in turn will enable them to write 'true' expositions as the learning outcome for writing short answers in first-year Biology. (See Veel 1997 and Coffin 1997 for discussion and exemplification of genre continua in secondary school science and history respectively.)

Achieving mastery of exposition genres in first-year Biology

Although the learning outcome of the first year may be expository writing, this, in fact, is not achieved by all students and some appear to remain at the level of report writing with which they began the year. To illustrate this problem, examples of student writing from the last short-answer writing task in the first year will be given. Due to lack of space, only the first paragraph in answer to the first question will be exemplified. The question is as follows: 'Write a brief description of the field characteristics which you would use to distinguish the Cactaceae from species of Euphorbia'. Student answers are based on field observations they make in the Sydney Botanic Gardens and, on the surface, the task appears a straightforward one of contrast. However, as will be seen below, it is not as unproblematic as it seems. The following extracts illustrate the range of student answers.

Text 1

In the species *Euphorbia,* leaves were sometimes found present. These leaves were large, green-yellow in colour, and had tinges of red on them. *Euphorbia* were woody shrubs and trees, that were distinguishable by their tall, thin appearance.

Text 2

One of the differences observed between Cactaceae and *Euphorbia* was the presence of leaves. In the Cactaceae species no leaves were observed, but many of the *Euphorbia* species had leaves present. The other major difference observed between Cactaceae and *Euphorbia* was the way in which the spines were arranged. In all of the Cactaceae species observed, spines were arranged in large clusters and were thickly distributed, whereas in *Euphorbia*, the spines were usually arranged in rows and often were just singular or arranged in pairs. Euphorbia millii was an exception with its spines scattered at random.

Text 3

On close examination of field records, there do not appear to be any characteristics that enable the family Cactaceae to be distinguished from the genus *Euphorbia.*
Both succulents have spines and fleshy stems for water storage, may grow as either trees or shrubs and both may or may not flower at the same time.

Text 1 is simply a written version of the student's own field records. Since it does not generalize, its generic status is that of a description, tied to observations made at one specific time in the past. No attempt is made in this text to contrast Cactaceae and *Euphorbia*; they are simply described as they appeared on the day. Text 2 develops the purpose of contrast, although it too ties this activity to a specific occasion in the past. It is only Text 3 which attempts to generalize from the field data. However, it goes further than this to establish a thesis, given in the first sentence, about the possibility of distinguishing between the Cactaceae and *Euphorbia* based on available field data.

This is in fact closer to a 'true' thesis because the writer is questioning the validity of the taxonomy, unlike the thesis statements of the comparison text on stems and roots. Text 3 above, the most highly valued of the three, could be said to represent the target genre for students graduating from first year. Having observed, described and classified life forms and communicated this knowledge through reports, students need to be able to make comparisons and contrasts within and among taxonomies and to account for variations and commonalities. Finally, they need to be able to question the validity of taxonomies based on detailed observations, descriptions and comparisons.

The ability to challenge biological knowledge through such an activity as the final short-answer writing task is a strong basis for continuing studies into second and third year.

Conclusion

The work reported here has implications for genre research as well as the approach to teaching genres across the curriculum. It highlights the problematic nature of a strict typological approach to genre identification and classification where a text has to be seen to 'belong' to a certain type based on its macro- and micro-level characteristics. The comparative text discussed in this paper poses a further problem in that it could even be given generic status on its own since it has a different purpose to that of a report or an exposition. Clearly, there is a need to research widely a number of texts within and among what are considered to be genre norms so that topological variations can be investigated and incorporated in the modeling of the schematic structure and the exemplification of the discourse semantics and lexicogrammar. (See Martin and Matthiessen 1991 for a discussion of typological and topological approaches in SFL analysis, and Lemke 1987 and Unsworth 1996 for discussions of typological and topographical approaches to genre analysis.)

At present this lack of research poses problems for the development of appropriate models and exercises for the pedagogical context, in particular pedagogical resources that support students' progressive acquisition of genres. A richer generic description would make explicit the transitions between genres – in this case from report, through comparative text to exposition – and would enable students to see the relationships between the different genres. These linguistic insights are invaluable in enabling students to effectively respond to the writing tasks they are set and to master the increasing complexity of these tasks in their undergraduate studies.

Introductory textbooks and disciplinary acculturation: a case study from social anthropology

Alison Love

Introduction

Studies of the genre of introductory textbooks at tertiary level have generally concluded that they provide 'representations of disciplinary orthodoxy' (Hyland 2000: 104). Johns (1997) gives a useful overview, suggesting that textbooks only present agreed, and therefore inevitably outdated, formulations of disciplinary knowledge, avoiding disciplinary conflicts and offering definitive information. MacDonald suggests that textbook writers need to negotiate the possible tension between the three competing goals of 'transmitting knowledge, engaging students in inquiry, or initiating students into the discipline' (MacDonald 1994: 180).

Introductory textbooks, by definition, assume no prior disciplinary knowledge. Moreover, in most cases the topics covered in a number of introductory textbooks are broadly similar. However, I should like to suggest, following MacDonald, that where such texts differ is in the degree to which they induct students into the epistemological issues of the discipline, as opposed to presenting them with 'accepted' disciplinary knowledge. This is a crucial issue in the social sciences, since there are few areas which are free of interpretive contestation (Giddens 1993: 21). Hence the textbook writer in a discipline such as social anthropology has to decide how much to expose their 'initiate' readers to the complexity of observed data within a topic and the extent of contestation of interpretation, weighing this against the desire to provide a clear and relatively simple overview of unfamiliar concepts. I shall suggest that decisions on these questions influence the textbook discourse, and realise the 'expectation level' of the textbook, which is likely to be of concern to lecturers selecting recommended texts for their students.

Case study: Cheater's 'alternative introduction'

In this case study I shall examine an introductory textbook, entitled *Social Anthropology: An Alternative Introduction* (Cheater 1986), which is the set text for the 'Introduction to Social Anthropology' course at the University of Zimbabwe. The text was originally produced for this course when the author was herself teaching it. The text has, subsequently, been published in an international edition (Cheater 1989) and is used in some UK universities (Street, personal communication). The book is, significantly, subtitled 'an alternative introduction', and Cheater explains:

> The Zimbabwean origins of the book mean that the book has a perspective that is subtly yet sharply different ... 'other cultures' were not something remote or exotic but familiarly real and living, changing and above all changeable. (Cheater 1989: x)

This suggests that Cheater is concerned to 'engage' her readers rather than 'inform'.

I shall then make a brief comparison with a North American textbook, *Contemporary Cultural Anthropology*, by Howard (1989). This author makes explicit his awareness of the problems of expectation level:

> Many [textbooks] approach the material at a level above the comprehension of most introductory students; those with a more accessible style often offer an overly simplistic approach. (Howard 1989: v)

Howard is also explicit about the need to focus on problems of interpretation:

> while we may not be able to arrive at answers for why people believe and act as they do, we can hope to understand the complexity of those forces that influence belief and behaviour. (Howard 1989: v)

The following analysis attempts to show how each author's concerns lead to different expectation levels in the texts.

Discourse cycles in textbooks

This analysis will be based on the idea that within an extended text such as a textbook information will be organised in discourse cycles which show particular repeated characteristics. These will include 'moves', which may be obligatory or optional (Hopkins and Dudley-Evans 1988; Dudley-Evans 1994), patterning of general and specific (Love 1991, 1993) and typical lexico-grammatical features (Love 1993). Such cycles are likely to reflect the fundamental epistemological concerns of the discipline. In the case of the Cheater text, I shall suggest that the cycles are organised in terms of the author's approach to the relationship between theory and data in anthropology. This relationship functions to introduce students to her view of disciplinary methodology and argument. The cycles also realise Cheater's presentation of the discipline as extremely complex (Love 1999) and subject to conflicting arguments and contested interpretations.

The analysis will examine an excerpt from the textbook which deals with small-scale agricultural societies. I shall examine this excerpt (which is representative of the approach of the whole textbook) in terms of the overall textual organisation of the excerpt, showing how this realises both the interaction of theory and data in anthropology and the complexity and contested nature of the data. I shall then show how this textual pattern is reinforced by the internal structuring of each cycle. Finally I shall discuss how the pattern is further realised at sentence level by lexicogrammatical choices.

Discourse structure of cycles

The excerpt from Cheater's textbook to be discussed here covers the first three sections of chapter 3, which is entitled 'Relations of Production in Peasant and Commercial Agriculture': these sections cover 'peasant agriculture' (Cheater 1989: 64–73). They include a short untitled introduction (paragraph 1), a section entitled 'Land as "object of labour"' (paragraphs 2–5) and a longer section entitled 'Land tenure and land rights' (paragraphs 6–26). The discourse structure of the section, however, seems slightly different from this division, with some overlap between sections and some internal subdivisions. Figure 1 suggests the discourse structure of the excerpt.

The overall structure of the section under discussion thus appears to be:

theory → data → theory.

Cycle 1 is concerned primarily with expounding a broadly Marxist/Neo-Marxist interpretation of the development and characteristics of peasant

Figure 1 Discourse structure of Cheater (1989) extract

Cycle 1: (paragraphs 1–5)

basic Marxist theory of development of agriculture
exemplification (Torbel)
generalisation of development of peasant agricultural societies
problematisation of theoretical interpretation

Cycle 2: (paragraphs 6–20)

review of African tenurial systems (6–8)
assertion of complexity ('ownership' vs 'use')
author's classification

2a: Ethiopia (9)	2b: Gikuyu (10–12)	2c: Ibo (13–20)
'feudal'	'lineage'	'village'
relatively simple	differing 'established' inter-pretations	problematic process of interpretation

Link between Cycles 2–3: (paragraph 21)
parallel between Ibo and Torbel

Cycle 3: (paragraphs 22–26)
principles of understanding land tenure systems:
importance of political systems
specific African examples
discussion of Gluckman's classification
author's classification system

agriculture. It therefore focuses on theory. Cycle 2 is primarily classificatory and descriptive. It establishes three categories of African tenurial systems, and then includes three subcycles (2a, b, c) which each describe an example of the category. Thus Cycle 2 is primarily concerned with data. Cycle 3 is concerned with establishing 'principles of understanding' of the kind of data presented in Cycle 2: it problematises the 'neat' theory of Cycle 1 in terms of the Cycle 2 data, and introduces new 'principles' based, to some extent, on the perspectives of the societies described, and incorporating the author's attempts to accommodate what she sees as the extreme complexity of African data. Thus the cycles move from discussion of apparently accepted theory, through detailed description of data to problematisation and attempts at fresh theory construction.

Intra-cycle discourse structure

However, the discourse structure of the text is more complex than this. The suggested theory →data → theory pattern is also present as a structural feature *within* each cycle. Here the pattern tends to be realised as:

introduction to theory → exemplification → problematisation of interpretation.

Cycle 1 opens with exposition of the theory of 'land as the object of labour' and the issues emanating from this (paragraphs 1–2). There follows a detailed exemplification, drawn from published research on a Swiss village (paragraph 3). Paragraph 4 generalises from the example about the consequences of change in peasant societies, thus moving back towards theory. There then follows an explicit problematisation of the 'classic' Marxist interpretation, claiming that 'this evolutionist assumption is in fact an oversimplification of empirical reality, at least in the 20th century, as a review of African systems of land tenure readily reveals' (Cheater 1989: 66). The cycle ends with further details from 'empirical reality' that increase the complexity of interpretation and further problematise it.

Cycle 2, while primarily concerned with empirical reality, also displays a theory → data → problematisation structure. The cycle opens with a subcycle which outlines the theoretical contestation of the classification of African land tenure systems: are they 'communal' (as generally assumed) or 'individual'? Cheater asserts the importance of distinguishing between 'usage rights' and overall 'tenure', and also of acknowledging the role of change. In other words, she introduces new elements to the theory behind classification of land tenure systems, emphasising their complexity. The subcycle continues with data exemplifying the kinds of forces which may result in this complexity, such as 'ecology or investment', illustrated from a number of African societies. The subcycle ends with an anaphoric summary of the apparent confusion between individual and communal land tenure in Africa, an acceptance that generally the systems had features which led to an (over-simplified) designation of communal, and a cataphoric proposal of three categories of quasi-communal systems. Thus the first part of Cycle 2 deals with theoretical interpretation and classification of land tenure systems, but even within the subcycle there is a theory → exemplification → problematisation mini-pattern.

The following three subcycles each deal with one of Cheater's three categories. The 'feudal' subcycle is straightforward, accepting (despite mention of some rather detailed exceptions) the *gult* system as an example of a feudal African system. The system itself is outlined briefly. The final theoretical comment raises mild problematisation, but does not elaborate on it:

> Whether or not the Ethiopian *gult* system and similar systems ... are identical to medi-aeval European fiefdoms, they have been described as examples of 'feudal' land owner-ship, since they depended on politico-administrative endowment from the monarch, while others held rights of usufruct to the land concerned. (Cheater 1989: 67)

The next subcycle, 'lineage-based' systems, is introduced as more problematic in its classification. Cheater deliberately chooses an example where the categorisation is contested:

> Lineage-based tenurial systems are most common in West Africa, but their ambiguity is perhaps best revealed by the Gikuyu of Kenya. Kenyatta (1938: 21) argued very strongly that 'every inch of land within (Gikuyu territory) had its owner', but not everyone would accept his characterisation of *mbari* (or 'family' land) as individualised. (Cheater 1989: 67)

The following description of Gikuyu practice is interspersed with differing voices interpreting the system. The subcycle ends with a summary of the problems:

> Even if we examine subordinate methods of acquiring land in an attempt to sort out whether or not the Gikuyu system was communal in the way the white Kenyan settlers assumed, the pattern is unclear. (Cheater 1989: 68)

Thus subcycle 2b, while illustrating one of Cheater's categories, also begins to emphasise the problems of interpretation.

Cycle 2c is introduced by a linking sentence:

> So the Gikuyu illustrate rather well the problem of determining the precise status of African systems of land tenure, as do the Ibo of Eastern Nigeria, whose landholding system, unlike that of the Gikuyu, was not materially affected by the intrusion of white agricultural settlers. (Cheater 1989: 68)

Thus the village-based system is introduced as even more interestingly problematic. There follows a long and detailed account of the Ibo system, shown as having three phases. The first phase is not portrayed as problematic. The accounts of the second and third phases, however, are interspersed with what one might call 'real-time' interpretation:

> We might then be tempted to think that this example merely supports capitalist notions of the individualisation of ownership under circumstances of increasing competition...

> But such thinking would be contradicted by the fact that.... (Cheater 1989: 70)

Thus in this subcycle the student is not only *told* that interpretation is contested, but is *actively involved in* (by the use of 'we') the problem of interpretation. The subcycle ends with a suggestion of a solution to the problem from the point of view of the described society:

> We can understand this pattern of development only by comprehending the Ibo principles on which all land use rested (Cheater 1989: 70).

Thus the long and complex Cycle 2, with its several subcycles, again shows a structural pattern of theoretical introduction, followed by detailed exemplification, leading through this exemplification to a theoretical conclusion. Within this, even within each subcycle the theory → data → problematisation pattern can be seen.

Paragraph 21 links Cycle 2 to Cycle 3 by pointing out the parallels between the Ibo and Swiss village systems. The theoretical point being made here is that the Ibo system is not specifically African, but generalisations can be made. This is then exemplified by further details from Torbel and a final generalising point from the original researcher (Netting).

In Cycle 3, the initial theoretical point involves a 'new' way of theorising land tenure systems:

In seeking to understand any system of land tenure, then, a useful place to start is with the political community which, in the widest sense, 'owns' the land falling within its boundaries. (Cheater 1989: 71)

The cycle continues with detailed examples, and reference to one model. This is critiqued and Cheater's own preferred classification outlined. The cycle – and indeed the section – ends with further complicating and problematising detail from empirical reality.

Each cycle and even subcycle appears to exhibit a pattern which leads the student from a theoretical opening, through description of empirical data and then back to theoretical implications, usually exposing the problems of the interpretive process. The central, data presentation section presents a number of subcycles which progress from simple classification, through contested classification to presentation of the real-time problems of the anthropologist faced with the classificatory task in relation to empirical reality. Students are left with an overall impression that a theory can be a useful starting point in interpreting tenure systems, but that great attention must be paid to the precise and changing details of any society, and perhaps new theoretical approaches adopted, drawing not only on the complexity of the anthropological observations but also on the principles of the societies observed.

Realisation of pattern at sentence level

As suggested above and elsewhere (Love 1993), the discourse pattern of cycles within a textbook is reinforced by lexicogrammatical choices. Most typically these choices reflect the author's shifts of focus between description of data and disciplinary analysis. Such shifts of focus correspond to features of the discourse structure of cycles in the Cheater text. A useful mode of analysis at sentence level is MacDonald's classification of the head-word of the grammatical subject in academic writing (MacDonald 1994). MacDonald makes a major distinction between 'phenomenal' subjects, which refer to the data under consideration and 'epistemic' subjects, which refer to 'the concepts, categories, abstractions, or methodological tools the researcher uses to reason about the subject' (MacDonald 1994: 157). Her argument is that such choice of grammatical subject realises the focus of the disciplinary writer on either the phenomenon being studied or on the research process itself. It will be seen that this has clear connections with the different elements in the discourse cycles of Cheater's text. Within her basic dichotomy MacDonald proposes a number of classes. Within the phenomenal group she distinguishes Class 1 'Particulars', Class 2 'Groups' and Class 3 'Attributes', the last including 'nouns referring to the attributes, properties, action, behaviour, or motivations and thoughts of the nouns in Classes 1 and 2' (MacDonald 1994: 158). Thus these classes refer to different levels of generalisation and abstraction of the data being described. The epistemic group contains Class 4 'Reasons', Class 5 'Research' (such as individual or groups of researchers), Class 6 'Isms' and Class 7 'Audience' (such as generalised 'we').

MacDonald's classification was designed to account for differences in mature research writing and she acknowledges that patterns may be different in what she terms 'intermediary texts' (MacDonald 1994: 179–89). Her discussion of the use of the classification in analysing textbook writing demonstrates the shifts of focus of a textbook writer and particularly what this shows about what I am terming the expectation level of the text. The presence or absence of epistemic grammatical subjects is of key interest here, as is the interaction between the Classes 1, 2 and 3, which reflects the degree of generalisation going on in the text. Accordingly, I shall examine the patterning of grammatical subject within the discourse cycles of the section from Cheater in terms of MacDonald's classification.

Detailed analysis of Cycle 1

A detailed analysis of the grammatical subjects in Cycle 1 (paragraphs 1–5) produces a clear pattern which reinforces the discourse pattern described above. The section begins with a cluster of (mainly) epistemic subjects. This is followed by a phenomenal cluster, within which there can be seen a progression from generalised subjects to more specific and then back to generalised. The final paragraph is a complex mixture of epistemic and phenomenal. (In the following analysis, the head-word of the noun phrase is italicised.)

The long opening subject, 'Most evolutionary *perspectives* on social and technical change' (E4: Epistemic, Class 4), reminds the student of the overall ideological position of the book. The next subject introduces the generalised topic of the chapter, 'Settled *agriculture*' (P3: Phenomenal, Class 3). The subjects then return to epistemic: 'All three *patterns*', 'The labour *theory* of value and Marxist *approaches* based on it' (all E4). Thus the first paragraph leads the student to relate to the topic under discussion in terms of explicit epistemic constructs. The second paragraph narrows this focus a little: the first sentence has specific groups of theorists as its subject: '*Neo-Marxists* such as Meillassoux (1981) as well as cultural *ecologists* such as Rappaport (1968)' (E5). The focus then starts to move towards the phenomenal: the next subject is 'this *process* of growth'. This subject forms an interface between the epistemic and the phenomenal: the head-word of the noun phrase, 'process', is epistemic, since it refers to a mental construct. However, the demonstrative 'this' refers back to the Rheme of the previous sentence, which included a detailed, concrete description of the implications of the concept of 'land as the object of labour'. The post-modifier 'growth' is a generalised phenomenal noun. Thus this subject forms an epistemic encapsulation (cf. Francis 1994: 85) of generalised phenomena previously mentioned, and so prepares students for the description of phenomena which is to follow. This interface between epistemic and phenomenal continues in the first sentence of the third paragraph, which describes the example of a Swiss peasant village. Here there is an extremely long subject which has an epistemic head-word followed by a long post-modifying clause whose nouns vary between highly generalised phenomenal and epistemic: 'The *extent* (E4) to which labour (P3) may be required to achieve an equilibrium (E4) between resource base (P3) and population (P3)'. Students are therefore led to enter upon processing the phenomena from a specific theoretical perspective.

The description of the Swiss village moves gradually from epistemic through generalised phenomenal to more specific and concrete. The next subject is post-modified epistemic, 'The production *system* in Torbel' (E4). This is followed by a generalised, abstract phenomenal subject, 'Torbel's *production*' (P3), which maintains the focus on abstract categories. This is then concretised by a number of group subjects: 'some mechanical *equipment*', '*People*' (repeated as subject of three consecutive sentences), 'Both *men and women*'. These phenomenal generalised subjects, combined as they naturally are (MacDonald 1994) with active material process verbs (e.g. 'maintain', 'repaired'), enable students to engage with the empirical reality which the introductory theoretical constructs are designed to interpret. This paragraph ends with a slight shift to generalisation, with a focus on phenomenal processes rather than people: 'these (*activities*)', '*Tilling* the grain and potato fields, the gardens and the vines', 'only *mowing, hay baling, milking and transport*'.

The fourth paragraph negotiates the shift back from phenomenal description to epistemic interpretation. The first subject is extremely long: *'redistribution* (P3) either of labour (P3) from those households (P2) with a surplus (P3) to those (P2) deficient in labour (P3), or of part of the product (P2) from its producers (P2) to those consumers (P2) who produce less than they themselves need'. While MacDonald restricts her analysis to the head-word of the subject noun phrase, it is interesting to look at the post-modifying elements in 'heavy' grammatical subjects. In this instance I would suggest that the shifts between the group (2) and attribute (3) categories could be said to enact the generalising process which is part of the interpretation going on in academic anthropology. The next two sentences move this generalisation to the epistemic level, with the subjects 'The *mechanisms* (E4) by which this redistribution (P3) is effected' and 'They' (i.e. 'mechanisms'). The paragraph ends with a phenomenal generalisation of such mechanisms: 'The *exchange* (P3) of gifts (P2)'.

The final paragraph in the cycle is predominantly epistemic, but interestingly complex. The first sentence is worth quoting in full, since its structure realises the author's problematisation of the previous interpretation:

> Fundamental to any understanding of how such redistribution works, however, are the issues of who is permitted to exploit what resources under which conditions: the class issues of ownership of, control over and access to the means of production.

The Thematised Comment is epistemic, since it evaluates the research process. The subject itself is also epistemic, 'issues' (E4), repeated in the appositional gloss, in both cases post-modified by phenomenal pronouns or nouns, P2 in the case of the head-noun, P3 in the case of the gloss. This complex sentence introduces the focus of problematisation. The second sentence makes this more explicit, with the grammatical subject 'a problem' (E4). Thus the discussion has shifted to an entirely epistemic focus. While the subject of the next sentence, 'pre-class or "gentile" *societies*', is superficially a group (P2) noun, the pre-modifying adjectives are technical Marxist terms, linked to the Marked Theme 'By Marxist definition...', and hence the focus remains epistemic. The next sentence maintains an epistemic subject, 'this evolutionist *assumption*' (E4). However, the final sentence shows that the epistemic 'problem' arises from the interaction of the interpretation with the phenomenal: the final subject is yet another heavy noun phrase consisting of two linked nominalisations modified by more specific objects of the preposition: 'the *ownership and control* (P3) of relatively high-tech equipment (P2), such as draught animals and tractors (P2), and of storage, processing and marketing facilities (P2)'.

The sentence-level pattern of grammatical subject and related features is essentially one of Epistemic → Phenomenal → Epistemic, culminating in a tension between epistemic and phenomenal. This reflects and reinforces the discourse-level structure of the cycle, which moves from theory to data and back to problematised interpretation. Students are required to begin with a focus on epistemic issues (theory) which inform their processing of the phenomenal. The cycle ends with the theory being problematised in terms of the available data.

Overview of Cycles 2 and 3

The pattern shown by Cycle 1 is also broadly maintained in the following cycles, though with some complications. Cycle 2, the central section of this chapter, opens with a primarily epistemic section which introduces Cheater's specific approach to land tenure issues. The subjects are primarily epistemic: '*It is necessary to note*', 'tenurial *systems*', '*It is also important to note*' (all E4). There follows some illustration of the epistemic principles with phenomenal subjects ('*ecology and investment*' (P3), 'Such *lands*' (P2)), after which this introductory section closes with linkage of the phenomenal to epistemic: 'concepts (E4) of rights (P3) to land (P2)'. Cycle 2a (Ethiopia) is seen as straightforward, and hence has entirely phenomenal subjects. Cycle 2b (Gikuyu) is presented as more complex, and this is reflected in the pattern of subjects. The two-clause first sentence shows this immediately: the first subject, '"Lineage-based" tenurial *systems*', is a clear epistemic generalisation, but it is followed by the interesting 'but their *ambiguity*' as subject. While 'ambiguity' could be seen as an attribute, and therefore phenomenal (P3), it seems in context to refer to an epistemic ambiguity – a problem of classification for anthropologists. The rest of the cycle reinforces this interpretation, since the phenomenal description is interspersed with reference to the proponents of different interpretations as subjects: '*Kenyatta* (1938)' (E5) appears several times as subject, occasionally contrasted with '*not everyone*' (E5), and 'The *descriptions* by non-Kikuyus' (E4). The positioning of references to other anthropologists as grammatical subject places the focus on the contrasting interpretations rather than on the descriptions themselves (Groom 2000). Thus Cheater introduces students to the contested nature of anthropological interpretation.

Cycle 2c (the Ibo) takes this involvement of students in the epistemic work of anthropology a stage further. The opening sentence has a specific phenomenal subject, 'The patrilineal *Ibo*' (P1), but this is the subject of what may be termed an epistemic verb, 'illustrate', which reminds the students that the specific society being described must be seen in epistemic terms. There follows a lengthy description, dominated by group phenomenal subjects (e.g. 'new *land*', 'All *households*' (P2)). However, towards the end of the cycle, when the interpretation becomes less simple, there appear what MacDonald terms 'Audience' subjects, '*We*' (E7), with such verbal processes as 'might be tempted to classify', 'might then be tempted to think': in paragraph 18 these feature in the first and last sentences, 'enclosing' the phenomenal description. Thus Cheater uses the inclusive 'we' to involve the students in struggling with the classificatory problem. The final paragraph of this cycle opens with a continuation of this audience involvement: 'We can understand'. This is followed by a series of related subjects: 'Each of these three *principles*', 'the basic *principle*', 'This second *principle*'. What is interesting about these subjects is the difficulty of categorising them as phenomenal or epistemic, for the simple reason that they are both: a 'principle' is clearly here an epistemic concept, but it is also in the context an attribute of the Ibo society. In fact, Cheater is emphasising the necessity of understanding the local epistemic foundation on which the phenomena observed are based.

The third cycle is the most complex in its patterning of grammatical subjects. It opens with a metaphorical epistemic subject, 'a useful *place* to start', which is followed by a series of phenomenal subjects (e.g. 'the *king or chief*', 'the political "*owners*" of the land' (P2)), although the use of 'scare quotes' for some terms suggests epistemic contestation. As the description progresses, it is interrupted by the author's comments on the classification, marked by the introduction of '*I*' (E5) as subject ('I personally find', 'I find it more useful') and the epistemic structure '*it should be quite clear*'. The final paragraph shows a complex interweaving of general and specific phenomenal subjects: 'these vertically-related *rights* of cultivation' (P3), 'salt *licks*' (P2), '*Rights* to depasture livestock, to build homes, ...' (P3, post-modified by specifying phrases), 'All of these different usufructuary *rights*' (P3). Thus the close of the section emphasises the difficulties involved for the anthropologist in reducing varied specific phenomena to a generalised epistemic system.

It can thus be seen that the sentence-level choices of grammatical subject reinforce the textual structure of the cycles: the use of epistemic subjects typically marks either cycle boundaries or places of methodological problematisation. The interplay between epistemic and phenomenal subjects realises the author's desire to introduce students to the processes of interpretation and categorisation in anthropology and the problematic nature of these processes when confronted with the variety of specific data.

Overview of Cheater

The above analysis of a section of Cheater's introductory textbook has attempted to show how the author not only provides the students with anthropological information, but also inducts them into her chosen disciplinary method of interpretation. This can perhaps be summed up as: approach phenomena with an analytical framework; describe (or read descriptions of) the data; question and problematise the analytical approach in terms of the data. This objective is realised at the level of the whole section, within cycles and at sentence level.

Students using this as an introductory text are actively involved in the struggle to engage with interpretation of anthropological data, to find analytical models which mesh with empirical reality. It is, however, clear that this introductory text has a rather high expectation level. It expects students to start from an analytical position – in this case a broadly Marxist one – and to use this as an approach to data. When data is introduced, examples are given which progress from ones which illustrate the analytical approach straightforwardly to ones which introduce conflicting interpretations, culminating in ones which introduce real-time, cutting edge problematisation and attempts to resolve it. The text treats students as mature thinkers, able to engage in debate and to be prepared to progress from the 'known' to the 'unknown' (Bernstein 1977: 97). This is not the expected characterisation of the introductory textbook, which is frequently seen as introducing students solely to what is 'already known'. It is perhaps interesting to reflect that Cheater wrote this text initially for mature students in a society coming to terms with recent political independence, who she saw as needing anthropology as a tool for interpreting their rapidly changing society, rather than as a body of information.

Comparison with another introductory textbook

The issue of expectation level can be explored further by a very brief comparison of the excerpt from Cheater with an excerpt covering broadly the same topic from a different textbook (Howard 1989). In this book, a much shorter section, within the chapter 'Patterns of subsistence', covers 'Small-scale farming societies' (Howard 1989: 107–9). In this excerpt there are two cycles, the first (paragraphs 1–8) incorporating an untitled introductory paragraph and a section entitled 'Food production practices'. The second cycle (paragraphs 9–12) deals with 'Social organization'.

Cycle 1 is organised as follows (numbers indicate paragraphs):

1   Transition from foraging to agriculture, with implicit positive evaluation of 'sedentary lives'.

2   Definition and characterisation of small-scale farming.

3–5   Focus on 'shifting cultivation' as typical:
description with embedded interpretation;
examples, qualified positive evaluation in terms of adaptation to environment.

6   Introduction of complexity: deviations from norm;
examples; complex evaluation.

7–8   Further descriptive detail:
augmentation of diet by foraging and hunting;
role of domestic animals: interpretation and example.

Cycle 2:

9   Generalised description of size of settlements, related to adaptation to environment.

10   Generalised description of social organisation.

11   Generalised description of specialisation of labour;
example.

12   Assertion of lack of differentiation by wealth;
example; interpretation.
'Undeveloped' assertion of complexity.

It will be clear that Howard's treatment of the topic is much less concerned with theory than Cheater's, although it does maintain an analytical position – the role of adaptation to environment in the interpretation of societal patterns. However, there are some similarities in the cycle structure between the two texts. There is a progression from a generalised portrayal of the type of societies to a detailed and exemplified description and, to some extent, an introduction of complexity. However, in this text the complexity is either acknowledged as an exception to the general pattern (related to atypical environmental conditions) or merely noted without any attempt at interpretation. Thus the overall pattern is one of 'canonising discourse' (Brown 1993, cited in Hyland 2000: 105), which interprets differing societal patterns as a gradual modernising progression, varying only in response to varying environmental conditions. There is no problematisation or invitation to students to participate in interpretation, which is presented as given.

The difference between the two texts is clearest when the pattern of grammatical subjects in Howard is analysed. There are relatively few epistemic nouns, and those there are tend to be generalised categories. A brief analysis will be made of Cycle 1. It opens with two highly generalised group nouns ('most of the world's *cultures*', 'many *societies*' (both P2)). Then follow a number of process nouns as subjects: '*Production* of domestic plants and animals', '*cultivation*' (P3). Thus the general topic is introduced. The opening subject after the subheading is a specific group, 'Subsistence *farmers* in small-scale societies' (P2), which is followed by a series of epistemic subjects: 'This *type* of production', 'A common *method* of food production...', 'this *type* of agriculture', 'other agricultural *techniques*', 'Its *range*' (all E4). Thus here Howard emphasises classificatory principles. There then follow two paragraphs of increased specificity, using both P2 and P3 subjects, for example 'Burning', 'fields'.

Paragraph 6 marks the introduction of complexity into the account, and this is marked by a different pattern of subjects. First occurs the negative group subject 'Not all small-scale *farmers*', introducing an alternative group. An exemplifying Marked Theme leads into the epistemic subject 'a modified *pattern*' (E4), with the pre-modifying participle interestingly suggesting an exception from an established pattern. This is fleshed out by a succession of phenomenal subjects ('*land*' (P2), 'Limited *use* of animal waste...' (P3)). The author then intervenes with an epistemic subject in the form of a thematised comment: '*It is important to recognise*', which casts doubt on the appropriacy of 'modified systems'. The high-level generalisations of '*costs*' and '*effort*' (P3) are the next subjects, with a final epistemic subject, 'the less intensive *pattern* of shifting cultivation' returning students to the 'accepted' interpretation. After this paragraph, complexity is introduced in the form of additional detail about such societies: the pattern of subjects moves from general phenomenal to increasingly specific (e.g. 'Many small-scale subsistence *farmers*', 'The *Munduruku* of the Brazil interior', 'domesticated *animals*', '*pigs*').

Thus Howard's text is mainly concerned with introducing students to a generalised account of a type of society, with specific examples. Complexity is acknowledged, but marginalised as explainable exceptions from a normal pattern. Very little attention is paid to epistemic issues, and this is realised in the infrequency of epistemic subjects, and the fact that those that occur tend to be basic categories, such as 'type', 'method'. This is not to suggest that interpretation does not occur in this text, but it is generally implicit in phenomenal description, for example:

> Most tropical *soils* are very poor and rapidly lose nutrients. *Burning* produces a layer of ash that provides needed nutrients for crops. The soil *fertility* is rapidly depleted, however, and after one or two plantings the *plot* is left alone for a number of years until natural growth has again become lush enough to be burned. (Howard 1989: 107)

Thus students are led to see the implicit interpretation as common-sense understanding of phenomena, rather than constructed by epistemic interpretation.

These differences suggest that Howard's text has a very different expectation level from Cheater's. It sets out to present students with an unproblematised, though complex, account of the societies being described, with no attention being drawn to the epistemic construction of the interpretation. Thus Howard presents students with a body of information and an implicit interpretation. Clearly the expectation level of this text is considerably less demanding than that of Cheater.

Conclusion

This analysis of an excerpt from Cheater's introductory anthropology textbook has attempted to show that the text is organised in terms of cycles which incorporate shifting focus between analytical/theoretical elements and descriptive elements. This organisation is realised at several different levels. Moreover, it realises Cheater's concern to introduce students to the essential interplay between theory and data in anthropology, and the problematisation which this implies. The comparison with Howard's text demonstrates that this is a departure from the more typical introductory textbook which does not involve students in direct engagement in analytical processes.

Each textbook represents a different expectation level for new students. Thus the patterns of textual structure and sentence-level lexico-syntactic choice examined in this paper suggest a way of analysing introductory text-books which may provide a heuristic for assessing the expectation level of a textbook. In particular, it provides a way of examining the degree to which an introductory textbook works to engage students in the epistemological issues of a new discipline.

Cyberdiscourse, evolving notions of authorship, and the teaching of writing[1]

Diane Belcher

Probably few today would argue that computers have not been beneficial to students and teachers of writing at least to some extent. Computers have obviously provided 'considerable technical support' (Rodrigues and Tuman 1996: 4) for the teaching and learning of writing as process, in that they have, as Tuman (1992) has pointed out, eased for all writers, whether novice or expert, 'the arduous task of working through the writing process ... using the electronic editing power of word processing to facilitate the recursive revising that underlies the writing process' (p.109). What is less clear is the extent to which networked computers and hypertext support the traditional writing class goal of empowering students as authors. Some have argued that the Internet and hypertext are actually undermining the print literacy notions of authorship that many writers and writing teachers subscribe to: our sense of authors as creators and authorizers of their own rhetorically motivated text, through which they are able, at least potentially, to exercise some influence over readers. Before either racing to embrace or digging our heels in to resist greater presence of technology in our classrooms, it may serve us well to take a balanced look at both the apparent problems posed and those that seem to be solved by electronic discourse.

Cyberproblems

Perhaps most worrisome to some writing teachers are the abundant textual borrowing opportunities presented by networked computers. Bloch (2001) reminds us how easily Internet connections and the 'cut and paste' functions of computers can subvert our efforts to nurture independent authors. Bloch notes that 'the World Wide Web allows for the easy copying of electronic source texts, whose numbers are growing as the supply of electronic magazines and journals expands'. In other words, these are source texts that student authors can easily 'pass ... off as their own' (p.209, but see also Pennycook 1996 on plagiarism as a form of resistance). Bloch calls our attention to an even 'more insidious problem' (p.209), websites such as www.schoolsucks.com and www.termpapers4u.com, where papers can be purchased or sometimes simply downloaded. Field-specific term paper sites are available now, too, some of which even offer customizing services: 'With experience dating back to 1994 A.D., our staff of contracted researchers and writers GUARANTEES that if we don't already have a paper on your topic, we'll write a new one as quickly as you need!' (www.theologypapers.com, which 'gladly accepts' Visa and MasterCard).

Yet more troubling to some than attribution problems are the many questionable sources of information on the Internet, which student writers may accurately enough provide attributions for, with the assumption that they are citing authorities. Tannen (1998) has noted with dismay that 'the Internet makes it more difficult ... to distinguish the veracity and reliability of information' (p.250). This is indeed what Hirvela (personal communication, 10 February 2001) found when he came across students who, having been asked to compose reader-responses to Elie Wiesel's poignant Holocaust-inspired *Night*, uncritically cited 'data' from Holocaust denial websites. These students, impressed by the face validity that Internet 'publication' lends in some readers' minds, resisted their teacher's attempts to promote the type of critical literacy that many writing teachers see as essential to academic (or any) literate practices (e.g. Rea and White 1999).

Some disturbing gender-related problems have also surfaced via the Web. Pagnucci and Mauriello (1999) have noted that the Web would seem to be supportive of novice authors, offering as it does the possibility of authorial anonymity (or pseudonymity), and hence a relatively secure environment for experimentation and self-expression 'shield[ed] from public criticism' (p.142). However, Pagnucci and Mauriello observed a curious phenomenon when students in their program were allowed to post their composition class essays on a website under pseudonyms. While none of the men chose female pseudonyms, some of the women did opt for male pseudonyms. Furthermore, the texts with male names attached to them received approximately 37 per cent more responses from other students than those with female identities. How empowering could this be for young women writers, how helpful to the development of their self-identities as authors? Pagnucci and Mauriello suggest that in face-to-face classrooms 'dismissive readings of female work, low response to genuine female identities, [and] consistent alteration of female personas' (p.146) would likely not be tolerated. Not surprisingly, Pagnucci and Mauriello's findings have tempered their enthusiasm for electronic discourse: 'In our [i.e. not Pagnucci and Mauriello's exclusively] haste to teach writing using the Web ... we may have taken a step backward' (pp.146–7).

Email too may not be especially conducive to the nurturing of novice authors insofar as it may not offer much incentive for the production of 'considerate' texts (Kantor *et al.* 1983: 62). Biesenbach-Lucas and Weasenforth (2001) found that when a group of ESL students were given similar prompts and asked to compose their responses for the same recipients, namely their composition teachers, the same students wrote very differently with a word-processing program than when composing their responses as email messages. Even though the students were given exactly the same amount of time to compose, their email texts were significantly shorter and contained much less text-initial contextualization than their word-processed responses. Thus, much of what we teach as the responsibility of the author – reader-friendly contextualization, introductions that provide some context for a topic – seemed unnecessary to students in this particular cohort when the medium was email. (See Hawisher and Sullivan 1998, and Tannen 1998, for discussion of the still more reader-unfriendly email practice of 'flaming' – i.e. unrestrained verbal attack – an outcome, Tannen suggests, of the increasing technology-induced isolation of authors.)

When we turn to hypertext, it becomes still less clear how electronic literacy helps students think of themselves as authors. Both reading and creating hypertext can make the role of the author rather murky for students. Landow (1997), as have others (e.g. Howard 1999; Kramsch *et al.* 2000), remarks that 'hypertext embodies many of the ideas and attitudes proposed by Barthes, Derrida, Foucault, and others [such as Lyotard 1979]' (p.91); that is, other postmodernists who have described and indeed wished for the death of the author, or the decentering of the authority of a single, unitary self over a text. Hypertext, as non-linear, interactive text (though some question if it is 'text' at all, e.g. Tuman 1992), seems to accomplish this goal. Heim (1987) views hypertext as having eroded the rights of the author 'as a persistent self-identity' (p.221). Lanham (1993) finds that with 'unfixed and interactive' digital text, the 'reader can ... become writer' (p.31). And Bolter (1991) goes so far as to say that with hypertext, 'the reader may well become the author's adversary, seeking to make the text over in a direction that the author did not anticipate' (p.154). Given the dynamic interactive nature of hypertext (for a description of hypertext's standard features, see Jonassen 1991), clearly its authors have limited control over the path that readers take through their text. Readers may or may not click on the links provided, may or may not read all of the verbal text written by the author, may be totally distracted by the 'eye candy' (Rea and White 1999: 427), e.g. color, graphics, even video, or they may become completely engrossed in the texts of other authors whose works the hyperlinks lead to. Similar claims about reader autonomy can be made for print literacy (see, for example, Paulson 1988), but obviously the distractions and freedom afforded readers are more extensive in hypertext. Unlike the traditional printed word, hypertext, Tuman (1992: 59) points out, can actually make the boundaries of individual texts 'disappear' – and by implication, the boundaries of individual authors too.

Hypertext has, in fact, been seen as a great boon to student readers, 'truly engag[ing] students, lifting them out of the passivity and lethargy associated with being only the receivers of other people's prepackaged ideas' (Tuman 1992: 66). Some Web pages allow student readers to add their own comments and even links to an 'ever-expanding web of information' (Tuman 1992: 66). But how helpful is this interactivity and all the bells and whistles of hypertext for students as writers? Tuman (1992) has suggested that hypertext can make it difficult for readers to see the forest for the trees, that is, to develop any sense of hypertext as coherent text (which, of course, it may not be; see Lanham 1993 on coherent vs chaotic hypertext design). Screen size too can contribute to the obstruction of the reader's view of hypertext, or any electronic text, as a whole entity (see Bloch and Brutt-Griffler 2001; Haas 1996). Begeman and Conklin (1988) remark, 'Traditional linear text provides a continuous, unwinding context thread as ideas are proposed and discussed – a context that the writer constructs to guide you to the salient points and away from the irrelevant ones. Indeed, a good writer anticipates questions and confusions that you may encounter and carefully crafts the text to prevent them' (p.260). Hypertext, to reiterate, is anything but linear. Tuman (1992), as have others, reminds us that 'few writers, professionals or students, relish the task of organizing their thoughts into a single linear form' and that hypertext 'frees them from this responsibility' (p.77). Birkerts (1994) wonders what may be lost as a result of this new freedom:

> This 'domination by the author' has been, at least until now, the point of writing and reading. The author masters the resources of language to create a vision that will engage and in some ways overpower the reader; the reader goes to the work to be subjected to the creative will of another. The premise behind the textual interchange is that the author possesses wisdom, an insight, a way of looking at experience, that the reader wants. (Birkerts 1994: 163)

Once a reader feels liberated from such authorial domination or guidance, is s/he likely to see much value as a writer in taking on the responsibility of providing such guidance for other readers? If writing in the discourse universe of hypertext means not necessarily assuming this responsibility for the reader, or not being 'reader-based' as Flower and Hayes (1981: 48) would say (but see Hinds 1987, for a very different perspective on reader/writer responsibility), will 'liberated' readers even see much value in being writers when the likelihood of engaging, if not overpowering, other readers with their own vision may be greatly diminished?

Cybersolutions

So far our focus has been on problems posed by electronic literacy for student authors and their teachers. A case can just as easily be made for technology as a means of enhancing students' developing sense of themselves as authors. In fact, in some respects, computers seem better suited to support the goals of writing classes than almost any other material means.

Networked computers can be especially helpful in transforming a writing class into a community of readers and writers. Bloch and Brutt-Griffler (2001) and others (e.g. Braine 1997; Panferov 2000) have noticed, for example, how well computers can facilitate peer responding (but see also Handa 1990). Bloch and Brutt-Griffler found that when students were encouraged to engage in peer-responding dialogue using collaborative writing software that provided special columns not just for student-reader comments but also for student-author responses to those comments, the authors seemed to be more comfortable receiving feedback. They had 'a sense of voice and the ability to question the judgment of the reviewers' (p.323) which, Bloch and Brutt-Griffler felt, promoted student responsibility and autonomy. Such dialogue can, of course, also take place in face-to-face peer-responding sessions, but online peer review escapes the temporal and spatial confines of the classroom and the hovering physical presence of a possibly judgmental teacher. The result may be more extended peer interaction, hence more attention given to the student-authors' text.

Authors can also greatly benefit from online class discussion groups, whether listservs, newsgroups, chat rooms, or MOOs (multi-object oriented MUDs, i.e. multi-user domains). Class discussion groups can serve as relatively safe sites, or 'safe houses', as Canagarajah (1997: 173) puts it, for brainstorming, use of others as sounding boards, rehearsal of articulation of ideas, and hence sharing of those ideas – a sharing that might otherwise not occur, especially not among language minority students who may be hesitant to call attention to themselves, or their spoken English, in a classroom (see Belcher 1999; Warschauer 1999).

Online access can also empower authors by giving them easy access to far more resources than can be found in their local or institutional libraries. Warschauer (1999) sees this as especially beneficial to those in developing countries where expensive new books and periodicals may be out of reach. Canagarajah (1996) has pointed to lack of access to current publications as one of the main constraints on authors in developing countries who wish to join the global conversations in their disciplines through publication of their own work. The Internet (when accessible), Warschauer (1999) and others have noted, not only enables such would-be authors to stay current, but also offers them the opportunity to become content-providers themselves, to add their voices by way of listservs and websites, where their contributions can be made public without the gatekeeping obstacle course of formal academic publication.

Online access to information, as well as the cut-and-paste function of word processing, can also help novice academic authors experiment with intertextuality, one of the hallmarks of academic prose (Landow 1997). Landow has pointed out how academic discourse can be seen in Bakhtinian terms: with its quotes and citations used 'for refutation ... for confirmation and supplementation', resulting in 'a dialogic interrelationship among directly signifying discourses' controlled by the author (p.88). Computer-facilitated insertion of quotations and references to other authors can ease the burden of construction of this dialogic interrelationship, encouraging the use of source texts, and thus strategic juxtaposition of the author's own ideas with those of others to enhance the rhetorical power of an argument. As more and more electronically savvy students realize the ease with which anyone, including their teachers, can utilize metasearch engines, such as www.dogpile.com, or electronic plagiarism detecting services, such as Glatt Plagiarism Services at www.plagiarism.com, to locate source texts, the temptation of unattributed textual borrowing from the Web may also become less attractive (but for a critique of use of plagiarism-checking software, see Howard 1999).

Hypertext, furthermore, enables not just enhanced and possibly more enlightened source text use, but also opens up options for argument construction that are simply unavailable within the constraints of linear verbal text. These new text-construction options have, Landow argues (1997), some rather profound implications:

> ... as Derrida emphasizes, the linear habits of thought associated with print technology often force us to think in particular ways that require narrowness ... and intellectual attenuation, if not downright impoverishment. Linear argument, in other words, forces one to cut off a quoted passage from other, apparently irrelevant contexts that in fact contribute to its meaning. (p.98)

In Landow's view, hypertext liberates the author not just from the constraints of linearity but from the necessity of creating a single text at a time. As hypertext allows readers a plurality of paths through the text, it thus makes it possible for authors to create a plurality of interconnected texts simultaneously, relieving them of the 'frustrations' of 'closing off connections and abandoning lines of investigation' (p.97) inherent in single, linear text generation.

Electronic technology, however, also offers the author resources, means of expression, far beyond the strictly verbal – visual, auditory, iconographic resources – the 'eye candy' mentioned earlier (Bowden 1999; Fortune 1989; Rea and White 1999). Bowden (1999) catalogues some of these extra-verbal resources that online composers have access to: various print styles, formatting styles, scrolling, color schemes, graphics, movement, and embedded sounds and video. One predictable yet striking example that Bowden cites of a field in which authors have already greatly benefited from such resources is film studies. Authors of film analyses with hypertext software can now illustrate and support their points with still images, digital sound and video, and links to other cinema sites, and thus are no longer confined to unsatisfying verbal approximations of cinematic scenes.

While, as noted earlier, hypertext clearly cedes some power to the reader,

Kramsch *et al.* (2000) help us understand how it can empower student authors by enhancing their awareness of audience. Kramsch *et al.* found students in a Spanish-language class energized by the prospect of producing multimedia texts on Latin American culture for a real audience of future undergraduates and their instructors. However, when several of the student-authors realized that their future audience could 'read' their hypermedia projects however they wished, Kramsch *et al.* noticed that they 'work[ed] hard to regain some authorial control and predict the reception of the work' and 'they repeatedly looked for ways to guide the readers through a set path while giving the semblance of absolute interactive freedom' (p.88). These two particular students 'consciously sought out ways to assert a feminist rendition of the Virgin Mary in Latin America' despite the fact that the navigational frame employed had no explicit references to gender or feminism (p.89). This hypertext design experience made the students intensely aware of an author's power and, consequently, more critical consumers of the Internet. In the words of one, 'Before working on this project I was very uncritical about what I saw on the Internet. Now I know, and not because someone taught it to me, but because I lived it myself, that behind every page there is someone just like me, imperfect and a little prejudiced, manipulating the information' (p.86; see also Faigley 1997).

Another goal that has seemed unattainable to many teachers in the context of the traditional second-language (L2) writing classroom may in fact now be within reach with the help of networked computers: support for development of students not just as L2 writers but as bi- or multiliterate writers as well. What the Internet offers, among other things, is a forum where growth as literate users of more than one language can be facilitated with relative ease. Warschauer (1999) informs us that 'the narrowcasting multichannel feature of the Internet means that it can allow communication in hundreds or thousands of languages at the same time' (p.19) and thus online connection of isolated groups of speakers of various languages all over the world. Kramsch *et al.* (2000) describe the transformation that can occur when a student overcomes a feeling of isolation and finally connects with a real-world audience through the Internet. Almon, a Hong Kong immigrant living in California, who felt frustrated and discriminated against as a Chinese learner of English, saw himself in an entirely different light, Kramsch *et al.* report, after designing his own English-language website devoted to Japanese pop music and connecting with email pals with similar interests, some of whom were fellow Asians that he could communicate with in both English and Chinese. As a result of his online experience, Almon found his interest in and attitude toward English as well as his ability to communicate in it greatly changed: 'Before I was the type who hated English .... Maybe it was a kind of escapism, knowing I was not doing well at it, and so I used hating it as a way to deal with the problem. But I think it's easier for me to write out something now ... [and] express better' (p.90). Kramsch *et al.* assert that Almon's own self-motivated use of the Internet accomplished what no English teacher had been able to do for him – given him a sense of himself as a successful user and author of global English.

Conclusion

Ultimately, how do the many pluses and minuses of electronic technology compute for the writing teacher? It seems highly unlikely that the world will become less digital as time goes on. Although print literacy will probably be with us for the rest of our lifetimes, electronic literacy, judging from the past few years, will likely play an increasingly dominant role in all communication. Rea and White (1999) have pointed out that while writing, especially the types of academic writing that many writing teachers attempt to teach, may not play a large role in the lives of some number of students after they leave school, it is very probable that all of them will find 'knowing how to communicate in electronic contexts' valuable in their future lives (p.423). Warschauer (1999) suggests that we should feel an even greater obligation to empower our students as electronic authors given the global digital divide, the current domination of the United States on the Internet and the exclusion of huge parts of the world from Internet use, with Latin America and Africa, for example, each having less than 1 per cent of the world's Internet sites, and in Africa, 98 per cent of those sites in only one country, South Africa. Warschauer argues, though, that being 'wired' is not enough: 'For students of diverse cultural, linguistic, and class backgrounds to have a voice, they need more than an Internet account. Rather, they need knowledge of the languages and discourses of power and opportunities to reflect critically on whether, when, and how to use them...' (p.177). Johnson-Eilola (1997) similarly argues that 'we must teach students to appropriate the technology, to construct more active and critical roles as users' (p.186; see Rea and White, 1999: 428, on development of an evaluative Web 'hyperheuristic', and Richards 2000: 5, on the need for a 'rhetoric of design'). Yet helping students appropriate, rather than be appropriated by, technology as users, especially as authors, could be a tall order for those of us who are teachers if we are not active and critical users of technology ourselves.

Note

1. An earlier version of this paper was presented at the 25th Annual TESOL Convention, St. Louis, MO, USA, March 2001.

Exemplification strategy in Adam Smith's *Wealth of Nations*

Willie Henderson[1]

Adam Smith's *Wealth of Nations* (1776) is, in the annals of the history of economic thought, a work of major significance. It has been analysed and re-analysed over many decades with particular attention paid to the consistency of Smith's theoretical constructs; the origins and impact of his writing and the methodological and other links between Smith, his predecessors, his followers and so on. Hardly a month goes by without some new perspectives on this work appearing in learned journals or in collected volumes. In all of this, Smith's rhetoric has been analysed, though it would be true to say that the attention given to Smith's rhetoric (how Smith argues) has been signifi-cantly less than to more specifically content issues (what Smith argues). And within the concerns about Smith's rhetoric, the search has been either to match Smith's writing to 18th-century notions of persuasive argument, including Smith's own, or to explore the system and invisible-hand metaphors. Such 'canons of correct taste' include notions of 'order, symmetry, balance ... harmony and love of system' as well as an 18th-century preoccupation with irony (Brown 1997: 291; Harrison 1995: 99).[2] More recently, Brown has looked at Smith's writings in terms of 'dialogical' ('novel-istic') and 'monological' rhetoric. The *Wealth of Nations* is, in contrast to *The Theory of Moral Sentiments*, seen, in Brown's analysis, as 'monological' (Brown 1994: 31).

Smith's writing, especially in the *Wealth of Nations*, exhibits a number of interesting features not the least of which is, I find, a sense of reading some-thing that has been already spoken and the recurrent use of examples. It is this recurrent use of examples which creates a balance between theoretical propositions and social possibilities.[3] In approaching Smith's work, it should not be forgotten (the 'death of the author' not withstanding) that he had earned his living for a substantial part of his working life as a successful university teacher and personal tutor. Smith is also known to have dictated parts of his manuscript: he often experienced difficulties with the physical aspects of writing and resorted to clerical help (Ross 1995). Smith was both a teacher and rhetorician and, as pedagogy grew out of rhetoric, it seems likely that Smith would know how to convince his readers. It would be surprising if there were no traces, in the structure of Smith's discourse, of a systematic and 'teacherly' approach, based on an understanding of what a lecture is and what is required pedagogically to convince others of the effectiveness of an argument.

In all the sophisticated literature that has grown up around Smith's seminal text, there is little concerning what might be called the mechanical aspects of Smith's writing. Some studies, particularly by Endres, have taken specific chapters and attempted a textual analysis though such works have often been motivated by study of Smith's *Lectures on Rhetoric and Belle-Letters* (*LRBL*) (Endres 1991, 1992, 1995) rather than simply making a direct response to the text, as recommended by Brown (Brown 1994: 18). Smith, though evaluating, synthesising and developing the work of other theoreticians, was not writing a theoretical text for the sole attention of other theoreticians (the work as a whole is a complex of theory, historical analysis, narrative episodes and reflections on policy and practices). For most of his readers, apart from a few *philosophes*, the *Wealth of Nations* was, in effect, an introductory text, a novel reading experience. In this context, can a descriptive examination of Smith's writing help us take a different view of what Smith wrote?

This paper will examine samples of Smith's writing drawn from the opening chapters of the *Wealth of Nations* in order to establish how Smith develops and uses examples. Smith goes to great lengths to illustrate his ideas with examples drawn from contemporary events and situations or from historical circumstances (Endres 1992). Perhaps his most well-known example is that of the pin factory which he uses to illustrate a key concept in his theoretical system, that of the division of labour. But his whole work is packed with exemplifications and these are often presented within a wider pedagogical strategy that we could think of, initially at any rate, as 'planned repetition' or even 'extensive familiarisation techniques'. Smith re-states and repeats key ideas throughout the text, e.g. his treatment, some would say satire, of landlords and their expectations, behaviours and 'predelictions' for the support of unproductive rather than productive workers is one such recurrent theme treated at various points in the work.

Modern-day, first-year economics textbooks spend much of their time in defining, exemplifying and familiarising (by repetition and variation) technical terms required for the analysis of more complex economic problems. The use of definitions and examples in modern-day economics textbooks was analysed by Henderson and Hewings several years ago, testing a model developed by Bramki and Williams (Henderson and Hewings 1987). The research itself grew out of cooperation between Willie Henderson, a development economist by training, of the, then, Department of Extramural Studies and colleagues, Tim Johns and Tony Dudley-Evans in particular, of the Department of English, University of Birmingham.

Since that time of close cooperation, I have been making application of a variety of discourse techniques to 19th-century writers marginalised by the mainstream economics canon. In making a further extension of discourse analysis to a canonical text in the history of economic thought, this time from the 18th century, it is fitting that work undertaken during a period of close subject–language cooperation should form a basis (perhaps in the extensive familiarisation techniques identified by Henderson and Hewings) for the chapter published here (Henderson and Hewings 1987: 125). At that time, and under the influence of Tony Dudley-Evans, the degree of subject–language cooperation at Birmingham was certainly innovative and probably unique. The hope is that by undertaking an analysis of the way in which Smith textually develops examples, a systematic pedagogical strategy will be found that may or may not be similar to that found in modern-day, introductory economics writing. The corpus is an 18th-century text and the analysis of examples, and the methodology used, will have to adjust to the text itself. Since exemplifications are intended to assist readers understand and extend an argument, the relationship between the proposition and example and the role of exemplification in the wider discourse, is also of significance.

Some general notions of Smith's writing in the *Wealth of Nations*

There is a literature on Smith's 'rhetoric', though the literature within the field of study known as the history of economic thought does not tend to approach the analysis of Smith's discourse through either details of language or the establishment of textual moves or patterns. Brown has surveyed a variety of critical approaches to the study of Smith's writing (Brown 1997).

Some of this literature tends to approach the *Wealth of Nations* through the principles that Smith himself outlined in his *LRBL*. This is a method of approaching the *Wealth of Nations* that Brown is sceptical about, though no one would wish to deny that Smith understood what was required to secure the attention of different kinds of lectors and readers (Brown 1997: 285). He had explored the issue in both theoretical and practical terms (if what we know about his teaching is allowed). The literature has also established that Smith understood what was required, rhetorically, for the development of a scientific argument (Campbell 1971: 29). Brown's scepticism is based on a desire to read text as text, and respond to it as text rather than as authorial product. Although the methods of analysis in general are not the type that will be pursued here, for the method used is closer to, though different from, Brown's, nonetheless, the existing literature has drawn attention to a number of features of Smith's text.

At the 'macro' level of textual organisation, it is generally held that the first three books of the *Wealth of Nations* are concerned with 'generalised description' (i.e. 'the analysis of the market economy and its vicissitudes through history'). The last two books are concerned, then, with 'generalised prescription' (i.e. 'alternative systems of policy and the functions of the State') (Robbins 1981: 7, quoted in Endres 1991: 76). Thus, different sections of the *Wealth of Nations* are doing differing kinds of work, building a different kind of relationship with the reader or perhaps identifying different kinds of (implied) readers. Within each of these broad sections, differences in the style of writing have been recorded. Chapter five in the first book is widely regarded as a rhetorical failure and the whole of book four has been described as 'propagandist'. Endres has tested out such insights in relation to chapter five, book four by investigating what he calls the 'compositional rules'. His conclusion is that Smith's chapter on bounties conforms to Smith's 'compositional rules' and is therefore best seen as 'a disciplined exercise in advocacy rather than as a crude polemic' (Endres 1991: 94).

It is also clear that Smith's *Wealth of Nations* is didactic in the sense that it is a teacherly text but also in the sense that it attempts to evaluate propositions by balanced argument (though this has been subjected to qualifications). It is also clear that it is based, like some of his other writing, on the development of 'a system comprised of a few core principles capable of accounting for manifold observed appearances' (Endres 1991: 82; Skinner 1972: 311–14). This is a central feature of Smith's writing and it may be a consequence of his understanding of the demands of Newtonian science, as he and other figures of the Enlightenment understood that science. But the textual implication is, of course, that there will be many textual repetitions of principles and their application as well as many different instances (examples) leading to the same result. Any 'planned repetition' in Smith cannot be, therefore, a simple consequence of an educational strategy as it is also implied by the preference for working with a few simple predictive or explanatory concepts. The rhetorical underpinnings suggest 'extensive familiarisation'.

The work undertaken here, initially at any rate, will not examine *LRBL* as a means of examining passages from the *Wealth of Nations*. It will as far as possible look at the first three chapters of the work simply as text, though given the subject-knowledge of the researcher there will be some constraints on this. The text will be analysed in terms of structure and language in order to establish generalisations about the use and purpose of exemplifications in Smith's discourse. Its primary aim is to describe the text, account for its coherence and so illustrate how examples are used, in the hope that such a description will allow for the development of an informed critical appreciation, capable of revealing something new about Smith's method of argument.

Initial classification of examples

There are probably three broad categories of examples to be found in Smith's text: current examples drawn from contemporary economic experience and written about in the present tense; historical examples; and, for the want of a clearer expression, 'hypothetical examples'. Current examples are likely to consist of two kinds. First, those which are directly observable and within the experience of the target reader, e.g. everyday examples of economic behaviour. Examples are found in references to 'carpenters', 'smiths' and 'tanners'. Second, those that are contemporary but which would be more difficult to directly verify. This is either because they are drawn from a different geographical environment ('France', 'Poland') from that of the target reader but which are in principle verifiable by observation or because they are drawn from some 'macro' economic experience. The use of current examples, written in the present tense, in the section on the division of labour must have given the text an 'up to-the-minute' quality for its first readers.

Another set of examples is historical, such as the economic conditions in the classical world or in medieval England. These are drawn from Smith's reading and understanding of historical texts. It is to be expected that Smith will make a special effort to select and shape the historical examples to assist the reader understand the concept, analysis or 'policy' that is being investigated, proposed or evaluated. As it happens, historical examples in the sense of located historical events, circumstances or policies are relatively unimportant in the three chapters under detailed consideration. From what is know about the 'macro' structure of the work (see below), historical examples can be expected to be significant in books four and five.

There is yet another set that can be called 'hypothetical examples'.[4] These may or may not have an authentic existence in the world beyond Smith's text and they are often 'stylised' in ways that are not always easy to describe. For example, the text may refer to a location such as the Scottish Highlands and make statements about conditions in 'a' remote village. The context is not specific – no definite village is being referred to though the example is within the bounds of social possibilities but, nonetheless, the example is not 'outside' the text. Such examples are therefore 'imaginary' or 'hypothetical' (and have an equivalence in the modern-day first-year economics textbook). When faced with such examples, the question of textual location and function perhaps needs to be explored in detail. In modern-day textbooks such examples are frequently located within a small-scale text pattern of situation-problem-solution-evaluation, signalled by imperatives such as 'assume', 'suppose' or 'take'. The 'hypothetical examples' provide a setting for a small-scale application of a concept (Henderson and Hewings 1986, passim). In Smith (see below) they tend to be located within a dynamic narrative. Such examples tend to illustrate a theoretical principle or extend a principle to a dimension of economic life that would be difficult or impossible to 'observe' (e.g. the process of change) or where specific detail is irrelevant (e.g. 'a' highland village).[5] They also tend to appeal to the shared cultural experience between the text and the reader such as with commonplace examples ('farmer' or 'merchant' in some given context) drawn from 'commonsense' or 'everyday experience', though the common sense that is appealed to is one that is heavily influenced by other Enlightenment writers. Such examples can give rise to problems of interpretation concerning their status and significance.

However, these are for the time being at any rate to be thought of as broad categories only as, given 18th-century referencing conventions, some examples will appear to the modern reader as vague whereas others will be more precisely located. The example of the pin factory is a general example that is not precisely located as a given pin factory. Nor is it uniquely located in that sense either for it has been 'often observed'. Smith, however, supplies us with evidence that he has seen just such a factory. Such a pin factory did exist but, whether it existed or not, it remains an example. The classification of examples cannot be expected to be clear cut; judgements will depend on how they are presented to, or interpreted by, the reader. So the schema set out here can only be taken as provisional. It may be, say, that the notion of 'vague examples' is a better way of approaching a whole set of exemplifications, but this remains to be seen. As 'evidence', Smith's 'examples' are both 'qualitative' and 'quantitative', and the 'qualitative' (sometimes based upon third-party observation) evidence can also be 'vague'.

Contextualisation of examples: overview of opening moves and development in the first three chapters of the *Wealth of Nations*

Smith is concerned with illustrating the 'causes of improvement in the productive powers of labour' (Smith [1776], 1952: 3). He concentrates on the concept of the division of labour in the first three chapters of book one of the *Wealth of Nations*. The discourse structures of the three chapters are themselves interesting. Each chapter begins with an assertion of analytical or practical significance. Even without detailed knowledge of economic thinking prior to Smith's work, it is clear from the language that the assertions are bold. Chapter one, paragraph one:

> The greatest improvement in the productive powers of labour, and the greatest part of the skill, dexterity, and judgement with which it is everywhere directed, or applied, seem to have been the effects of the division of labour.

Chapter two, paragraph one:

> This division of labour, from which so many advantages are derived, is not originally the effect of any human wisdom, which foresees and intends that general opulence to which it gives occasion. It is the necessary, though very slow and gradual consequence of a certain propensity in human nature which has in view no such extensive utility; the propensity to truck, barter and exchange one thing for another.

Chapter three, paragraph one:

> As it is the power of exchanging that gives occasion to the division of labour, so the extent of the division of labour must always be limited by the extent of that power, or, in other words, by the extent of the market. When the market is very small, no person can have any encouragement to dedicate himself entirely to one employment, for want of the power to exchange all that surplus part of the produce of his own labour, which is over and above his own consumption, for such parts of the produce of other men's labour as he has occasion for.

Each one of these opening paragraphs conveys a striking proposition to the reader, though the detailed linguistic construction of each differs in detail. In a way, Smith has already signalled the boldness of his plan: the first sentence of the *Wealth of Nations* has already been provided in the 'Introduction And Plan of the Work'. It reads:

> The annual labour of every nation is the fund which originally supplies it with all the necessaries and conveniences of life which it annually consumes, and which consist always either in the immediate produce of that labour, or in what is purchased with that produce from other nations.

This striking sentence has, given knowledge of economic thinking prior to Smith, the force of a cannon shot. According to early economic doctrines, the 'fund' was a monetary fund consisting of gold and silver, either as money or as plate. But even without such insider knowledge, the paragraph's textual location underlines its importance. The linguistic construction of the sentence itself also signals its importance as a significant, formal proposition. It is in fact two definitions, one concerning the nature of the 'fund' ('annual labour') and another of the 'annual' consumption defined as the produce of the 'fund' of labour. The relationship between the rest of the 'Introduction' corresponds to the structures revealed by the analysis of the first three chapters (below).

The opening sentences in each of the three chapters considered here follow the same formal pattern and suggest an origin in Smith's lecturing style or in other formal, scientific texts. The propositions (topics?) are all, in effect, key analytical statements, central to the development of Smith's economic analysis and must be, in a sense, conclusions that Smith has already reached. Indeed the structure is found in various places in the *Wealth of Nations*, to a greater or lesser degree. The lead sentences are presented as assertions and what follows in each chapter is a justification for, and extension of, the key ideas. Extra-textual evidence, from chapter two, part two of *The Theory of Moral Sentiments*, and comments by John Millar (one of Smith's students) suggest that Smith's method of lecturing in Moral Philosophy consisted in presenting distinct 'propositions' and then proving and illustrating them (Smith [1759], 1976; Raphael and Macfie (eds.), Introduction, 4).

Chapter one, paragraph one relates increases in the productive powers of labour (whose annual application gives rise to the means of consumption) to 'the effects of the division of labour'. The pin factory is such a well-known example that it is difficult at first sight to be certain that there is anything new to be said about it. However, when looked at from the point of view of the development of Smith's argument in writing, several interesting things emerge. Smith does not offer, for example, a definition of the division of labour but merely highlights the link between the division of labour and increases in productivity. Instead he opts for an example: 'the effects of the division of labour, in the general business of society, will be more easily understood by considering in what manner it operates in *some particular manufactures*' (my emphasis). Smith then reverses the order of treatment: the text deals *first* with the question of *illustrating* what is meant by the division of labour before it explores the analytical link between the division of labour and increases in labour productivity.

In paragraph three, Smith introduces his famous (though not innovative) example of 'the trade of the pin-maker'.[6] But before working through his example, Smith considers some methodological issues. He first challenges the erroneous notion that the division of labour is carried further in 'trifling' occupations than in bigger undertakings. This notion arises from the capacity to observe small-scale operations, under 'the view of the spectator'. Smith lays great stress on the capacity to observe economic processes: 'the view of the spectator'; 'seldom see more'; 'not near so obvious'; 'I have seen a small manufactory of this kind ...'; 'I have seen several ...'; or have them confirmed by other people's observations, 'I am assured ...'; '... must frequently have been shown ...'. Such instances, right at the start of the work, attest to the Baconian influence on Smith and to the active nature of his researches. Smith is envisaging something more systematic than mere idle curiosity. He is very much concerned that evidence should support his argument and it is clear from samples of his writing that he both practised direct observation and encouraged others to do so (see Skinner 1972: 309). He uses similar phrases elsewhere in the *Wealth of Nations*, e.g. in chapter five, book four (Endres 1991: 88).[7] But some 'great manufactures' cannot be readily observed.

Smith, then, is careful to justify his example and stress that it is suggestive of a greater process found in other types of enterprises and economic activities of even greater significance. This is important for Smith never defines the division of labour itself. His approach, here, is inductive. He merely illustrates it in the pin factory by spelling out the processes involved and extends it, by informal analogy or by metaphorical extension, to a whole series of other simple examples that call upon the implied readers' existing but unorganised knowledge of economic life or on their capacity to observe it. Smith works to reorganise their experience of observing such life. These examples are: 'farmer'; 'manufacturer'; 'linen and woolen manufacturers'; 'growers of flax'; 'bleachers and smoothers of linen'; 'dyers and dressers of cloth'; 'carpenter'; 'smith' – also, later, in the context of 'a common smith' who 'has never been used to make nails', and so on. In this sense, the pin trade is taken as a case study from which the organisational and productive features of the division of labour can be extended to other economic contexts, subject, as in the general case of agriculture, to certain provisos. In short, Smith is saying that the principles that operate in example 'X' also operate in example 'Y', and by this process unlike things can be reduced to one common process: the division of labour. It is up to the readers, for most of the examples, to spell out the process for each type of work. McCloskey has drawn economists' attention to a similar process of metaphorical extension found in modern-day economic argument, e.g. a 'child' is just like a 'durable good' and so in explaining 'family size', notions of investment can be applied (McCloskey 1994: 327–8). An aim of Smith's rhetoric of repetition is to fix the underlying principles in the reader's mind and relate them to diverse social practices and historical contexts.

In the sixth paragraph, Smith initiates discussion of the circumstances that give rise to the increases in productivity. The textual structure repeats the pattern, generalisation-exemplification. In each paragraph a generalisation is supported by evidence. In two out of the three paragraphs the evidence is supplied from contrasting situations. One passage is adequate by way of illustration:

First, the improvement of the dexterity of the workman necessarily increases the quantity of the work he can perform; and the division of labour, by reducing every man's business to some one simple operation, and by making this operation the sole employment of his life, necessarily increases very much the dexterity of the workman [*theoretically backed empirical generalisation*]. A common smith, who, though accustomed to handle the hammer, has never been used to making nails, if upon some particular occasion he is obliged to attempt it, will scarce, I am assured, be able to make above two or three hundred nails in a day, and those too very bad ones [*authentic empirical example without benefit of dexterity*]. A smith who has been accustomed to make nails, but whose sole or principal business has not been that of a nailer, can seldom with his utmost diligence make more than eight hundred or a thousand nails in a day [*authentic empirical evidence with some benefit of dexterity*]. I have seen several boys under twenty years of age who had never exercised any other trade but that of making nails, and who, when they exerted themselves, could make each of them, upwards of two thousand three hundred nails in a day [*authentic empirical evidence with high levels of dexterity*].

As nail making was a significant activity in Smith's home town, extra-textual evidence suggests Smith had engaged, once again, in direct observation. The comparative method (i.e. 'compare and contrast' or even, in formal economics terms, some sort of 'comparative statics') is taken to a high degree in this extended example or mini-case study. Several examples, in the sample of text considered, exhibit this pattern. Elsewhere in the *Wealth of Nations* other contrasting examples are to be found, e.g. 'rude' and 'civilized', 'improved' and 'unimproved', 'servant' and 'slave'. The opening paragraph of part one of book one chapter ten contains five paired examples of contrasting conditions that systematically, in Smith's estimate, influence the structure of wages.[8]

The long final paragraph of chapter two consists of a narrated series of intellectual speculations and examples in which readers are invited to work with Smith ('let us consider', 'we should be sensible that ...' and the use of the exclamation mark to signify a sense of intellectual excitement), to enter, as it were, his world of economic wonder and explore the remarkable social and economic consequences of the division of labour.[9] The specific example, this time of a compound product rather than of a simple manufacturing process relying on individual dexterity, that gives rise to a sustained narrative, is that of 'that very simple machine, the shears with which the shepherd clips the wool'. The consideration of the inputs and other specialisations gives rise to a long list of occupations and activities, tied together in a mutual dependence of interlocking exchanges. The examples are set within the framework of a great economic drama that starts with a consideration of the number of people involved in preparation of the accommodation of 'the most common artificer or day-labourer' and ends with:

> Compared, indeed, with the more extravagant luxury of the great, his accommodation must no doubt appear extremely simple and easy; and yet it may be true, perhaps, that the accommodation of a European prince does not always so much exceed that of an industrious and frugal peasant as the accommodation of the latter exceeds that of many an African king, the absolute master of the lives and liberties of ten thousand naked savages.

In between comes the long list of examples with the associated danger of incoherence. Smith's closure must be judged little short of masterly, for it guarantees the coherence of the paragraph. Smith has a capacity for generating memorable images and the creative or imaginative aspects of his writing should not be underestimated. The *Wealth of Nations* is a blend of fact and fiction. And to think that Ruskin was accused of a romantic approach to economic life! The long list of economic specialisations united round consideration of one product became a staple of Victorian economic story telling, Smith's 'shears' being dropped in favour of the 'Christmas pudding'. A modern-day literary manifestation of a list of economic activities contributing to a final product is satirised in David Lodge's *Nice Work*, an 1980s reworking of themes from the Victorian socio-economic novel (Lodge 1988).[10] The evidence from 'outside' the text is that Smith's wondrous nature of economic life had a huge impact on his readership and those influenced by it.

The opening paragraph of chapter two signals an insight that is of fundamental importance to Smith's approach to the whole of economic life: the principle of natural propensities in human nature which give rise to unintended consequences. The organisational and productive implications of propensities 'to truck, barter and exchange' emerge slowly over historical time, the unintended consequences of individual human beings trying to better their position through trade. Here it is, clear and plain and located at the core of his fundamental principle of productivity, central to his theory of economic growth.[11]

Smith then develops the theme of human nature by a series of exemplifications, developed within the context of 'truck, barter and exchange', which contrast (in the manner of David Hume in his *Treatise of Human Nature*) human nature with animal nature. Smith's examples are also formed within the general framework of wider enlightenment thinking. Fawning is presented as an attribute of both human and animal nature. However, humans 'stand in need of the cooperation and assistance of great multitudes' (Smith [1776], 1952: 7) and need to gain that cooperation (instinctive in animals, through the 'accidental concurrence of their passions') by other means. The exemplifications lead up to the following observation:

> It is not from the benevolence of the butcher, the brewer or the baker that we expect our dinner, but from their regard to their own interest. We address ourselves, not to their humanity but to their self-love, and never talk to them of our own necessities but of their advantages.

'[A]ddress' and 'talk' serve to remind the reader that Smith has opened the discussion with a speculation that the human propensity 'to truck, barter and exchange' may be located in 'the faculties of reason and speech'.[12]

The lead sentence in the third paragraph in chapter two is:

> *As it is by* treaty, by barter, and by purchase that we obtain from one another the greater part of those mutual good offices which we stand in need of, *so it is this same* trucking disposition which *originally* gives occasion to the division of labour. (my emphasis)

This is, as far as I can see, the first use in the text of the construct 'as it is ... so it is', a construct Smith uses in the following chapter to present implications to the reader. I have italicised 'originally' because Smith's thought was developed within the context of vision of the historical evolution of society and accounting for origins is a significant aspect of his social thought. The rest of the paragraph consists of examples designed to illustrate 'origins' within the conceptual framework of the division of labour. Thus 'In a tribe ...' introduces a set of stylised, i.e. 'hypothetical', examples of growing specialisation that allow an individual 'to cultivate and bring to perfection whatever talent or genius he may posses for that particular species of business'. The individual examples have, in context, a kind of plausibility with 'realistic' narrative touches helping to paint an idealised picture of the developmental process. The division of labour is arrived at on a voluntary or natural basis. The specialisations are in making arrows, frame building and cover making for 'their little huts or moveable houses', smithing, skin dressing, dressed skins being presented as 'the principal part of the clothing of savages'. In this narrative passage Smith uses the present tense: this gives immediacy to the examples, in keeping with the 'of the moment' approach found elsewhere in the sample. Furthermore the details of the narrative appeal to a shared body of knowledge concerning the nature of the 'rude' or 'savage'. Although a story of 'origins', the specialist members of the tribe learn the lesson in one generation. The paragraph that follows corrects the impression that these differences are entirely innate: they are themselves 'the effect of the division of labour'.

The final paragraph opens with '*As it is this disposition* which forms that difference of talents, so remarkable among men of different professions, *so it is this same* disposition which renders that difference useful' (my emphasis). The exemplifications, most of which are stylised, again a series of contrasts, tracing out distinctions between animals and men, are designed to illustrate the utility of the 'general disposition to truck, barter, and exchange'.

The opening paragraph of the third chapter is more complex but just as bold as those of the preceding chapters. It is an analytical proposition presented as an *implication* of what has gone before : 'As it is the power of exchanging ... so the extent of this division'. This in itself signals that Smith's argument has already progressed, the principle of exchange having already been explored in the preceding chapter. The reader has something to build upon. And this is reflected within the organisation of the paragraph. The second sentence is an exemplification of the 'hypothetical' type, designed to illustrate the analytical statement. It is an exemplification but it is not located in any given concrete situation and the reader is supplied, given what has gone before, with just enough information to make sense of the proposition. The two sentences together follow the 'rule–example' pattern found in modern-day introductory economics writing.

What follows in the rest of the third chapter is at first sight (and especially for the modern reader) rather dreary, considering the dramatic opening. Closer reading shows it to be otherwise. It is in fact a series of carefully contrived more or less concrete examples illustrating the analytical relation-ship in a series of linked sets of contrasting examples, rising from the village up through cities and so to the whole world. Overall for the rest of the third chapter taken as a whole the pattern is 'specific-general' but there are varia-tions within this. Smith, however, continues to use the same basic pattern of subsets of analytical propositions with implications. He does this, strikingly, in paragraphs three and four.

In paragraph two the contrast is between town and country and the paragraph develops from the 'hypothetical' example of a general nature, becoming progressively more detailed in terms of specific trades. In other words a 'general-specific' text structure within the paragraph. It terminates with the example of the impossibility of a 'nailer' finding the means of specialised employment in a remote part of the Scottish Highlands. Again the example is hypothetical but it serves the purpose of re-applying a key concept by exercising the imagination. The 'nailer', a parallel example to that of the pin maker and already treated as such, and in some detail, by Smith in chapter one, requires only a thumbnail case study as the process is close to that already examined in the first chapter. This textual variation must also count as a kind of deliberate repetition that at the same time extends, without too much intellectual effort, the reader's experience.

Paragraph three opens 'As by means of water-carriage ... so it is upon the sea coast and along the banks of navigable rivers'. In fact it is useful to set out the whole of the complex lead sentence in this paragraph:

> **As by means of water-carriage** a more extensive market is opened to every sort of industry than what land-carriage alone can afford it, **so it is upon the sea coast, and along the banks of navigable rivers**, that industry of every kind **naturally begins to subdivide and improve itself**, and it is frequently not till a long time after that those **improvements extend themselves to the inland parts of the country**. (my emphasis)

The first part of the sentence illustrates an application of the idea through a means of extending the market and the implication relates the general principle to the world beyond Smith's text 'sea coast and banks of navigable rivers'. The bold type picks out language that is consistent with Smith's concept of 'natural' behaviour and unintended consequences, 'improvements' 'extend themselves'. The pattern of development is not planned. Rather it evolves, under the influence of competition, as each individual pursues his interests in trucking and bartering. Smith's ideological position is here found within the details of the language choices that he has exercised while writing. His overall system is founded upon a notion of 'natural liberty', operating in this example at the 'macro' level. The rest of the paragraph consists, again, of a series of teacherly contrasts between the movements of goods on land and sea. It is in such 'compare and contrast' exercises that the didactic nature of the text is manifest. The comparisons start with the detailed domestic example of London and Edinburgh but extending to the international arena by the addition of a question: 'What goods could bear the expense of land-carriage between London and Calcutta?' (Smith [1776] 1952: 9). Smith explicitly justifies his choice by pointing out that London and Calcutta in fact carry out 'a very considerable commerce with each other'. The comparisons cannot be extended to London-Calcutta because the land alternative is impractical: its absence is used to effect.

Paragraph four maintains the general form of the argument and opens with:

> *Since such, therefore are* the advantages of water-carriage, *it is **natural** that* the first improvements of art and industry should be made where this conveniency *opens the whole world for a market* to the produce of every sort of labour, and that they should always be much later in extending themselves into the inland parts of the country. (my emphasis)

Smith continues to demonstrate reasoning by moving from, in this case, an empirical generalisation based upon comparative costs, to a 'natural' implication. In the previous paragraph, the pairing, Edinburgh-London and London-Calcutta has given way to 'the whole world for a market'. But the position of the 'sea coasts' and 'navigable rivers' is contrasted with that of inland parts whose development is limited by local conditions. Once again the paired contrasts, this time 'inland-coastal', is maintained. The text repeats a basic pattern but the variation maintains the interest.

The final series of paragraphs, in a sense, focus on more or less concrete examples that treat 'the whole world' in terms of what has gone before. Again the textual pattern is 'general-specific'; the general concept 'the whole world' is then divided into its component parts: China, India, Central Asia and Africa. Considerable emphasis is placed on exemplifying, further, the consequences of the division of labour for economic well-being, in the contemporary and historical world as known by Smith, and in relation to access to coastal or riparian navigation. This principle, based upon comparative costs, is used to explain the lack of development in interior locations or on continents, such as Africa, with few navigable waterways. Thus, through a careful pattern of exemplifications, Smith effectively illustrates that his theoretical insight is valid, over time, and in local, regional, national and international contexts.

Conclusions

The primary purpose of this paper was to explore Smith's use of examples and to relate his use of examples to the wider discourse. A number of interesting aspects of Smith's writing have been revealed. First, the general scheme for considering examples has proved to be useful in context. In the passages under consideration, the 'hypothetical' example, essentially an appeal to the active reasoning power of the implied reader predominates though there are several instances of the more-or-less authentic case study. 'Hypothetical' examples are sometimes set within plausible if somewhat idealistic narratives. Second, the macro structure of each chapter considered seems to follow a pattern. This consists in a single-paragraph introduction that sets out the topic or proposition that is to be explored in the chapter. The rest of the chapter consists of the justification of the proposition, by exemplification, some of which corresponds to styles of exemplification found in modern-day economics textbooks, and its extension, again usually by exemplification, to other contexts. Third, it has also been revealed that the use of examples is not accidental or incidental but, for at least two of the chapters concerned, fundamental to the development and justification of the proposition that is being presented. Considerable effort has gone into the specification and selection of examples (used inductively and deductively) and into their textual organisation and presentation. It is by weaving a simple principle or set of principles in and out of largely contemporary examples (in the case of the sample considered here) that a few simple propositions are demonstrated to have a powerful explanatory and predictive role. Even in this small sample of writing, Smith's hierarchy of examples aims for universal appeal. Fourth, it would seem that the implied reader has, sometimes, to activate the knowledge of certain working environments and apply the principle to the understated examples, real or imaginary. Fifth, the cohesion of the chapters is secured by recurrent patterns in the structure and handling of examples within the framework of simple text patterns such as 'general-specific' and 'compare and contrast' and by details of the language used. This textual organisation, which a quick check shows to be found elsewhere in the text, would seem to correspond to a pattern most likely found in scientific discourse (either written or spoken) of the time. Sixth, the analysis has also revealed a linguistic pattern 'As it is .. so it is' for the presentation of any theoretical or empirical implications of key propositions. A quick look in the introduction to book two shows that there it is reduced to 'as ... so', a construct suggestive of the 'if/then' formula found in elementary modern-day positive economics (Mead and Henderson 1983). The construction is in evidence also in *The Theory of Moral Sentiments*. Further work is required to see if this pattern is found elsewhere in Smith's writing.

It would seem, however, that a primary interest in textual description gives rise to interesting possibilities for textual exploration by other (extra-textual) means. It provides detailed evidence for existing propositions about Smith's text and suggests additional ways of understanding Smith's economics writing.

Notes

1. I thank Vivienne Brown, Ann Hewings, Warren Samuels and Sebastian Mitchell for comments on earlier drafts of this paper.
2. Contemporary judgements were not always favourable. Walpole, no great lover of Scottish philosophers, found the work, according to Ross, badly written and repetitive (Ross 1995: 250).
3. There is a very special quality to Smith's use of examples. It is the business of the rest of this paper to make that quality explicit. But there is nothing to match it in, say, the economics writings of Hume, another very clear writer. Hume was engaged, however, in writing essays on economic topics and not a complete discourse. Smith pays the same attention to examples in his *The Theory of Moral Sentiments* where he is concerned with the relationship between philosophy 'and ordinary life' (Griswold 1999: 22).
4. This use of examples is complex and may be developed within a framework that is referred to in the wider literature on Smith as the method of 'conjectural history'. This method is one in which 'principles established on the basis of observed facts' are used to explore 'events where facts were not readily available' (Skinner 1972: 308). However, 'hypothetical examples', in the sense used here, can be contrived out of direct evidence; i.e. they can have an iconic quality.
5. Most of Smith's readers will never have seen a highland village so in this respect he is providing a substitute experience of 'observation' (Brown 1994, chapter seven).
6. Both Deleyre and Diderot had already published on the 'Pin' in the *Encyclopèdie* (Still 1997: 71).
7. Indeed the notion of social life as a 'spectacle' and the individual as both 'spectator and spectacle' has been seen as a significant metaphor in Smith's other major work, *The Theory of Moral Sentiments* (Brown 1997: 286; Griswold 1999, passim). In the passages analysed here from the *Wealth of Nations*, the notion of economic life as a wondrous spectacle can also be found, so that once again, 'spectator and spectacle' are brought together.
8. 'Compare and contrast' is to be taken as a general descriptor of a repeated textual pattern.

However, each occurrence is adapted to the specific context or argument being made.

9. Smith in his *Philosophical Essays* points to the role of 'wonder' and its temporary consequence of 'giddiness and confusion' in exciting philosophical investigation (Skinner 1972: 309; Skinner 1983, passim). The long last paragraph of chapter one with its exclamations and quick-fire list of examples suggests a rhetoric of wonder, excitement and perhaps even giddiness.

10. Smith's formal text influenced a number of creative writers. Harriet Martineau produced in 1832 her first tale illustrating political economy, *Life in the Wilds*, in which the theme of 'economic progress' is considered from the perspective of a 'modern' group that has fallen on hard times in 'the south of Africa'. One of the manufacturing processes that helps the group discover the significance of specialisation and the division of labour is the making of arrows. This is both an example, and a developmental context, suggested by her reading of Smith on the division of labour, chapter two paragraph two in particular. This is further evidence of the forcefulness of Smith's examples for his initial readers.

11. Keynes, in 1936, used the language of natural propensities, in the form of psychological propensities to set up a relationship between increases in income and increases in consumption. The meaning of Smith's 'propensity to truck, barter and exchange' is open.

12. Smith's example points up the significance of rhetoric for economic life in a specific context of exchange (i.e. the language of buying and selling, though in modern-day capitalism the emphasis is on the language of selling) but the idea is perfectly general. The division of labour and the emergence of specialist roles implies the emergence of specialist languages, e.g. think of the consequences of the application of the division of labour to the work of 'philosophers'. The English language expanded its vocabulary during the 18th century as a result of international trade.

Active verbs with inanimate subjects in scientific research articles

Peter Master

Animate subjects include humans and animals, whereas inanimate subjects embrace all other categories of nouns, including abstract nouns. Inanimate subjects, being devoid of animate life in the common sense of the word, are generally considered to be incapable of acting on their own and are therefore primarily associated with the passive voice. However, some languages in the world, including English, allow inanimate subjects to act on their own accord in certain circumstances and thus be associated with an active verb. An example of a sentence with an inanimate subject is 'A thermometer measures temperature'. This usage is particularly prevalent in modern scientific text wherein priority is given to facts (Gopen and Swan 1990), usually in the form of complex nominalizations. In contrast, the avoidance of such usage may lead to wordiness.

Non-native English speakers of languages that do not allow inanimate subjects with active verbs have particular difficulty accepting the fact that this structure is possible in scientific English, even desired under some circumstances, because they interpret such a structure as an unacceptable anthropomorphism (perhaps analogous to the response English speakers would have to a sentence such as 'The thermometer ran up the stairs'). Kojima and Kojima (1978) showed that Japanese writers of English, for example, often employ the personal *we* to avoid using an inanimate subject with the active voice.

In a sentence such as 'We make temperature measurements with a thermometer', the use of *we* as a main subject in English sentences is partially explained by the fact that in Japanese this pronoun would typically be dropped, with the effect that the sentence is perceived as being depersonalized. Since English cannot drop pronouns in this way (it is not a pro-drop language), *we* must be supplied, which casts the sentence in an undesirably personal or subjective light and thus detracts from the 'directness' of the sentence. (Master 1991: 17)

In Master (1991), I investigated the phenomenon of active verbs with inanimate subjects in the annual listing by field of reported scientific and technical discoveries (the 'Science News of the Year' column that appears every December) over a 10-year period in a sophisticated popular science magazine called *Science News*. Analysis showed that concrete inanimate subjects were almost equally likely to take an active or a passive verb, whereas abstract subjects were almost twice as likely to take an active than a passive verb. In other words, the structure was widespread, a finding that ran counter to the notion that scientific prose was characterized by primary use of the passive voice.

There are, however, levels of prose. Huddleston (1971) referred to scholarly journal articles as 'high-brow', to undergraduate textbooks as 'mid-brow', and to popular science for the general reader as 'low-brow'. In Master (1991), I argued that *Science News* was 'more akin to a survey paper than to a journal article, especially as the corpus consists entirely of synopses of the year's discoveries. With a ratio of 77 per cent active/23 per cent passive, the 'Science News of the Year' column is similar to the ratio of active to passive verb forms in general 'mid-brow' scientific discourse' (p.22). The purpose of the present study was to determine if these findings also applied to 'high-brow' prose, specifically scientific research articles, the primary genre to be analyzed in the ESP literature.

The study

The object of the present analysis was to determine the frequency of occurrence of active verbs with inanimate subjects as well as the nature of the verbs with which the structure is associated in formal scientific research articles in contrast to popular scientific prose. The scientific research articles (RAs) selected represent the fields of cell biology, chemistry, clinical psychology, computer science and geology. Faculty at a major metropolitan university were asked to identify the top journals in these fields, and two articles were selected in each field from these journals, three in the case of computer science as the articles were somewhat shorter. Full citations for the articles appear in the reference section.

Each sentence in the 11 articles was analyzed for the following information, which was then entered into a computer database with the following categories:

a) field;

b) page and sentence number;

c) status of the clause: main or subordinate;

d) the bare subject of each clause;

e) the classification of each subject as animate, inanimate concrete, or inanimate abstract;

f) the verb in each clause (including nonfinite verbs with a recoverable subject);

g) the classification of each verb as active, passive, or stative/intransitive (the latter category in order to parallel the original study and to separate out verbs in which the active or passive voice is not a true choice);

h) the classification of each verb as cause and effect, change of location or state, presentation, or explanation;

i) notes on particularities of the example.

Results

The results were first analyzed in terms of verb types in the entire corpus of 4,300 subject-verb pairs, almost twice the number investigated in Master (1991). Table 1 compares the analysis of *Science News* with the results of the present study.

Table 1 Comparison of verb forms in *Science News* and the science RAs.

Verb Form	Science News		Science RAs	
Active	1,407/2,979	47.2%	1,418/4,300	32.98%
Passive	613/2,979	20.6%	1,322/4,300	30.74%
Stat/Intrans	959/2,979	32.2%	1,560/4,300	36.28%

It shows that the percentage of stative/intransitive verbs was fairly similar, but that there was a substantially greater percentage of passive verbs and thus a lesser percentage of active verbs in the research articles. The corpus was then analyzed in terms of active/passive verbs alone. The ratio of active to passive was 1,418/2,740 = 51.75 per cent active and 1,322/2,740 = 48.23 per cent passive compared to 69.7 per cent active and 30.3 per cent passive in *Science News*. The greater proportion of passive usage in the journal articles is characteristic of 'high-brow' prose, though it contrasts markedly with Tarone *et al.* (1981), who found a percentage of 81 per cent and 89 per cent active voice in two astrophysics journal articles.[1]

The subjects of each clause were then analyzed in terms of the voice of their corresponding verbs (see Table 2).

Table 2 Subjects and voice (excluding stative verbs).

Subject Type	Voice	*Science News*		Science RAs	
Inanimate	Active	310	52.01%	192	40.00%
Inanimate	Passive	286	47.99%	288	60.00%
Inanimate	(Subtotal)	596	(29.50%)	480	(17.52%)
Abstract	Active	490	65.77%	835	46.31%
Abstract	Passive	255	34.23%	968	53.69%
Abstract	(Subtotal)	745	(36.88%)	1,803	(65.80%)
Animate	Active	607	89.40%	391	85.56%
Animate	Passive	72	10.60%	66	14.44%
Animate	(Subtotal)	679	(33.61%)	457	(16.69%)
TOTAL		2,020	(100%)	2,740	(100%)

Table 2 shows that the distribution of the subjects and their verbs in *Science News* differs substantially from that in the science RAs. The proportion of abstract subjects is nearly half that of the science RAs, while the proportions of both animate and inanimate subjects is approximately double. The only categories that are somewhat similar in the two databases are the animate active and passive verbs.

The next consideration is the extent to which the presence of active verbs with inanimate subjects is different in various scientific fields. The figures for each field (cell biology, chemistry, clinical psychology, computer science, and geology) are compared to the closest category in *Science News* in Table 3.

Table 3 Distribution of active and passive verbs in five disciplines.

Field (SN)	n	Active	Passive	Field (RAs)	n	Active	Passive
Biology	227	67.8	32.2	Cell Biol.	238	37.4	62.6
Chemistry	188	78.2	21.8	Chemistry	431	41.1	58.9
Medicine	314	71.0	29.0	Clin. Psych.	485	59.6	40.4
Technology	150	87.3	12.7	Comp. Sci.	831	60.0	40.0
Earth Sci.	206	73.8	26.2	Geology	755	48.2	51.8

Table 3 shows that every field represented in the five science RAs has a far greater proportion of passive usage (20–30 per cent higher) than did *Science News*. Technology/computer science showed the highest percentage of active verbs in both data sets, while biology/cellular biology showed the lowest.

The use of active verbs with inanimate subjects, both concrete (InConc) and abstract (InAb) is compared in the five disciplines in Table 4.

Table 4 Distribution of subject types with active verbs in five disciplines.

Field (SN)	n	An	InConc	InAb	Field (RAs)	n	An	InConc	InAb
Biology	154	56.5	17.5	26.0	Cell Biol.	89	36.0	27.0	37.0
Chemistry	147	44.9	27.2	27.9	Chemistry	177	46.3	9.1	44.6
Medicine	223	38.6	26.4	35.0	Clin. Psych.	289	44.3	.03	55.4
Technology	131	44.3	22.9	32.8	Comp. Sci.	499	20.0	11.2	68.7
Earth Sci.	152	36.2	19.1	44.7	Geology	364	13.5	26.1	60.4
TOTAL	807	43.6	22.9	33.5	TOTAL	1,418	27.6	13.5	58.9

Animate = 43.6% Inanimate = 56.4%   Animate = 27.6% Inanimate = 72.4%

Table 4 shows that the proportion of inanimate subjects with active verbs is higher in the scientific RAs, comprising almost three-quarters of the total, compared to those in *Science News* (SN), which comprise almost two-thirds of the total. However, the proportion of concrete and abstract inanimate subjects is quite different. The science RAs show far more abstract than concrete inanimate subjects with active verbs, with a ratio of 4.4:1 for the science RAs as compared to a ratio of 1.5:1 in *Science News*. The cellular biology and geology RAs had the highest proportion of concrete inanimate subjects with active verbs, whereas in *Science News* the two closest areas (biology and earth sciences) had the lowest proportion. While there is little correlation between the two databases in terms of individual fields, the science RAs show an even greater proportion of inanimate subjects with active verbs than *Science News*.

This study differed from Master (1991) in that a record was also kept of whether the subject occurred in a main or a subordinate clause. In the entire corpus, 52.7 per cent of the subjects occurred in a main clause, 47.3 per cent in a subordinate clause, i.e. in roughly equal proportions. Within the sub-category of active verbs, these proportions were reversed, with 47.2 per cent of the subjects with active verbs occurring in main clauses, 52.8 per cent in subordinate clauses, though they can still be said to be roughly equal. This rough equivalence holds for inanimate subjects in general (both concrete and abstract) with active verbs, with 50.4 per cent occurring in main clauses and 49.6 per cent in subordinate clauses. However, it does not hold for animate subjects with active verbs, where 38.6 per cent occurred in main clauses and 61.4 per cent in subordinate clauses, nor for concrete inanimate subjects, where 39.6 per cent occurred in main clauses and 60.4 per cent in subordinate clauses, in remarkably similar proportions. It thus appears that, with active verbs, concrete inanimate subjects behave much like animate subjects as far as subordination is concerned.

Kojima and Kojima (1978: 221–5) identified 10 environments in which inanimate subjects occurred: cause-effect, explanatory statement, factual statement, judgment/opinion, possibility/potentiality, maintenance/prevention, necessity/requirement, function, presentation, and change/movement. In Master (1991), I consolidated the environments in which inanimate subjects occurred in *Science News* into two large categories: causal and explanatory. The causal environment pertains to the instigation of an event, while the explanatory environment (e.g. *suggest, show, describe, compare*) pertains to the explanation of an event. The causal environment was further divided into cause and effect (e.g. *cause, produce, prevent, allow*), change of state or location (e.g. *change, increase, dissolve, convey*), and presentation (e.g. *give, produce, contribute, provide*). The two databases are compared in Table 5.

Table 5 Instrumental subjects with active verbs in the environments.

Database	Science News		Science RAs	
Environment	n	%	n	%
1 Causal	519	64.9	810	78.9
a cause and effect	262	32.8	176	17.1
b change of state/location	153	19.1	349	34.0
c presentation	104	13.0	285	27.8
2 Explanatory	281	35.1	217	21.1

Table 5 shows that the causal environment dominates in both data sets. However, the explanatory environment occurs less frequently in the science RAs. Within the causal environment, change of state/location and presentation occur substantially more frequently in the science RAs than in the *Science*

News database, with cause and effect occurring correspondingly less.

The most frequent verbs in the environments found in the *Science News* corpus were then compared to the most frequent verbs found in the science RA corpus. Table 6 gives the results for verbs taking both concrete (Conc.) and abstract (Abs.) inanimate subjects.

Table 6 shows that many of the verbs identified in the *Science News* corpus occurred frequently in the science RA corpus as well. For example, in the cause-and-effect subset, *cause* occurs in both lists, and while *create* occurs in the *Science News* list, the synonyms *make* and *form* occur in the science RA list. In the change-of-state-or-location subset, *reduce* is the most frequent verb on both lists, and *increase* occurs on both lists as well. In the presentation subset, *provide* is the most frequent verb on both lists, and *give* occurs on both lists as well. Finally, in the explanatory subset, the first three verbs *show*, *indicate*, and *suggest* are the most frequent verbs in both lists, and *reveal* and *explain* occur on both lists as well.

There are some notable differences in the nature of the subjects associated with these verbs, however. While in the cause-and-effect subset *cause* occurs in both lists, it is associated more with concrete inanimate subjects in the *Science News* corpus, whereas it is associated exclusively with abstract subjects in the science RA corpus. Similarly, in the change-of-state-or-location subset, *reduce* occurs with both concrete and abstract subjects in the *Science News* corpus, but exclusively with abstract subjects in the science RA corpus. In the presentation subset, *provide* occurs more frequently with concrete inanimate subjects in the *Science News* corpus, but again exclusively with abstract subjects in the science RA corpus. Finally, in the explanatory subset, *show* and to a lesser extent *reveal* occur with comparable frequency with both types of inanimate subjects in both corpora. However, *suggest*, *indicate*, and *explain* occur, once again, exclusively with abstract subjects.

Discussion

The findings suggest that the corpus from *Science News* magazine analyzed in my earlier paper (Master 1991) was not as representative of scientific prose as I had thought and that the passive voice does indeed play a greater role in scientific research articles. However, the greater proportion of inanimate subjects with active verbs in the latter confirms my earlier finding that inanimate subjects with active verbs occur frequently and should therefore be the subject of focused pedagogical attention.

Table 6 Most frequent verbs with inanimate subjects in the two environments.

Science News			Science RAs			
A Most frequent verbs in the cause-and-effect subset						
Verb	Conc.	Abs.	T	Verb	Conc.	Abs.	T
cause	12	7	19	use	6	36	42
kill	6	3	9	allow	0	24	24
affect	4	4	8	make	4	15	19
prevent	6	2	8	form	8	10	18
create	3	4	7	affect	1	13	14
protect	5	1	6	cause	0	8	8

B Most frequent verbs in the change-of-state-or-location subset

Verb	Conc.	Abs.	T	Verb	Conc.	Abs.	T
reduce	3	4	7	reduce	0	26	26
bring	1	5	6	follow	6	13	19
open	2	3	5	increase	7	2	9
revolutionize	3	2	5	take	0	8	8
increase	0	3	3	fill	5	0	5
decrease	1	2	3	modify	0	5	5

C Most frequent verbs in the presentation subset

Verb	Conc.	Abs.	T	Verb	Conc.	Abs.	T
provide	13	10	23	provide	0	38	38
produce	3	6	9	give	0	20	20
support	0	8	8	require	0	12	12
yield	1	5	6	generate	0	9	9
offer	2	3	5	predict	0	9	9
give	1	3	4	specify	0	9	9

D Most frequent verbs in the explanatory environment

Verb	Conc.	Abs.	T	Verb	Conc.	Abs.	T
show	10	44	54	show	18	61	79
indicate	5	38	43	suggest	0	33	33
suggest	5	37	42	indicate	0	28	28
reveal	6	17	23	characterize	9	2	11
find	0	14	14	determine	0	9	9
raise	1	10	11	reveal	3	5	8
confirm	0	6	6	raise	1	4	5
explain	3	3	6	explain	0	4	4

The results in Table 2 suggest the possible nature of popularized scientific text compared to academic research articles: fewer abstract subjects and a greater number of animate and inanimate subjects, perhaps because they are more accessible to the layman. The active/passive ratios for animate subjects are about the same, but for the inanimate subjects, the ratios show higher percentages of passive constructions in the science RAs.

It is clear from Table 3 that *Science News*, sophisticated as it is, is still a popular science magazine, and the nature of the prose therein is only partially representative of scientific writing in general. In general, the science RAs showed a far smaller proportion of concrete inanimate subjects with active verbs, but they did show many more abstract inanimate subjects with active verbs, which is also a difficulty for students whose first languages only allow animate subjects to perform actions or directly cause things to happen.

The finding that concrete inanimate subjects behave much like animate subjects as far as subordination is concerned is an interesting one that would be a good topic for further research. Since the animate subjects in the research articles were almost entirely human beings (primarily researchers, often as pronominal *we*, other authors, and patients in the case of clinical psychology), it is not surprising that they would tend to be more subordinated, given the understanding that facts are meant to speak for themselves in scientific research articles. That concrete inanimate subjects should be subordinated to almost exactly the same extent may be sheer coincidence. However, it raises the unexpected notion that the human agency implied in such structures (we are, after all, aware that a thermometer is in fact being used by a human being to measure temperature and that it has not in any real sense been imbued with this capacity) tends to be subordinated just as human agents are in scientific text.

The corpus used in the analysis of *Science News* was the annual listing by field of reported scientific and technical discoveries. Each discovery was described in a sentence, sometimes two. The science RAs, on the other hand, were full-fledged research articles. While scientific sentences may have features in common, the rhetorical nature of the two corpora were completely different. It is thus not surprising that, as shown in Table 5, inanimate subjects would occur much more frequently in the explanatory environment in the *Science News* corpus (more than a third compared to less than a quarter in the science RAs) since the objective of the 'Science News of the Year' columns is to explain a series of new discoveries. The causal environment overall is proportionately higher in the science RAs, although change of state/location and presentation predominate while simple cause and effect accounts for less than a fifth. This is also not surprising since the 'Science News of the Year' presents a list of discovered causes and their subsequent effects, whereas a research article is concerned with a limited number of causes and effects and is clearly more concerned with changes of state or location and presentation.

As far as specific verbs are concerned, there are fewer differences between the *Science News* and the science RA corpora. Table 6 shows that in a few cases the most frequent verbs found with inanimate subjects are the same in both. The most marked similarity is in the explanatory environment. This is no doubt because explanation is a function that is required in many areas of inquiry, as corpus linguistics is beginning to reveal, and that the level of 'brow' does not seriously alter the means by which this function is accomplished in formal text.

It is interesting to note that concrete inanimate subjects appeared to occur with greater frequency in the *Science News* corpus than in the science RA corpus. Another interesting subject for further study would be to determine if popularized science in general makes greater use of this grammatical structure than formal research articles, which appears to be the case in this study. The finding that concrete inanimate subjects tended to be subordinated to the same extent as human subjects in the science RAs studied also suggests that 'humanness' must at least be subordinated in formal scientific text. On the other hand, perhaps it is this very factor that popularizers of science use to make difficult material more accessible to the layman.

Pedagogical implications

It is clear from the findings of this study that popularized scientific prose, even when it is fairly sophisticated, remains 'mid-brow' and does not represent the 'high-brow' proportions of inanimate subjects with active verbs in formal scientific research articles, confirming in a general way Tarone *et al.*'s (1981: 136) statement that 'different rhetorical functions are required in [*Scientific American*, a popular science magazine, and astrophysics research articles]'. The analysis shows that concrete inanimate subjects in science RAs are somewhat more likely (at a ratio of 3:2) to take a passive than an active verb, whereas abstract subjects were almost equally likely to take an active or a passive verb. Even though they occur with somewhat less frequency in the science RAs, inanimate subjects that 'act' are still a prominent feature and they therefore warrant attention in the EST classroom.

In Master (1991), I suggested analyzing 'Earthwatch', a column in many US newspapers that describes the significant environmental occurrences of the week all over the planet, as an engaging way to have students discover inanimate concrete subjects with active verbs. An example of the kind of exercise that an EST student should be able to do after appropriate instruction (from Master, in press) is the following:

Directions: Change the following causes and effects into sentences containing inanimate subjects and active verbs.

Example: the catalyst is present → reaction rate is increased
Answer: The catalyst increases the reaction rate.

1 glaciers existed → many valleys were changed from a V shape to a U shape
2 penicillin is effective → dangerous bacteria are destroyed
3 a seismometer is a machine → it is used to measure earthquakes
4 a meteorite was present → the Arizona desert was struck 30,000 years ago
5 Hurricane Fifi was formed→ 8000 Hondurans were killed in 1974
6 welding is used → sometimes metallurgical changes in materials are produced
7 nitrogen is deficient → leaves become yellowed and plant growth is stunted
8 using fire to polish the sharp edges of a new glass tube (Fire polishing...) → the edges are softened by this process
9 a solution is hypertonic → blood-cell shrinkage occurs
10 a force acts on a rigid body → a reaction force in the opposite direction is generated.

The ultimate goal is to provide EST (English for Science and Technology) teachers (and students) with a solid foundation for understanding and teaching this phenomenon, the avoidance of which, largely due to interference from the first language, may lead to unnecessarily wordy scientific prose.

Note

1. Tarone *et al.* (1981: 137) found that 23 per cent of the total verbs were active *we* verbs, which rose to 37 per cent when existentials (what I have labelled 'stative/intransitive' verbs) were omitted. In the science RA corpus, only 4.7 per cent of the total verbs were active *we* verbs, which rose to 6.4 per cent when statives are not included. The highest percentage of active

we verbs occurred in chemistry RAs (13.7 per cent), followed by clinical psychology (8.0 per cent), cellular biology (7.6 per cent), computer science (4.5 per cent), and geology (3.0 per cent). The high percentage of active verbs in Tarone *et al.* (almost three times higher than the highest percentage found in the RAs) may be a consequence of the speculative nature of astrophysics journal articles, in which the use of *we* + active verb perhaps plays a greater role in establishing authorial stance.

Research articles analyzed

Cell Biology

Lee, M., Van Brocklyn, J. R., Thangada, S., Liu, C. H., Hand, A. R., Menzeleev, R., Spiegel, S. and Hla, T. (1998) 'Sphingosine-1-Phosphate as a ligand for the G protein-coupled receptor EDG-1', *Science* 279, 1552–5.

Otto, F., Thornell, A. P., Crompton, T., Denzel, A., Gilmour, K. C., Rosewell, I. R., Stamp, G. W. H., Beddington, R. S. P., Mundlos, S., Olsen, B. R., Selby, P. B. and Owen, M. J. (1997) 'Cbfa1, a candidate gene for cleidocranial dysplasia syndrome, is essential for osteoblast differentiation and bone development', *Cell* 89, 765–71.

Chemistry

Hall, H. K. Jr and Padias, A. B. (1990) 'Zwitterion and diradical tetramethylenes as initiators of "charge-transfer" polymerizations', *Accounts of Chemical Research* 23(1), 3–9.

Miller, R. E. (1990) 'Vibrationally induced dynamics in hydrogen-bonded complexes', *Accounts of Chemical Research* 23(1), 10–16.

Clinical Psychology

Bennett, P. and Carroll, D. (1990) 'Stress management approaches to the prevention of coronary heart disease', *British Journal of Clinical Psychology* 29(1), 1–12.

Jack, R. L. and Williams, J. M. (1991) 'The role of attributions in self-poisoning', *British Journal of Clinical Psychology* 30(1), 25–35.

Computer Science

Bohr, M. (1998) 'Silicon trends and limits for advanced microprocessors', *Communication of the ACM* 41(3), 80–87.

Pease, D., Ghafoor, A., Ahmad, I., Andrews, D. L., Foudil-Bey, K., Karpinski, T. E., Mikki, M. A. and Zerrouki, M. (1991) 'PAWS: A performance evaluation tool for parallel computing systems', *Computer (IEEE)* 24(1), 18–30.

Stunkel, C. B., Janssens, B. and Fuchs, W. K. (1991) 'Address tracing for parallel machines', *Computer (IEEE)* 24(1), 31–8.

Geology

Abu Zeid, N. and Vuillermin, F. (1997) 'Geochemical characterization of the outcropping rock masses in the immediate vicinity of Wadi El-Kaffrein Dam Site (Jordan)', *Bulletin of the International Association of Engineering Geology* 55, 3–17.

Boyer, B. W. (1997) 'Sinkholes, soils, fractures, and drainage: Interstate 70 near Frederick, Maryland', *Environmental & Engineering Geoscience* 3(4), 469–485.

There'll be some changes made: predicting future events in academic and business genres.[1]

Meriel Bloor and Thomas Bloor

Introduction

Writing about future events and future action is not generally considered to be a major function of academic discourse, and English language courses for international students offer little advice on how to undertake such a task. Most academic writing courses focus on the reporting of past events, the expression of generalisations, rules and hypotheses, or accounts of the present or ongoing state of affairs. This is not surprising in the teaching of general academic English since it reflects the most common functions of textbooks, lab reports and research articles in many disciplines. However, in some disciplines, a central concern can be the prediction of future events or possible future states.

Some branches of economics, particularly monetary economics, business and actuarial studies are partly or wholly concerned with forecasting financial, demographic and/or social trends, and, although it is rare to find whole texts with a future focus, many texts include some element of forecasting. The forecasting element does not take up a large proportion of the text in terms of number of words but has a rhetorical significance in that other parts of the text are there to support or explain the predictive function. Pindi (1988) identified predicting future events and economic trends as the most important function of the economic reports and articles in his corpus, and the whole field of econometrics is concerned with devising better models and methods for predicting events and trends. In addition, town planning, urban renewal and traffic management are fields which are inevitably oriented towards future action, and a significant proportion of written texts in these disciplines contain accounts of planned procedures.

In this chapter we consider the nature of predictions[2] and other expressions of the future in a selection of academic texts from economics, business and town and country planning, in terms of their lexical and grammatical features.[3] We then briefly discuss some of the implications for teaching English to international students of the relevant disciplines.

On form and rhetorical function

One problem in text-based work of this type is that one cannot employ concordancing tools to look for predictions in a corpus because no one has yet fully identified the range of lexical forms or grammatical structures that are used to realise futurity in English. In fact, a glance at a newspaper is enough to indicate a wide variety of forms available to writers for the expression of predicted futures, some of which may not be at all obvious. The following headlines, for example, refer to events that had not taken place when they were published:

Legal threat to Kiley tube deal (O)
Bond issue pips Orange float (O)
Co-op movement set for radical shake-up (O)
Blair to put price tag on Tory tax cuts (O)

Such forms are not often discussed in pedagogic grammars and are not associated with futurity in most descriptive English grammars either.

The expression of future acts or future behaviour is most often said to be realised by the use of *will* or *shall* and the infinitive of the lexical verb, as in *will develop,* or the use of *going to* with infinitive, as in *going to develop* (see, for example, Hurford 1994: 76–7, 123; Leech and Svartvik 1994: 71–3). These standard grammars usually also mention the possibility of using the present progressive or present simple tense in some contexts. Other future indicators mentioned are *be about to, be on the point of,* and Palmer (1979: 48) makes the point that modals such as *can* are sometimes used to express futurity.

Frequency analyses of verb tenses can be of little help in understanding the function of these tenses in text. Some early analysis of tenses in academic texts demonstrated that verbs in the present simple tense far outnumber other tenses and that the *will+infinitive form* (until recently called 'the future tense' in most pedagogic grammars) is relatively rare at about 3 per cent of the total number of verb phrases (see, for example, Barber 1962; Wingard 1981). Such analysis might appear at first to support the view that we need not take the expression of future events too seriously in the teaching of EAP. However, as we attempt to show here, the expression of futurity, in academic writing as in newspapers, is not limited to the use of *shall* and *will*. We find a variety of types of verbal group, including present tense verbs and infinitive forms, and a range of associated lexical items, such as *threat* and *set for* in the headlines cited above.

In their discussion of 'key grammatical forms' for ESP teaching, Dudley-Evans and St John (1998: 75), referring to the high frequency of present tense forms, stress the need to consider the distribution of tenses across genres and sub-genres. Their point is that, for teaching purposes, it is not enough to know the frequency of a grammatical form; we need to consider the use of the form in its rhetorical and discourse context. That is to say, we need to know what notions are realised by the present tense forms and what rhetorical functions they help to fulfil. Prediction and forecasting are not genres as such but rather rhetorical functions appearing in certain genres. However, the same principle applies: we need to know how a function is realised in text and where, say, present tense forms or even untensed forms represent processes taking place in other time frames. Approaching this problem from a different direction, we take the functions of prediction and forecasting and seek examples of how writers convey them in text.

The rhetoric of prediction and forecasting

Our examples are instances of language in use that in part or whole predict or describe an event that is expected to take place at a specified or unspecified time in the future. Such predictions may be qualified or unqualified depending on the strength of commitment being made by the author/s. Examples (i) to (vii), from a business text, illustrate typical degrees of commitment to a future proposition. The examples have been selected because they use the clear verbal indicator of futurity *will* + *infinitive* (except in vii). All are taken from a business document (CSG). The first example expresses unhedged complete commitment:

> i. y will occur
> *Share prices will be listed daily in most national newspapers.*

However, many predictive texts also describe or discuss past or present events that have a bearing on the future, as represented in (ii) and (iii):

ii. x has occurred – therefore y will occur

At the time of writing, BG Group plc has proposed a further demerger which will be put to shareholders on 16 October next.

iii. x is the case – therefore y will occur

Changes in legislation are expected soon which will make it possible for us to communicate with you electronically rather than by post.

The future event may be seen as dependent on some hypothetical condition:

iv. if x occurs/does not occur, y will/will not occur

If shares are sold before the record date or bought after it, you will not be entitled to that dividend.

The prediction in the last example is presented as the inevitable consequence of events or behaviour more or less under the control of human beings, but the condition could refer to an externally motivated event or even to an existing state as in the next example:

v. If shares are held solely or jointly by two or more shareholders, the register will show the names of all the shareholders together with a registered address.

Thus we can establish a range of alternative kinds of prediction, more or less supported by pre-existing states.

Any propositions may be hedged with some expression of modality, as in (vi), where *it is anticipated* and *increasingly* modify the strength of the proposition.

vi. x will probably occur

It is anticipated that in future shareholders will increasingly deal in shares electronically via the internet and that gradually share certificates will be phased out.

Alternatively, the modality may be conveyed by the finite verb as in (vii).

vii. x may occur

You may at some point wish to transfer some or all of your shares to someone else (for example your partner or other members of your family).

Features of modulation in economics forecasting

The use of adverbs like *probably*, *possibly*, *likely* and *presumably* to modify the author's commitment to a proposition is a common feature of academic writing in English. It is one of a range of hedging devices that have been widely researched and discussed over the past 15 years (see, for example, Bloor and Bloor 1993; Dudley-Evans 1993; Hyland 1996, 1998a; Myers 1989; Salager-Meyer 1994; Skelton 1989). With the exception of some work of the present authors (Bloor and Bloor 1988; Bloor and Pindi 1990; Pindi and Bloor 1987), this body of research has focused either on the hedging of propositions in general or more specifically on the hedging of authorial claims rather than on the hedging of predictions and forecasts.

Much discussion of hedging in the literature concerns the use of hedging as a politeness strategy in academic writing, where a writer seeks to mitigate a knowledge claim that may be face-threatening to other researchers (see Dudley-Evans 1993:134–6 for a concise exposition). The predictions in our data do not, in the main, fall into this category of claim since they are not general observations or hypotheses about the truth or falsity of a research finding. In science, general claims are thought of as having a predictive ability – at least until they are refuted by subsequent research – but this is very different from a prediction in economics or planning where the future event is not governed by natural or scientific laws but by human decisions and behaviour. It may be then that the hedging of predictions in most instances is best accounted for by the more traditional 'lay' explanation of the writer's tentativeness or reluctance to commit fully to the strength of the prediction, knowing as we do that the future is always uncertain.

Academic economists base their predictions on what they consider to be rational deductions from research in the light of their understanding of economic laws. Business economists could be accused of tempering their predictions with some degree of optimism when they wish to attract investment or otherwise present their company in a favourable light. Nevertheless, it is rare to find economists who express unequivocal commitment to a forecast. Thus in a corpus of economic forecasting texts, Pindi and Bloor (1987) found unmodulated propositions only in supporting observations, not in forecasts themselves. In the forecasts with *will*, the strongest marker of authorial commitment, clauses like those in (1) and (2), were hedged, often with adjuncts. (The adjuncts are in bold italicised typeface):

(1) The reduction in the total public sector deficit as a percentage of GNP from 16.5% to 16.1% *will **probably** be repeated* in **1983** down to say 15%. [Written before 1983.] (P)

(2) **Next year** non-oil trade *is **likely** to* deteriorate further. (P)

In terms of modulation, these follow the model of (vi) and (vii) above rather than (i) and they each contain, in addition to the hedging adjuncts, explicit adjuncts signalling future time.

There are various strategies for varying the degree of modulation. Pindi (1988) claims that *probably*, as used in (1), signals a fairly confident prediction from the authors whereas in (3) the double hedge indicates that they are less certain of their position. Here the authors are hedging both the prediction that the acceleration will continue and also the statement of the conditions that give rise to the prediction. Neither is given total commitment:

(3) ... **it looks as though** in most of the OECD area there has been a gentle acceleration and **it seems likely** that this will continue. (P)

Other hedging of verbs in Pindi's data includes *will very likely*, *will almost certainly* and *will no doubt*.

Adjuncts of future time

As we have seen in the examples above, unsurprisingly, one major linguistic indicator of futurity in English is a future time adjunct. This is realised as a single word or, more commonly, a phrase (e.g. *in the future*) or clause (e.g. *when you receive your user ID number*). A time adjunct may be used alongside a verbal indicator of futurity or the latter may stand alone.

In economics forecasting, the most common time adjuncts appear to involve the use of dates as in (1) above: *in 1983*, which was later than the time of writing. The following phrases are also common: *next year*, *during the forecast period*; *over the next few months*; *the remainder of (year date)*.

Similar time adjuncts appear in planning data, with *by+date* being favoured as in (4) and the addition of the expression *beyond that* as in (5):

(4) ...some schemes now in the pipeline will be completed **by 2010.**
[These schemes are then listed.] (TCP)

(5) It (i.e. *the ten-year public transport plan for London)* goes on to set priorities **beyond that.** (TCP)

Very often, of course, a time adjunct may appear towards the beginning of a section of discourse and apply to a number of sentences in the subsequent text. Occasionally, the future time may be indicated lexically as a modifier in a nominal group as in (6). The fact that *ten-year* here refers to the future (from time of writing) is, of course, only clear from the larger co-text:

(6) At its heart is a **ten-year** public transport **plan** for London. (TCP)

Epistemic modals and conditions on forecasts

As mentioned earlier, grammar books usually link futurity to *will/shall* or *going to* with the lexical verb, but there is no requirement for these forms to appear. As long as the period or point of time is established or understood the verb can take many forms. It is well recognised that modal verbs reduce the degree of authorial commitment to a proposition and function as a type of hedge. This seems to be the reason for the choice of such modals as *could, may, should* or *can* in preference to *will* in the economics forecasts:

(7) Overall foodstuff prices **could** well **fall over the next few months.** (P)

(8) The austerity policy **should continue to affect** household demand ...**during the forecast period.** (P)

(9) I interpret these ... calculations as suggesting that in the US economy the adoption of a balanced-budget rule, if not accompanied by a change in the stance of monetary policy, **may lead** to the loss of the nominal anchor. (JME)

In (9), in addition to the hedge inherent in *may*, we also find the conditional clause 'if not accompanied by a change in the stance of monetary policy'. Pindi and Bloor (1987) pointed out that although conditional clauses are not normally regarded as hedges, they resemble hedges in that they modify major propositions. This type of modification is referred to by Pindi and Bloor as a 'specifying condition'. They observe that such clauses can provide some authorial support for the prediction as in (10) where we find an additional embedded prediction that the condition will be realised:

(10) If, as we anticipate, the strike is not extended, prices will rise only slowly in the final quarter. (P)

Bloor (1998) identifies four types of conditions, normally expressed as conditional dependent clauses, that appear with predictions:

A   *The sufficient condition*, where the fulfilment of the prediction follows from the realization of the condition but could result from other conditions.

(11) At the same time the economic recovery now underway may not be sufficiently vigorous if real rates of interest persist. (P)

B   *The necessary condition*, where the fulfilment of the prediction needs the condition to be met. (Typically 'only if'.)

(12) Therefore, a fall in Dutch money rates or the dollar can be affected only if US interest rates fall further or the dollar starts its long awaited downtrend. (P)

C   *The enhancing condition*, where the chances of the fulfilment of the prediction would be increased by the condition being met. (Typically 'especially if'.)

(13) From their present level of around 11% some further modest easing in long term rates is possible especially if the election result leads to a further strengthening of the exchange rate. (P)

D   *The concessive condition*, where the realisation of the condition would fail to block the fulfilment of the prediction, notwithstanding its contrary force. (Typically 'even if'.)

(14) Even if some deterioration in the payment occurs, the treasury will have no difficulty in the next few months in financing its deficit in the capital market. (P)

The difference between the rhetorical implications of conditions A to D is of importance to both readers and writers of forecasting texts.

The fact that conditional clauses, like clauses of time, do not normally incorporate *shall/will* verb forms even when they refer to future events or behaviour, is well known and well described in grammars of English, but the further classification of types of conditionals in terms of their rhetorical implications does not match the classification of conditionals that we usually find in English language textbooks with their emphasis on grammatical considerations. Forecasting data does not, for example, include the so-called third type of conditional, counterfactuals, as a condition on predictions, since economists cannot make a forecast contingent upon something which they say did not happen.

The modal *would*, in a main clause, seems to be mainly used where there is an implicit condition or when alternative futures are presented. These cases are discussed further below.

The present tense and lexical indicators of futurity

Any word which incorporates meaning relating to a change of state or time can imply a future event. Words like *plan* and *project*, whether used as nouns or verbs, come into this category as do mental processes like *intend*, *expect* and *promise*. We can see this phenomenon illustrated in (15a) from a popular planning article. This simple, one-clause sentence contains a high density of lexical information some of which undoubtedly predicates possible future events even though there is no direct verbal or adverbial future marker. The sentence could be paraphrased as in (15b).

The initial nominal group (*italicised*) has the head noun *scheme* followed by two (tenseless) infinitives.

15a)   *The scheme to allow the country to expand from the narrow fertile strip of the Nile's banks* poses major headaches. (TCP)

(15b)   There is a scheme which will allow the country to expand from the narrow fertile strip of the Nile's banks. This scheme is likely to cause problems in the future. (Constructed example)

Sometimes, a change of state word, together with a future time adverb or a comparative such as *further,* is used for a prediction. In (13) above there is a present tense verb used with nominalised processes indicating a change of state (*easing* and *strengthening*) modified by *further.*

We have already seen examples where the present tense is used for possible future occurrences in conditional clauses (11 to 14), but, more interestingly, we find that authors often choose to use present tense forms in main propositions in matrix clauses usually, but not always, where the future time is overtly marked with an adverb or other time adjunct. Thus in (16) we find a present tense *is* followed by an infinitive (tenseless) verb with the clear future indicator in the adjunct *next year*. Further elaboration on the present tense finites are seen in (16) and (17):

(16) **Next year** non-oil trade **is** likely **to deteriorate** further. (P)
      [Present simple tense]

(17) In conjunction with Lloyds TSB Registrars we **are looking at being able to offer** to shareholders the opportunity of updating their registered details electronically. (CSG)
      [Present continuous tense; active voice]

(18) World demand for metals **is** generally **expected to continue to improve during the remainder of 1984**... (P)
      [Present simple tense; passive voice]

In data such as (18) where present tenses are found, the futurity is indicated lexically by the use of such words as *expect, forecast, predict* or *project* with or without a time adjunct. Such lexis is forceful as a future marker, indicating that a present state by its nature projects a future state or event. *Is expected to continue to improve* in (18) is particularly interesting in this regard since both *continue* and *improve* are verbs which imply change of state over a period of time, as is *deteriorate* in (16). The present simple passive *is expected* leads the reader to anticipate future processes that are then realised in the two infinitives *to continue* and *to improve*. The gradual change of state is reinforced by the use of *during* in the adjunct.

Verbal group complexes and clause complexes

A number of the predictions exemplified above contain examples of *verbs in phase*, a form that we had not expected to play such a significant role in predictive and forecasting text.

This type of verbal group complex, sometimes known simply as 'phase', has received some attention in a Hallidayan model of grammar (for example, Halliday 1994: 278–91; Young 1980: 137–42), and in the Collins COBUILD English Grammar (1990: 184–9). The latter describes verbs in phase as 'two actions or states that are closely linked'. Both grammars agree that it is the 'primary group that carries the mood of the clause' and that the secondary group is always non-finite.

Halliday identifies five possible relationships between the verbs in phase: time-phase (e.g. *keep on doing*); reality phase (*appear to do; is done*); conation (e.g. *try to do; succeed in doing*); and modulation (e.g. *venture to ask; help to build*). Four of these types were identified in the data, for example from (15) to (17) above:

continue to improve (time phase)

looking at being able to offer (conation)

is to determine (reality)

allow to expand (modulation)

Francis *et al.* (1996: 90–93) identify at least a further five types, some of which clearly have the potential to be used in prediction. Two of these groups are described as being concerned with ideas or attitudes 'about what is going to happen in the future' (1996: 84): (1) *dread (I dread meeting him); face; look forward;* (2) *anticipate; consider; intend; plan on,* etc.

One issue is the time relationship between the verbs in a verbal group complex. Halliday distinguishes between 'expansion', where the second verb is said to always carry the same time reference as the first verb, and 'projection', where the time reference of the two verbs in the complex may be quite distinct. Expansion would apply to (16) where the time reference *next year* governs the whole of the verbal group complex *is to deteriorate.* Projection is seen in (18) where *is expected* has a present time reference (now, at the time of writing) and *to improve* has a future time reference (*during the remainder of the year*). The verb *to continue* appears to provide a linking, durative reference, implying that the improvement has already begun. This is much more complex than Halliday's or Francis *et al.*'s examples, which have only pairs of verbs in phase, but such lengthier verbal structures are by no means rare. Young (1980) points out that there is 'no limit' to the number of predicators there may be and gives a constructed example with three dependent infinitives. In the similar example (16), (*We are looking at being able to offer*), *being able* provides a link between *are looking at* and the predicted offer. In this way, writers use infinitives (*to offer, to improve, to affect, to deteriorate*) to express processes at various degrees of proximity to the time of writing. Infinitives are tenseless and hence were traditionally thought of as a timeless form. However, they are often used in newspaper headlines to express a predicted future event without any finite verb or other marker of futurity, as in the example earlier (*Blair to put price tag on Tory cuts*).

When they are used in phase with another verb they can imply that the process takes place at a later time than the verb they follow. Thus, if I report the information in (18) as in the (constructed) example (19), the infinitive verbs express past events in relation to the time of writing (2001) but we understand that they were seen as future events at the time of the original expectation:

(19)   World demand for metals was generally expected to continue to improve during the remainder of 1984. The expectation was proved correct.

Change of state verbs do not express 'pure' futurity but imply processes that are beginning or have begun at the time of writing and will continue into future time. Where the text is being read after the projected events have taken place, as in (19) the interpretation of the relative time scale requires complex re-adjustment. A parallel situation was referred to by Houghton (1996) in her analysis of the problems faced by overseas students reading business case studies.

It seems that non-finite predicators in phase are most frequently infinitives and this is the case in our data, but instances of -*ing*-form verbs were identified. In Table 1 there is an example: *Centrica is considering offering... .*

The hypothetical and the real

In forecasting and planning texts, we find the presentation of alternative futures. These seem to attract the conditional form of the verb. In the next example we find verbs in phase (*poised to take*) as a post-nominal qualifier which could be paraphrased as 'about to' thus carrying a future time implication but without a definite prediction. Instead, alternative forms of action follow, each presented in some detail.

(20)   However, with the government **poised to take action** on the issue, it is now time for a long hard think about the best method of regulation. **One way** to do it **would be to withdraw** the exemption in Section 55... (TCP)

In the data of prediction, we can identify a cline from the definite predicted event to the hypothetical. This is very roughly indicated in the examples (i) to (vii) above but does not precisely parallel the use of hedging. One major feature of predictive texts seems to be the easy transition from the expression of a planned actual event to the hypothetical or possible event. In one sense, the outcome of *any* prediction is unknown, but writers can still present future events as definite intended acts or as conditional possibilities. The short text (from CSG) that is analysed in Table 1 illustrates this type of transition; all future indicators are in bold type.

Table 1

Text	Comment
Some shareholders hold their shares in PEPs or ISAs or in other financial arrangements. In these circumstances the shares are held in what is known as a nominee holding.	Non-predictive. Explaining existing state of affairs.
The underlying individuals **will not be named on** the register and **will not have** a share certificate but **will have** a statement of holding and **will be able** to vote at general meetings and receive annual reports ...	Predictive. Non-hypothetical.
It is anticipated that **in the future** shareholders **will** increasingly **deal** in shares via the internet and that gradually share certificates **will be phased** out thereby *eliminating paper from the share dealing process.*	Predictive. Non-hypothetical but hedged.
Dealing with share certificates **might** then **become** more expensive.	Predictive. 'Might ' is epistemic, expressing possibility but not certainty.
Centrica **is considering offering**, at the appropriate time, a service that **would enable** shareholders **to hold** their shares electronically....	Predictive. Implicit conditional.

Tenseless structures and implied predictions

On occasion, one or more predicted events can be presented in non-finite clauses as in the example in the table above: *eliminating paper from the share dealing process.* This non-finite dependent clause carries with it the futurity indicated in the previous finite clause. The scope of a future *will* or time adjunct can extend over nominal groups as well as over non-finite clauses. Example (21) from town-planning literature shows how a writer indicates futurity in an initial clause and then follows this with a list of four planned developments realised by nominal groups and one non-finite clause.

(21) Some schemes, now in the pipeline, **will be completed by 2010** – improvements to the A13 and A206 in east London, as part of the Thames gateway project; stage two of the channel tunnel rail link, via Ebbsfleets and Stratford to St Pancras; Thameslink 2000, bringing trains from Peterborough and Cambridge under London to destinations in Sussex and Kent; and the Docklands light railway extension to London City Airport. (TCP)

The subsequent paragraph (22) has a similar structure but lacks the future indicator (*will be completed by 2010*), the meaning of which is 'carried over' from the earlier paragraph. The verbs here are present and non-finite.

(22) For rail, it **proposes** two schemes. One, relatively cheap and simple, **is** Ringrail: an orbital link for London **running** on average one or two miles further out than the present Circle line. (TCP)

From a different planning text, we find (23) where the single verb *suggests* governs three *ing*-form, tenseless non-finite verbs.

(23) It (the report) suggests making all agricultural buildings and land subject to planning consent; removing the protected status of BMV farmland; and relaxing rules about the change of use of former agricultural buildings to commercial purposes. (TCP)

On the teaching of predicting on EAP courses

The matters we have discussed in this chapter have implications for the teaching of the expression of futurity in English. Textbooks on academic reading and writing do not generally pay much attention to this aspect of the language since it is not considered a priority in academic 'core' language, and certainly for many students it may be of peripheral concern. However, for students in the relevant disciplines, prediction can prove to be difficult to handle and such students may need special help with this area.

Jordan (1980: 59) is one of the few books that mentions predictive statements, which are introduced under the heading of 'Generalisation and qualification'. The example given is the constructed and somewhat strange sentence: 'A few students are unlikely to obtain all their course books from libraries'. But Jordan also provides a useful list of adverbs and modal verbs associated with probability (p.60).

Most EAP textbooks inevitably present a simplified account of how futurity is expressed in English even when the topic is introduced at all. The best books focus on four forms: the use of *shall/will* + *infinitive*; the use of *going to* + *infinitive*; the 'formal' use of the present simple (e.g. *The president arrives tomorrow*) and the 'informal' use of the present continuous (e.g. *We are leaving next week*), essentially following Palmer (1974: 36–8). It would be surprising to find much about verbal group complexes in learners' textbooks since it is only since the development of corpus linguistics that such forms have begun to receive much attention in accessible literature (such as the Collins COBUILD English Grammar 1990 and Francis *et al.* 1996).

Currently, the use of verbs in phase, we suspect, is rarely taught except in so far as students' attention may be drawn to errors in the use of verb patterns, as for example when a student writes 'enjoy to go'. Students underuse complex verbal groups in their own writing and may have problems interpreting them in reading.

The use of hedging and attribution in relation to predictive statements is a further area that often needs attention in student writing, as is the expression of hypothetical futures.[4] As Hyland (1994) shows, hedging is not normally taught in English language textbooks, and even though some more recent books do include discussion of how authors can distance themselves from the strength of propositions, they do not associate such hedging with prediction. Swales and Feak (1994: 86–9), for example, give a relatively detailed account of 'qualification' (probability, likelihood) but this is conceptually linked to the expression of claims and generalisations rather than to forecasts or predictions.

In the short term, the EAP teacher can raise students' awareness of the rhetorical structure of prediction, making sure to provide appropriate reading texts that illustrate the clear use of adjuncts, complex verb groups in phase, the use of hypothetical futures and the other features we have outlined above. It is also important that students are exposed to the use of hedges in these contexts. In writing tasks, they can be given the opportunity to draft plans or forecasts based on data given in the form of graphs or diagrammatic drawings or whatever may be appropriate in their specialist discipline.

In the long term, there is a case for reconsidering the whole approach to the teaching of tenses and the expression of time in English, not only when English is taught for academic purposes. Predicting, promising, expecting and other future-oriented functions are important to all language users, and the forms discussed here appear, more or less frequently, in other genres.[5] Generally, students are given the impression that there is a one-to-one correspondence between time and tense. In fact, this is not the case, and temporality is often communicated in clauses which are tenseless. Students are, perhaps, overprotected from the complexity of the expression of time in English and would benefit from explicit attention to a wider range of temporal indicators.

Notes

1. Retiring from academic life is an experience that leads one to look forward to the future and perhaps make some predictions. The title of this chapter is taken from an old jazz classic in honour of Tony's work past and future for jazz in Britain, and Birmingham Jazz in particular.
2. The examples given in this chapter are from the texts listed under *Sources of data* below.
3. We exclude from our discussion consideration of textual prospective signals of the type investigated by Tadros (1985) and others, which are also labelled 'prediction'.
4. Writing about hypothetical worlds is of particular importance in some branches of philosophy (see Bloor 1998).
5. Forecasting has been discussed as a feature of the discourse of newspapers (Bell 1991; Bloor and Bloor 1988; Zuck and Zuck 1984).

Sources of data with their code

O   *The Observer.* 4 February 2001

CSG   Centrica plc: *Shareholder Guide.* October 2000

P   Data from Pindi 1988 (including various financial surveys from British banks, OECD Economic Outlook and reports from the Association of European Banks)

JME   *Journal of Monetary Economics* 45 107–28; 211–46 (2000)

TCP   *Town and Country Planning* (Journal) Feb. 2000

Anticipatory 'it' in academic writing: an indicator of disciplinary difference and developing disciplinary knowledge

Ann Hewings and Martin Hewings

Introduction

Academic text is often seen primarily as a vehicle for transmitting information in an objective and impersonal way. However, this view neglects the fact that scholars need also to persuade a frequently sceptical readership of the validity of the information that they present. Academic text therefore not only contains propositional content, but also devices having textual and interpersonal functions. These devices are often referred to as *metadiscourse*, by which readers are helped to organise, to interpret and to evaluate this content. The study of metadiscourse has received growing attention in recent years (e.g. Crismore and Farnsworth 1990; Crismore *et al*. 1993; Hyland 1997, 1998a/b, 1999a/b; Vande Kopple 1985), mainly because it provides a means of investigating the relationships between scholars and their readers. The focus of this paper is one linguistic feature which has predominantly a metadiscoursal role, *it*-clauses with extraposed subjects; for example, 'it is by no means certain that...', 'it is worth pointing out that...' and 'it is tempting to...'. In particular, we examine variation in the use of *it*-clauses, first in texts taken from different academic disciplines and, second, in texts produced by students near the beginning of their undergraduate studies and those near the end.

We see this study as significant in a number of ways. First, evidence of variation between academic disciplines helps to refute the notion of a homogeneous academic writing and refines our notions of functional variation. Second, different language choices reflect different meanings to be exchanged. Through the identification of areas of disciplinary difference, we are able to uncover the epistemology – what is valued as significant and how those values are signalled – of different academic areas. The academic pursuit of knowledge and understanding is perceived differently by different subject areas and finding ways to contrast those differences helps to highlight their significant identities. Third, apprentices to a discipline, both undergraduate and postgraduate, native speaker and non-native speaker will benefit from making explicit the demands of writing for a particular disciplinary culture. Such display of the foundations of thought and its manifestation in writing is becoming the norm in postmodern academic literature and it is also of value pedagogically as students become more generalist and less specialist in their subject areas. Students learning to write in more than one disciplinary area can benefit from work which demonstrates how and why writing in one field varies from that in another. Finally, by focusing on one element within the broader area of metadiscourse, we hope to reveal further areas for fruitful investigation.

We begin by considering the major functions of *it*-clauses with extraposed subjects and in our first study explore variation in their use in published research articles across a range of disciplines. Our second study examines how they are employed in student writing in a single academic discipline, Geography, considering their use in relation to developing maturity in disciplinary writing norms and negotiation of the reader-writer relationship.

It-clauses with extraposed subjects

The grammatical focus of this paper is clauses in which the subject, normally a non-final element, is moved to the end of the clause and *it* inserted in the normal subject position. For example, the sentence:

> That the costs are so high is surprising.

has a congruent form:

> It is surprising that the costs are so high.

The terms *extraposed subject* and *anticipatory 'it'* are used to refer to these two elements (after Quirk *et al.* 1985). Excluded from consideration are clauses in which initial *it* fulfils other grammatical functions, including as pronoun, in cleft sentences (e.g. 'It was on examination of the corpus that differences were observed...'), as dummy or prop *it* (e.g. 'It's raining'), and instances in which *it* anticipates a following object clause where there is an intervening necessary clause element (Biber *et al.* 1999: 155) (e.g. 'I put it to you that the argument is incorrect') as in such cases there is no alternative to extraposition. However, we include constructions such as *It seems* and *It appears* which, while having all the appearance of clausal extraposition (Quirk *et al.* 1985) have no non-extraposed version. For convenience, the term *it-clause* will be used below to refer to anticipatory *it*-clauses with extraposed subjects.

Both non-rhetorical and rhetorical motivations for the choice of *it*-clauses over congruent non-extraposed forms, where they exist, can be identified. A *non-rhetorical* motivation rests on the assumption that longer subjects are more commonly located at the end of the clause. Quirk *et al.* (1985: 1392) claim that 'for clausal subjects the postponed position is more usual than the canonical position before the verb', while Bloor and Bloor (1995: 167) observe that 'other things being equal, the longer and more complicated the clause, the more likely it is to be extraposed'. Evidence is also put forward by Tarone *et al.* (1998), whose finding that long equations are frequently placed at the ends of clauses is attributed to a desire not to disturb the usual pattern of end-weighting.

A number of *rhetorical* motivations for the selection of *it*-clauses have also been identified. Quirk *et al.* (1985) note the use of comment clauses – including *it*-clauses such as *It is said, It is reported, It has been claimed* – as hedging devices. The *it*-clause distances the writer from the content expressed in the following *that*-clause and choice of the reporting verb allows great freedom in accepting, rejecting or remaining neutral about the proposition expressed (Thompson 1994). Second, *it*-clauses with adjective complementation (e.g. *It is surprising, It is important*) allow the writer to provide an evaluation which influences how the subsequent clause is to be interpreted (Francis 1993). Third, the choice of *it*-clauses over a construction with a personal pronoun (e.g. *It is proposed*, rather than *I propose*) can also allow the writer to deperson-alise opinions. By this means, the writer can present an opinion as objective, not associated with the writer, suggesting that it is less open to negotiation (Martin *et al.* 1997).

A classification of it-clauses

The classification of *it*-clauses having a metadiscoursal function used in the two investigations described below is presented in Figure 1. Excluded from consideration were *it*-clauses that presented propositional content (e.g. '...Hughes *et al.* (1996) show that *it is possible* to reconstruct continental-tohemispheric-scale snow variability...') and those with a text-organising purpose, referring to other parts of the text (e.g. 'In Section 3 (above) *it was shown* that...'). (For more details on how this was arrived at, see Hewings and Hewings, in press.)

Figure 1 Classification of *it*-clauses.

Interpersonal functions of it-clauses	Sub-categories	Example realisations
1. hedges	1a likelihood/possibility/certainty; importance/value/necessity etc.	it is likely; it seems improbable; it would certainly appear
	1b what a writer thinks/assumes to be/will be/was the case	it could be argued; it seems reasonable to assume; it was felt
2. attitude markers	2a the writer feels that something is worthy of note	it is of interest to note; it is worth pointing out; it is noteworthy
	2b the writer's 'attitude'	it is important; it was interesting; it is surprising
3. emphatics	3a the writer indicates that a conclusion/ deduction should be reached; that a proposition is true	it follows; it is evident; it is apparent
	3b the writer strongly draws the reader's attention to a point	it is important to stress; it should be noted; it must be recognised; it is essential to understand
	3c the writer expresses a strong conviction of what is possible/important/necessary, etc.	it is clear; it is impossible; it is safe to assume; it would be strongly desirable
4. attribution	4a specific attribution (with a reference to the literature)	it has been proposed (+ reference)
	4b general attribution (no referencing)	it is estimated (+ no reference)

The framework has four broad categories with sub-categories within each:

Hedges withhold the writer's full commitment to the content of the extraposed subject. Category 1a includes hedges in which the writer gives an indication of the degree of probability, value or necessity of the content. Realisations typically include a modal adverb (e.g. *(un)likely, possible, probable*) or modal verb (*might, would, may*). In 1b the non-factual status of a proposition is indicated by its being marked as the writer's suggestion, contention, argument, assumption and so on.

Attitude markers express the writer's attitude towards the content of the extraposed subject. A distinction is made between those (2a) in which the writer identifies information as worthy of particular attention and those (2b) which express an evaluation, indicate a value judgement or provide an assessment of expectations.

Emphatics emphasise the force or the writer's certainty in the content of the extraposed subject. We distinguish three sub-categories of emphatics. The writer may (3a) indicate that a conclusion or inference should be drawn, without mitigating this through hedging. Effectively, the reader is told that s/he, too, must reach this conclusion from the evidence provided. In 3b the reader's attention is forcefully drawn to some point. This is distinguished from items in 2a in which the writer simply identifies material as noteworthy. Typical realisations include a modal verb such as *must, should* or *need to*, or an adjective such as *important* or *essential*. We group items in which the writer expresses a strong conviction of what is possible, important, or necessary in category 3c. Typical realisations include adjectives such as *clear, impossible* or *necessary*.

Attributions are used to lead the reader to accept the writer's judgements as being soundly based. A distinction is made between specific attributions (4a) which have references to literature attached to them, and general attributions (4b) which have no such references. Typically, specific attribution is achieved using *it* followed by a past (perfect) passive form of a reporting verb, while general attribution makes reference to a generally held view.

While the classification was reasonably easy to apply, one consistent area of difficulty might be noted. Although we found it useful in general to distinguish between category *2b Attitude markers: the writer's 'attitude'* and *3c Emphatics: the writer expresses a strong conviction of what is possible/important/necessary, etc.,* placing particular instances in one or other group was occasionally problematic. We have taken adjectives such as *clear, impossible* and *necessary* as indicative of a 'strong conviction' and therefore in 3c, while adjectives such as *important*, *interesting* and *surprising* do *not* indicate such strength of conviction and are therefore in 2b. Clearly, the precise boundary between them is to some extent arbitrary and always context-dependent.

It-clauses as an indicator of disciplinary differences

In order to investigate potential disciplinary difference in the use of *it*-clauses, these clauses were identified in journal articles taken from four fields of study: Astrophysics/Astronomy, Business Administration, Geography/Environmental Sciences and History. These fields were selected in order to provide a wide spread across the sciences, social sciences and humanities. Three important international journals were identified from within each field and three articles selected at random from each of these journals. Details are given in Figure 2.

Figure 2 Details of the corpus used.

Sub-corpus	Journals	Number of articles	Total size of sub-corpus (words)	Average length of article (words)
Astrophysics/ Astronomy (Astro.)	*The Astrophysics Journal, The Astronomical Journal, Monthly Notices of the Royal Astronomical Society*	9	57,223	6,358
Business Administration (Bus.)	*Journal of General Management, Journal of Business Research, International Marketing Review*	9	45,563	5,063
Geography/ Environmental Sciences (Geog.)	*European Urban and Regional Studies, International Journal of Climatology, Environmental Research*	9	54,441	6,049
History (Hist.)	*Journal of Modern History, The Journal of Military History, Renaissance Quarterly*	9	73,381	8,153

Using the framework presented in Figure 1, *it*-clauses in the four sub-corpora were classified. Totals for each of the four categories and the sub-categories are presented in Figure 3. Figures in brackets give the number of occurrences per thousand words.

Figure 3 Classification of *it*-clauses in the four sub-corpora.

		Astro.	Bus.	Geog.	Hist.	TOTALS
1 Hedges	1a	17 (0.3)	4 (0.09)	4 (0.07)	17 (0.23)	42 (0.18)
	1b	14 (0.24)	7 (0.15)	9 (0.17)	13 (0.18)	43 (0.19)
	Total hedges	*31 (0.54)*	*11 (0.24)*	*13 (0.24)*	*30 (0.41)*	*85 (0.37)*
2 Attitude markers	2a	9 (0.16)	4 (0.09)	4 (0.07)	4 (0.05)	21 (0.09)
	2b	9 (0.16)	14 (0.31)	11 (0.2)	8 (0.11)	42 (0.18)
	Total attitude markers	*18 (0.31)*	*18 (0.4)*	*15 (0.28)*	*12 (0.16)*	*63 (0.27)*
3 Emphatics	3a	3 (0.05)	3 (0.07)	5 (0.09)	5 (0.07)	16 (0.07)
	3b	8 (0.14)	6 (0.13)	9 (0.17)	0 (0)	23 (0.10)
	3c	7 (0.12)	4 (0.09)	5 (0.09)	7 (0.10)	23 (0.10)
	Total emphatics	*18 (0.31)*	*13 (0.29)*	*19 (0.35)*	*12 (0.16)*	*62 (0.27)*
4 Attribution	4a	6 (0.1)	3 (0.07)	1 (0.02)	0 (0)	10 (0.04)
	4b	1 (0.02)	0 (0)	4 (0.07)	3 (0.04)	8 (0.03)
	Total attribution	*7 (0.12)*	*3 (0.07)*	*5 (0.09)*	*3 (0.04)*	*18 (0.08)*
TOTALS		*45 (0.99)*	*74 (1.29)*	*52 (0.96)*	*57 (0.78)*	*228 (0.99)*

This initial quantification of *it*-clauses suggests substantial variation in frequency, not only in their total occurrence (from 0.78 per thousand words in History to 1.29 in Business Administration) but within functional sub-categories (for example, total figures for hedging range from 0.24 in Business and Geography/Environmental Sciences to 0.54 in Astrophysics/Astonomy). Indeed, as both the highest frequency of occurrence and the greatest disciplinary variation is in category 1, Hedges, our following discussion focuses on this metadiscoursal function of *it*-clauses.

Hedging serves to qualify a writer's commitment to a proposition and, as such, can be a useful indicator of epistemic values in a discipline. It also has an affective purpose relating to how writers negotiate their claims and persuade their readers. These two functions are highlighted by the various functional descriptions of hedging in academic writing. It has been associated with strategies to denote deliberate vagueness or imprecision (Channell 1990, 1994; Lakoff 1972), politeness strategies to avoid threatening face (Myers 1989), and also as a way of signalling distance between a speaker and what they say (Nash 1990; Skelton 1988). These diverse functions are subsumed by Hyland (1998a: 5) who defines hedges as '...the means by which writers can present a proposition as an opinion rather than a fact'.

In the four sub-corpora investigated here, *it*-clauses as hedges are used most frequently in History and Astrophysics/Astronomy. This is perhaps not surprising given the nature of evidence in both disciplines. Historians make use of original sources, sometimes incomplete, possibly biased, and are often not only trying to describe past events but also to attribute causes to them or motivations to the protagonists. They are trying to construe their version of 'reality' on the basis of limited knowledge (McCabe 1999). In Astrophysics/Astronomy, unlike some sciences, it is not possible to test theories in a laboratory. Evidence is gathered through observations of distant bodies with equipment which is constantly evolving and improving. A theory is only as good as the data it is based on and the scientists are therefore cautious in claiming that their conclusions are definitive. This last point is illustrated in example 1 from an Astrophysics article (in this and following examples, the focus of attention is in italics):

(1) Regarding the first question, given the single slit position and relatively low spatial resolution for the high-redshift radio galaxies *it cannot categorically be stated that* the emission-line profiles of large radio sources are rotation profiles.

The *it*-clause hedges the proposition 'the emission-line profiles of large radio sources are rotation profiles' and the preceding clause gives reasons for this lack of a stronger statement both of which are related to the state of knowledge possible with the equipment available. In addition, this acknowledgement of the existing state of knowledge in the field and of these reasons is assumed by the writer to be shared knowledge. This assumption therefore has an affective function implying that the readers and the writer share this same understanding of the discipline. Creating such a shared understanding is an important part of establishing a writer's credibility and therefore helping to get her/his work accepted.

Example 2 from History, while withholding full commitment, is actually a fairly strong assertion of the writer's opinion. However, the writer does not have irrefutable evidence and there is in fact the denial of this view from one of the protagonists at the time. Therefore, the writer circumspectly hedges his views and uses an impersonal *it* construction to advance them:

> (2) Gressett … had several long discussions with General H.D.G. Crerar, the Canadian Chief of the General Staff. During the course of their conversations Gressett reiterated his views on the benefits of increasing Hong Kong's garrison. *It is likely* Crerar led him to expect that Canada might be able to supply forces for this task, although Crerar later denied that he had done so.

Examples 3 to 5 are also hedges, but this time their status is marked as suggestion, contention, assumption or argument; that is, as non-factual. In example 3, from Astrophysics, 'anticipated' points up that the proposition is not an established fact of the discipline. Its non-factual status is also flagged in the preceding sentence where it is labelled as 'assumption'. Such hypothetical constructs are common in disciplines where observation of the world and model building rather than results from experimentation are a common feature (see, for example, Henderson and Hewings (1990) on Economics). Within the *it*-clause, the status of hedge is marked by the modal 'might'. In addition the impersonal 'it' allows the writer to avoid saying 'I myself anticipate…', but rather to leave open the possibility of the reader feeling that the statement is indicative of their shared knowledge. Taken as a whole, the *it*-clause again acts to be inclusive of the reader. It could have read 'we might anticipate' given our shared understanding of the subject area.

(3) The assumptions made here have been chosen to be simple and to be the most favourable … For instance, *it might be anticipated that* mass might be lost more easily from the galaxy through the minor axis of the galaxy.

In example 4, from History, the *it*-clause functions in a similar way to the 'it might be anticipated' in example 3:

(4) The Alberti women could not have done what they did during the years of exile were it inconceivable behaviour in Quattrocento Florence. *It is, therefore, reasonable to suppose that* Alberti women and their patrician contemporaries always played a stronger and more active role in family and society.

It includes the reader in the logic of the viewpoint being put forward, again by assuming a level of disciplinary knowledge and understanding of how reasoning and deductions are arrived at in historical scholarship.

Example 5, also from History, does not have this affective function to such a degree:

(5) Bell … believed that troops could be entirely weaned from alcohol if their commanders replace their liquor ration with cocoa or fruit juice. *But it appears that* few if any officers heeded his advice.

It is taken from a paper on the problems of drunkenness and alcoholism in the British army and navy in the 18th and 19th centuries. The writer could not assert that officers didn't heed the advice to substitute cocoa or fruit juice because the historical record that was available to him did not give sufficient information. Instead, he is generalising from the evidence of continued drunkenness which is available. He thus feels it necessary to hedge the proposition with 'it appears'. Given the ideational content of these few sentences, the hedging may in fact be deliberately highlighting the unlikelihood of a suggestion to substitute cocoa and fruit juice for alcohol ever being implemented; the intent of the author may have been ironical.[1]

It-clauses as hedges are relatively less common in Geography/ Environmental Sciences and Business Administration than in Astrophysics/ Astronomy and History. Within the Geography/ Environmental Sciences sub-corpus it is noticeable that the majority of such clauses occur in the more scientific wing of the broad field of Geography represented by journals in Climatology and Environmental Sciences. They are similar to the

Astrophysics examples in that they are associated with deductions drawn from data which cannot be categorically proven. However, they are more often couched as assumptions (that is, category 1b) than assessments about probability, value or necessity (1a). Example 6 is from Environmental Science.

(6) To evaluate the potential for elevated blood-lead levels due to bone-lead mobilization, a two-compartment model is adopted for the transfer of lead between the blood and the bone tissue … *It is assumed that* the transfer of lead between the blood and the bone tissue and elimination of lead from the body follows a first-order kinetic relationship.

In Business Administration *it*-clause hedges are most often used to qualify conclusions from reports and statistics as in examples 7 and 8. These serve to highlight the problematic nature of data in the discipline. Like the Astrophysics examples above, trends and theories can only be as trustworthy as the available data. Use of hedging demonstrates an acknowledgement of the shared epistemic understanding between professionals engaged in the same disciplinary endeavour.

(7) Therefore, even in the case of significant results from these earlier studies *it is not clear that* inflation-adjusted disclosures are informative.

(8) In conclusion, *it appears that* a significant relationship exists because of the importance placed on marketing culture and the profitability of a firm. Table 4 indicates that 94% of the total variation in profitability is explained by marketing.

This close examination of *it*-clauses as hedges in a variety of disciplines helps to focus attention on their implicit epistemic norms. Surprisingly, it is History and Astrophysics/Astronomy that share characteristics most closely, with a concern to highlight the evolving state of knowledge within the discipline. All four disciplines also show the affective function of hedges in creating and maintaining a shared understanding between professionals, with the effect of making propositions harder to refute.

It-clauses in student writing: focus on a particular discipline

The second part of this study looks at the writing of undergraduate students taking Geography at a British university. We examine the types of metadiscourse conveyed in *it*-clause by student writers and compare the use of such structures in first-year writing and third-year writing. The aim is to discover whether this feature of the academic discourse of Geography was applied in a similar way by both groups or whether there was a change as the students were acculturated within the discipline.

The data consisted of 68 essays (32 from first-year and 36 from third-year students) with a rough balance between those receiving high and low marks. The essays were written in response to a variety of questions on physical and human geography topics. All the writers were single honours Geography students who had studied the subject up to 'A'-level standard (British examinations taken generally at the age of 18 before leaving school). They therefore had a common background of approximately seven years of school Geography before commencing their three-year degree courses. Essays ranged from about 1,100 to 3,000 words in length with a mean of 1,700, and the total corpus size was 115,894 words. (For more details, see A. Hewings 1999.)

Once again, the classification presented in Figure 1 was used to produce the totals given in Figure 4 below. Again, figures in brackets give the number of occurrences per thousand words.

		Yr 1	Yr 3	*TOTALS*
1 Hedges	1a	4 (0.09)	5 (0.07)	9 (0.08)
	1b	16 (0.34)	15 (0.22)	31 (0.27)
	Total hedges	*20 (0.43)*	*20 (0.29)*	*40 (0.35)*
2 Attitude markers	2a	0 (0)	3 (0.04)	3 (0.03)
	2b	12 (0.26)	13 (0.19)	25 (0.22)
	Total attitude markers	*12 (0.26)*	*16 (0.23)*	*28 (0.24)*
3 Emphatics	3a	12 (0.26)	16 (0.23)	28 (0.24)
	3b	5 (0.11)	18 (0.26)	23 (0.2)
	3c	7 (0.15)	19 (0.27)	26 (0.22)
	Total emphatics	*24 (0.52)*	*53 (0.76)*	*77 (0.66)*
4 Attribution	4a	11 (0.24)	18 (0.26)	29 (0.25)
	4b	6 (0.13)	5 (0.07)	11 (0.09)
	Total attribution	*17 (0.37)*	*23 (0.33)*	*40 (0.35)*
TOTALS		*73 (1.57)*	*112 (1.62)*	*185 (1.6)*

Figure 4 Classification of *it*-clauses in the two student corpora.

The total overall use of *it*-clauses with a metadiscoursal function in the two student corpora was broadly similar, with only a slightly higher number per thousand words occurring in the third year group. However, the distribution of types of metadiscourse used did show variation between the two year groups particularly in the categories of hedging and emphatics. First-year writers used more hedging, especially in category 1b (e.g. 'it appears that…', 'it seems as though…', 'it could be argued that….'), often combining hedges such as 'appear' with further markers such as modal verbs. In example 9:

> (9) *It would appear* that the volcano type and eruption type are integral to the kind of hazard generated.

the hedge appears in the final sentence of the essay and seems to represent a summation of the essay's arguments. However, these arguments have not been clearly or logically presented in the body of the text. The main proposition following 'that' may represent the view that the student has been encouraged to see as correct but she/he may not have found sufficient evidence for it during work on the essay. The hedging may therefore be seen as an attempt to conclude on accepted disciplinary wisdom and not to challenge it, or even as a cover for insufficient work on the topic to support this conclusion. The work received a relatively low mark of 52 per cent.

This tentativeness in first-year essays is in contrast to greater use of emphatics by third-year student writers. Categories 3b and 3c were noticeably more frequent. Thus both year groups used emphatics to emphasise a conclusion or deduction (3a), but first-year writers made much less use of them to draw attention to a particular point they were making (3b), as is done in the following example from a third-year writer:

> (10) As well as examining these two areas *it is also important* to consider the internal geography of the specific service activity in question.

or to express a strong conviction about possibility, importance or necessity (3c), as appears in examples 17 and 18, again by third-year students:

> (11) Thus it seems that an explanation of gender segregation in terms of women's domestic responsibilities is not sufficient. Instead, *it is necessary* to study the structure and operation of the labour market.

(12) In evaluating the influence of social disparities upon morphological characteristics *it is vital* to address two main issues.

A possible explanation for the increased use of *it*-clauses as emphatics by third-year students is as a device to make comments strongly but anonymously. This could be construed both as a politeness strategy and as an increased use of the objectivity they see as constituting academic writing. Student writers, who are urged to use published writing as their models, and also often told of the need to construct arguments and praised for having opinions, may use *it*-clauses as a mechanism for expressing opinion and arguing from a lower status position vis-à-vis the academic who will mark their work. They do not have original work to report, based on which they can make claims. Their main area of concern within essays (as opposed to research reports) is synthesis and evaluation of the published work of professional academic geographers and other researchers. In order to mitigate any face loss for themselves if their marker disagrees, they make their arguments as strong as they dare but using an impersonal construction to distance it from themselves.

This impersonal style is also in keeping with the general scientific academic style of apparent objectivity. Students are often criticised for using constructions such as 'I think' or 'In my opinion' on the grounds that any statement made is their opinion and does not need to be flagged as such (see also Myers, this volume). This is both a misunderstanding of the tertiary academic essay genre by students, and a rather unhelpful comment by academics. Student writers are concerned with the content and arguments of the discipline as seen by others, and may not see a role for their own voice. The information and opinions expressed in their writing are synthesised from others. They may well not yet be 'internalised', to borrow a Vygotskian concept (Vygotsky 1991). Also, they may not see that the synthesis that they produce is unique and construed as an argument by their markers. By the third year of study the approaching status of graduate may help to encourage student writers to employ rhetoric to a greater extent. However, they turn to impersonal *it*-clauses to help provide the necessary objectivity and yet allow them to introduce the rhetoric of argumentation. Professional academics who do have a point to argue can make more appearances in their own texts either through pronouns or through reference to their work, as in the following extract from a Geography journal:

(13) *In the present study*, first *we* conduct a simple statistical analysis...second, *we* focus on....

They can also assume that their peers will draw the necessary inferences from their work without flagging them quite so blatantly.

Conclusions

This paper has looked at metadiscoursal uses of *it*-clauses in published academic research articles taken from four disciplines, and in two corpora of undergraduate student writing in Geography. We have concentrated on this single lexicogrammatical feature partly on the basis that it is in itself an important component of the metadiscourse of academic text, but also on the assumption that variation observed in its use across the corpora is likely to be indicative of more general patterns of variation.

In the first study, the four disciplines examined showed greatest variation in their uses of *it*-clause hedges, with highest frequencies in History and Astrophysics/Astronomy. This was attributed to their particular epistemic concern with the intrinsically provisional nature of their findings. For Astrophysics/Astronomy this relates to the difficulties surrounding the collection of data from distant galaxies. For History, gaps in the historical record are significant together with the possibility that further sources could one day come to light. The analysis of metadiscoursal *it*-clauses in student writing in Geography provided contrasts which highlight the different rhetorical nature of student writing when compared with that produced by professionals. The struggle to develop a critical voice, yet maintain status differentials may account for the more frequent use of impersonal forms, particularly in conjunction with emphatics.

Both investigations highlight areas of reader-writer negotiation. The study of journal articles has enabled us to identify areas of interpersonal negotiation between readers and writers which reflect disciplinary choices and expectations. *It*-clauses are one of the linguistic devices by which writers attribute varying degrees of confidence to their statements in line with disciplinary norms. The exploration of student writing suggests a progressive change towards such norms but within the genre characteristics of the essay rather than the research report.

The findings we have presented have the potential to inform tertiary writing programmes. In that they give some indication of differences in how knowledge claims are presented in different disciplines, and how a student's voice develops as they move from novice to more experienced writer, the findings can help the instructor to explain more clearly what is required. Before this can be done with confidence, however, we need to confirm that these observations of the use of metadiscoursal *it*-clauses are representative of general trends in the use of metadiscourse, and it is clear that future research needs to address this task.

Note

1. We are indebted to Margaret Berry for this interpretation of the text.

Reflections on collaborative practice in EAP materials production

John M. Swales and Christine B. Feak

Introduction

Any quick review of the EAP literature, whether in the form of research articles, programmatic descriptions or actual published teaching materials, will show that collaboration – as expressed and ratified by co-authorship – is a fairly common phenomenon. Indeed, it is hard to think of a well-known personage in the EAP movement who has not co-written something over his or her career. These collaborative or collective endeavors can, of course, take many forms. Sometimes, they are the coming together of equals, or approximately so, even if the collaborating individuals may have different strengths and weaknesses. Sometimes, they reflect inequality at least in terms of position and experience. This is the craftsperson-apprentice model, sanctioned in Lave and Wenger's influential work (1991) as processes of 'legitimate peripheral participation' whereby relative newcomers are inducted into the mysteries of the profession by relative old-timers (Prior 1998). In our field, perhaps the most common outcome of this type of collaboration is a research article or book chapter co-authored by an academic and one or more graduate research students. A third variant, that of a cross-disciplinary collaboration, is perhaps less common, but occurs when a 'specialist informant' from some disciplinary area shares co-authorship with one or more EAP colleagues. And sometimes, these types of collaboration may themselves coalesce. An influential example of this last arrangement is the 1981 paper 'On the use of the passive in two Astrophysics journal papers' by Tarone, Dwyer, Gillette and Icke, where Elaine Tarone was a faculty member at the University of Minnesota, Sharon Dwyer and Susan Gillette, two of her graduate students, and Vincent Icke, a faculty member of the Department of Astrophysics (Tarone *et al.* 1981).

Tony Dudley-Evans, to whom this volume is affectionately dedicated, has been no stranger to such collaborations over his long and successful career.

Most of his collaborations have been of the first type, and the success of these can presumably be partly ascribed to his warm, supportive and outgoing personality. In terms of published output, there have been some landmark publications over the last 30 years. First came the *Nucleus General Science* volume published with Martin Bates and destined to become probably the most commercially successful EAP textbook in our short history (Bates and Dudley-Evans 1976). The origins of this are discussed in Bates (1978) and its structure and rationale analyzed in Swales (1985). A second important collaboration has been with Tim Johns, particularly involving their work at the University of Birmingham with subject lecturers on the co-teaching of international students in selected disciplines (e.g. Johns and Dudley-Evans 1980). A third has been with Maggie Jo St. John, eventually leading to their important and wide-ranging survey of ESP practices (Dudley-Evans and St. John 1998).

Collaborations with students, typically taking the well-known MA at Birmingham, have included an influential early paper with Andy Hopkins on discussion sections (Hopkins and Dudley-Evans 1988) and a first foray into business communications (Zak and Dudley-Evans 1986). In addition, and as a striking example of cross-disciplinary collaboration, he has worked for many years with an economist at Birmingham, Willie Henderson, on the evolution and structure of economics papers, one major result being the volume entitled *Economics and Language* (Henderson *et al.* 1993). Other collaborations have involved his co-editorship of *English for Specific Purposes* (Johns and Dudley-Evans 1993) and more recently with his colleague at the University of Birmingham's English for International Students Unit, Martin Hewings (e.g. Hewings and Dudley-Evans 1997).

In this contribution, we first explore an EAP materials collaboration between Tony and John that has not – as it were – hitherto seen the light of day. We use this as a backdrop to discuss the more recent collaborations between Chris Feak and John Swales, leading to *Academic Writing for Graduate Students-Essential Tasks and Skills* (*AWG*) in 1994 and to *English in Today's Research World – A Writing Guide* (*ETRW*) in 2000. We conclude with some lessons learnt, certainly for ourselves, and perhaps for the profession at large.

Birmingham, England, 1978–1979

In 1978, John returned from the Sudan to take up a senior lectureship at the

University of Aston in Birmingham, where he was to be in charge of the ESL section of the Modern Languages Department at this technological university. One important aspect of this work was the provision of pre-sessional and in-sessional EAP and ESP courses for the increasing numbers of international students being recruited by the various science and engineering departments. Meanwhile Tony (along with Tim Johns) had been conducting a similar program at the University of Birmingham since his return from Tabriz, Iran in 1976. John and Tony had got to know each other in Libya in the late 1960s, and had kept in touch ever since. As John owned a house in Leeds, his family remained there for a year or so while a house in Birmingham was obtained; in the meantime, John moved in with Tony. Although John and Tony have in fact published only one paper together, entitled 'Study modes and students from the Middle East' (Dudley-Evans and Swales 1980) and based on their shared experience in Libya and their different experiences in Iran and Sudan, and co-written at that time, sharing a house led to a very different type of collaboration.

As it happened, Tony was already teaching courses in Report Writing and Writing for Scientists and Engineers, and John took over a similar course from a predecessor at Aston, as well as a special course for graduate students in the Department of Physics. A pattern began to emerge whereby John and Tony would co-write (or revise) EAP materials of an evening, teach the materials at their separate institutions and then compare notes of what worked and what did less well. Among other things, John's residual and tattered file from those days contains an information-transfer task designed by John, on which is written in Tony's distinctive handwriting the cryptic comment 'muddled'! Some of these materials had their origins in *Nucleus*, such as generating change-of-state propositions from diagrams, such as this example:

steam → cooled → boiling point → condense → water
If steam is cooled to below boiling point, it condenses, changing to water.

Some others came from *Writing Scientific English* (Swales 1971), in particular the sections on linking-*as* clauses and compound nouns. However, there were some other and more interesting developments, three of which we illustrate here.

The first, which may have originated with Ian Pearson in Sudan in the mid 1970s, involved the generation of paraphrases. The rationale for this type of activity derived from the widely observed phenomenon that non-native speaker of languages, particularly for those with intermediate levels of proficiency, can often come up with one way of communicating something, but find themselves stumped when asked to find a different point of departure for what they want to say. Here is an extract from our jointly designed materials.

> E. Re-write the following sentences so that they have the same meaning as the base sentence.
> 1. This instrument can magnify up to a 1000 times.
> a. It is possible for _____
> b. It is possible to magnify _____
> c. It is possible to achieve a _____
> d. A magnification of _____

John in fact brought this type of paragraph task to Michigan, and a version of it was used in the ELI (English Language Unit) diagnostic re-assessment of incoming international students for a number of years, but it was eventually discarded because of difficulties in rapid and consistent scoring of the paraphrased propositions.

A second illustration from Tony and John's collaboration involved the 'beefing up' of their independently conceived Discussion of Results sections in their scientific writing courses. Their jointly written third unit on this topic focused on the discussion of the accuracy of the results and the explanation of any errors. Here are two extracts:

Explanation of Error
Some ways of explaining errors are given in the tables below.

This discrepancy	may be due to	incorrect calibration of the instruments.
		inaccurate measurements.
The error	can be attributed to	failure to control the variable humidity.
		the inexperience of the interviewers.
The differences between the two sets of figures	could be accounted for by	insufficient data on health standards.
		the long delay in the replication of the experiment.

Here are some test-retest results (i.e. the same test was given again and all variables were the same except those listed below). Offer *guarded* explanations of the discrepancy.

Test (85% correct answers)	Re-test (62% correct answers)
a. given on Monday morning	a. given on Friday afternoon
b.75 subjects	b. 15 subjects
c. administered by experimenter	c. administered by experimenter's secretary
d. examples gone through	d. examples not thought to be necessary

The first of these two extracts will be recognized by old hands as a substitution table, a sentence-generating machine (in this case 3x3x6 sentences) long out of favor because of its lack of contextual cueing and its inability to shape a meaningful, if subtle, relationship between linguistic form and communication function. Its very automaticity contributed to its fall from grace. That said, John recollects the excitement around the kitchen table in Tony's small terrace house in the unglamorous Selly Oak suburb as they slowly assembled their table together. These things do not come quickly and provide their own particular satisfactions when eventually no ungrammatical sentences can be produced.

The second table comes toward the end of the three-page handout. John cannot now remember how the idea of disparity between test and re-test came about, but he does remember both Tony and John trying it out in their respective classes and returning to the house broadly satisfied. And in fact both of these unpublished class exercises would cross the Atlantic and eventually morph into the Language Focus section entitled *Dealing with 'Problems'* from Unit Four of *AWG*.

By 1979, attention to the rhetorical structure of texts was beginning to emerge - and here it is worth remembering that Michael Hoey was a colleague of Tony's at that time. One text that we found and tended to use on a regular basis was entitled 'Metering Pumps', although its provenance, doubtless from some engineering textbook, is now lost. Here is the first part of the passage, with sentence numbers added, but with the diagram removed.

Metering Pumps

[1]Metering pumps are positive displacement pumps, driven by constant speed electric motors. [2]They are used where a constant rate of supply of liquid is required, irrespective of the pressure. [3]The motor, therefore, should be of such a power that it is not

appreciably retarded as the load increases. [4]The delivery is varied by an adjustment on the pump itself. [5]The metering pump is usually a plunger type pump (Fig. 5.22), incorporating one or more plungers and the delivery is varied by an adjustment of the length of the stroke. [6]In some cases, the plungers are replaced by a flexible diagram (Fig. 5.5), whose movement can be regulated.

As already intimated, we both used this passage for various purposes, but perhaps, as far as memory serves, not in exactly the same way. However, we both noted that it has an inimitable engineering style (as in the third sentence); that it is an excellent example of an expanded definition; that it serves well as a general-specific text, as can be seen from a comparison of the first four and last two sentences in the extract; and that it raises interesting questions for the students to answer about what the preceding and following texts might be about. In fact, 'Metering Pumps' at one period became a sort of joke solution to all problems – 'Well, we could always use metering pumps for that'.

The Birmingham collaboration between Tony and John in 1978–9 was one between two comparatively experienced ESP/EAP materials writers, who in the 1980s would extend their repertoires into more academic and more research-oriented roles. The serendipity of a shared house offset the fact that they were working at different institutions. Each had colleagues who would further contribute to a positive and productive materials-writing environment, such as Ray Williams at Aston and Tim Johns at Birmingham. Over that kitchen table and of an evening, we could plan next week's materials, spark and improve ideas, kill off weak or stray enthusiasms, and cobble together collages of photocopies and handwritten manuscripts to take to our secretaries for typing up. Yes, we still did that.

The University of Michigan 1992–2000

John and Tony's story as recounted above is probably close to what many ESP practitioners might envision as something of an ideal collaboration. Two like-minded friends with similar backgrounds putting their creative energies together come up with materials to be trialed in comparable but institutionally different environments. If only collaboration were always so effortless.

John and Chris have a different story to tell, one that began nearly a decade ago. It is fair to say that we did not begin as equals working from the same vantage point in our very first collaborative effort, *Academic Writing for Graduate Students*. About four years before starting this project, Chris had finished her degree program where she was fortunate to have gained experience in EAP materials development. In terms of teaching ability, she and John were quite similar. However, as a relative newcomer to the field, Chris lacked experience writing for a broader ESP/EAP audience, particularly with regard to how an instructor might transform an odd collection of handouts and ideas into a textbook to be used outside his or her immediate academic environment. And Chris certainly did not have the research and publication record that John did; moreover, John was Director of the English Language Institute and a full professor, while Chris was a lecturer on a renewable contract. Thus, although our situation was not entirely one of expert and novice, our collaboration can perhaps best be described, especially in the early days, as an instance of accidental professional mentoring.

In some ways John could very well have written *AWG* without a co-author. As we have seen, some of the roots of the book were deep, extending all the way back to his collaboration with Tony and including a collection of materials in the form of a course pack. Moreover, John had recently finished *Genre Analysis*, and had already developed teaching materials to illustrate some of the key points from this work. John's interest in having a co-author was in fact more pragmatic than altruistic. One important local factor was the existence of an arrangement, first established by Ronald Wardhaugh in the early 1970s, whereby ELI staff interested in writing textbooks could be released from certain teaching duties in exchange for a proportion of their eventual royalties. This has proved an outstanding win–win scheme, but as director John did not think he could apply it to himself – although he could to a co-author. Another factor was the amount of time he could reasonably devote to the project. A third was his admitted lack of computer savvy, especially as the University of Michigan Press had made it clear that they would eventually require a disk in *Pagemaker* format. Finally, typing in the units of *AWG* with only two fingers certainly would have delayed its publication, although as his doctoral students know, he may be a slow typist but he is quite a fast writer.

That there was any mentoring going on in the early stages of writing *AWG* was not apparent to either of us. There was no kitchen table where together we hammered out ideas, developed materials and then went our separate ways to try them out. In fact initial meetings to discuss the last week or two's work were somewhat tense for a number of reasons. We certainly did not know each other well and had no idea what we could reasonable expect from each other. At times, our short-lived project assistant found herself in the uncomfortable role of mediator, particularly in the very first meetings where we discussed issues of audience, content, and writing style. Also, it seemed very much to Chris that she was brought on board for John's project, even though it was not exactly clear what her role was; and to a great extent, Chris was not exactly sure how John, as the senior partner, viewed his own role. For the first couple of months it seemed as if we were spending a lot of time just figuring out how to work with one another, including understanding each other's strengths and weaknesses. A final difficulty is that both Chris and John are known for holding and holding on to pretty firm opinions; as Tony observed of John in *Other Floors, Other Voices,* 'I wouldn't necessarily say that you are a good listener, as you can be and usually are obstinate in argument…' (Swales 1998: 176).

Perhaps because of these tensions, *AWG* was actually written from the outside in, so to speak – the first and final units being written first, with Chris mainly responsible for units 1 and 2 and John for 7 and 8. Working from the outside-in had its advantages and disadvantages. One advantage, at least for John, was that he could take his recent work on article introductions and transform it into a coherent set of exercises and commentary. A major disadvantage, however, was that since this was Chris and John's first attempt to work together, Chris was far too deferential to John about what should be included in the final units, thinking that as the senior member he, of course, knew what he was doing. With time this deference faded, but its imprint can still be seen in unit 8, most notably in the Almosino text entitled 'High Angle-of-Attack Calculations of the Sub-Sonic Vortex Flow in Slender Bodies', which is used to demonstrate the moves in a research paper introduction. While the text is an excellent example of the move-step structure of article introductions put forth in *Genre Analysis* (and was indeed one of the main worked examples in that book), the difficulty of the content weakens its effectiveness as a model. The forthcoming revision of *AWG* will take this into account and the Almosino text will either be replaced by or supplemented with one from the field of Economic Psychology, which has proved more accessible to students in our writing classes.

On the other hand, having the more senior person take the lead on the perhaps more challenging units and the junior person focusing on the less challenging and more straightforward units was also at the same time advantageous for Chris; in effect, she was given full responsibility for part of the book project even before she herself thought she was really ready for it. Even more importantly though, this approach allowed a subtle, informal, and often indirect process of mentoring and of being further initiated into the broader arena of EAP textbook production to take place.

Not that this was an easy process. As luck would have it, we still happen to have some of the first drafts of most of the units in *AWG*. Looking back, we found there were no fewer than 14 drafts of unit 1 before we got it just about right. Getting it right for this and other units was initially largely a product of John's carefully worded comments and questions that made it clear that this was *our* project and that Chris was just as responsible for its success as John was.

> Do you think you could expand this explanation to address writing for publication? You might want to refer to our discussion in unit 8.

> This section seems too swift. Can you slow it down as you did in the previous section? Students will need time to digest this.

> Perhaps this task is given too early. It's too ambitious for the beginning of the unit. What about trying it on page 9?

> This term is clear to us, but to a broader audience?

> Some of these examples are too general given our purpose here. Try to find some others as those on page 15.

> This section needs a lead in; otherwise it seems to go against our earlier advice.

The use of *our, we,* and *us* certainly gave the impression that we were collaborating, when in fact this was John's subtle way of revealing the strategies of an old-timer and helping a newcomer understand the 'tricks of the trade' while making her feel a part of that trade.

As a result of this mentoring, the deference along with the unsupported claims, a perspective that was at times too narrow and at other times too broad, commentary and tasks that lacked depth or clear purpose, and difficulty in seeing how good research can be transformed into teaching materials gradually gave way to true collaboration. One month before the book manuscript was due at the publisher, we had one final unit to write – unit 3, eventually entitled *Problem, Process, and Solution.* Of all the units this one was clearly a collaborative effort, in which together we fleshed out ideas, decided on the types of tasks that would be most useful, and compromised on content, including certain elements that one of us liked and the other did not (for John this meant yielding to Chris on the change of state verbs discussion and for Chris agreeing to include the interview on bruised fruit). The four drafts necessary for the completion of this unit were a far cry from the 14 for unit 1.

Not long after we had finished *AWG*, John was already contemplating a sequel, since he was now teaching writing courses for senior rather than junior graduate students and had been accumulating mounds of trial materials. However, it was only when Chris began teaching at a comparable level, that the time seemed right for a second volume. In the end, it would be six years before a successor volume appeared under the title of *English in Today's Research World* (Swales and Feak 2000).

This time around, the book units were not divided as they were with *AWG*. Instead, since we had at best fragments of units in the form of either finished or 'in progress' classroom materials, we each were major contributors to each unit, with John exerting a little more influence here and Chris a little more there. Again, in contrast to *AWG*, in *ETRW* most, if not all of the tasks and commentary are the result of both of our creative energies. We still did not have a kitchen table, but the mentoring aspect of our relationship had become less central.

Task Two in the first unit on literature review writing is a good example of the kind of 'back and forth' that characterizes how much of *ETRW* was written. The checklist as a starting point for discussion was something that Chris wanted to try since an exercise of this kind can give one a sense of what the students already know (or think they know) about a sub-genre and what myths might need to be dispelled. The checklist started with 10 points and then grew to 15 or 16, a number which we both felt was too high to maintain interest and momentum. After considering the points we felt were most important, we were able to reduce the list to its final 12 – still maybe somewhat longer than what we had wanted, but adequate to cover the main points. The end-result of these discussions is illustrated below:

Task Two

Check your literature review knowledge. Make a check mark (√) next to the items that would seem to apply to your writing situation, that is, whether you are writing something for publication or preparing the literature review for your thesis or dissertation.

__ 1.   The preparation of a literature review is a three-step process: finding the relevant literature, reading, and then writing up the review.

__ 2.   Your literature review should be as long as possible to persuade your reader that you have read very widely.

__ 3.   You need to include all of the previous research that relates to your topic.

__ 4.   You can safely ignore literature that is not directly related to your topic.

__ 5.   Your literature review is important because it demonstrates that the findings, theory, or analysis that you will present are a contribution to a cumulative process.

__ 6.   Your literature review needs to explain clearly which potential areas for inclusion have not been covered in the review and why they have been omitted.

__ 7.   Your literature review should discuss problems and/or controversies within your field.

__ 8.   Your literature review should be presented in chronological order.

__ 9.   Your literature review can help you discover conceptual traditions and frameworks used to examine problems.

__ 10. Your literature review should focus on very recent publications because they are likely the most relevant.

__ 11. Your literature review should help you reveal gaps in the existing body of research.

__ 12. In your literature review you should critically evaluate each piece of work included.

Coda

The springboard for this short essay in honor of Tony Dudley-Evans was John's close collaboration with Tony more than 20 years ago. Twenty years later, that kind of collaboration seems finally to have been reached by Chris and John. Even so, while John and Tony had at that earlier time very much the same strengths and weaknesses, today Chris and John still differ in some respects. Chris has excellent computer skills, while for John a computer is really little more than a useful instrument for a bad typist; on the other hand, John does more primary research, sometimes in conjunction with doctoral students, into the discoursal and linguistic features of target academic and research genres. If our own experience is anything to go by, utilizing complementary strengths, as opposed to similar ones, requires a longer learning period. And certainly in our case a level of equality can in the long run be achieved. One small piece of evidence for this is our being able to jointly construct this very essay! Another and much more significant sign of a changed relationship is the fact that as we begin to undertake a comprehensive revision of *AWG*, it will be Chris who will take the lead and become the first author of the second edition.

Another conclusion that only occurred to us once we began to undertake this piece of writing is the remarkable durability of certain EAP materials production ideas. We have traced the origination, migration and modification of certain types of tasks designed by John and Tony over 20 years ago to their current deployment in *AWG*, and their likely retention in further modified form in the second edition. While John thinks that there are no direct traces of those old Birmingham days in *ETRW*, some of the activities, given the short history of ESP, have almost ancient timelines. The long language focus on '*this* + summary word' (p.44–9) goes back to some ideas originally developed by David Charles in Singapore in the early 1970s; indeed, the original key exemplification 'The students said they wanted more tests. This surprised the teacher' remains as the lead pair of sentences in only a lightly paraphrased version. Secondly, the idea of using a constructed collection of abstracts as a basis for writing a literature review goes back to materials developed by John for the Faculty of Architecture at the University of Khartoum in about 1976. In the hermeneutic cycle of EAP materials production, what goes around, comes around.

The final message is that successful EAP materials production is for most a hard-won achievement, but one that can be facilitated by two kinds of synergy. One is the synergy that comes from collaboration between people in one or more of the configurations that we outlined at the beginning of this chapter. The second derives from a synergy among teaching, materials writing and research that leads to a productive combination of institutional practice and knowledge of the relevant global literature. These two synergies have, we believe, had an important bearing on Tony Dudley-Evans' success as an ESP specialist, as editor, academic writer, consultant and materials writer.

References

Abbate, J. (1999) *Inventing the Internet*. Cambridge, MA: MIT.

Abbott, A. (1988) *The system of professions*. Chicago: University of Chicago Press.

Anderson, J. and Poole, M. (1994) *Thesis and assignment writing* (2nd edn). Queensland: Jacaranda Wiley.

ANSI (1979) *The American National Standard for Writing Abstracts*. ANSI publication, New York.

Applebee, A. M. and Langer, J. (1983) Instructional scaffolding: Reading and writing as natural language activities. *Language Arts*, 60, 168–75.

Aronowitz, S. (1988) *Science as power*. Minneapolis: University of Minnesota Press.

Askehave, I. and Swales, J. M. (2001) Genre identification and communicative purpose: A problem and a possible solution. *Applied Linguistics*, 22, 195–212.

Atkinson, D. (1999) *Scientific discourse in socio-historic context*. Mahwah, NJ: Lawrence Erlbaum.

Bäcklund, I. (1998) Metatext in professional writing: A contrastive study of English, German, and Swedish. *Texts in European Writing Communities 3.TeFa, 25*.

Bakhtin, M. M. (1981) *The dialogic imagination: Four essays by M. M. Bakhtin* (C. Emerson and M. Holquist Trans.) M. Holquist (ed.). Austin: University of Texas Press.

Barber, C. L. (1962) Some measurable characteristics of modern scientific prose. Reprinted in J. Swales (1985) *Episodes in ESP* (pp.1–16). Oxford: Pergamon.

Bargiela-Chiappini, F. and Nickerson, C. (eds) (1999) *Writing business: Genres, media and discourse*. London: Longman.

Barnes, B. and Shapin, S. (eds) (1979) *Natural order*. Beverly Hills: Sage.

Bartholomae, D. (1985) Inventing the university. In M. Rose (ed.), *When a writer can't write* (pp.134–65). New York: Guilford.

Bates, M. and Dudley-Evans, A. (1976) *Nucleus: General science*. London: Longman.

Bates, M. (1978) Writing *Nucleus*. In R. Mackay and A. Mountford (eds), *English for Specific Purposes* (pp.78–96). London: Longman.

Bazerman, C. (1989) *Shaping written knowledge*. Madison: University of Wisconsin Press.

Bazerman, C. (1999) *The languages of Edison's light*. Cambridge, MA: MIT.

Bazerman, C. (forthcoming) Nuclear information. *Written Communication.*

Begeman, M. L. and Conklin, J. (1988) The right tool for the job. *Byte, 13*, 255–66.

Belcher, D. (1999) Authentic interaction in a virtual classroom: Leveling the playing field in a graduate seminar. *Computers and Composition, 16*, 253–67.

Bell, A. (1991) *Language of the news media.* Oxford: Blackwell.

Benesch, S. (2001) *Critical English for academic purpose: Theory, politics, and practice.* Mahwah, NJ: Lawrence Erlbaum.

Berkenkotter, C. and Huckin, T. (1995) *Genre knowledge in disciplinary communities.* Mahwah, NJ: Lawrence Erlbaum.

Berners-Lee, T. (1999) *Weaving the Web.* New York: Harper.

Bernstein, B. (1977) *Class, codes and control: Vol. 3 Towards a Theory of Educational Transmissions.* London: Routledge & Kegan Paul.

Bhatia, V. K. (1992) Pragmatics of the use of nominals in academic and professional genres. In L. F. Bouton and Y. Kachru (eds), *Pragmatics and language learning,* Monograph Series Volume 3 (pp.217–30). University of Illinois at Urbana-Champaign, USA.

Bhatia, V. K. (1993) *Analysing genre. Language use in professional settings.* London: Longman.

Bhatia, V. K. (1994) Generic integrity in professional discourse In B.-L. Gunarsson, P. Linnell and B. Nordberg (eds), *Text and talk in professional contexts* (pp.61–76). ASLA: Skriftserie nr. 6.

Bhatia, V. K. (1995) Genre-mixing in professional communication: The case of 'private intentions' v. 'socially recognised purposes'. In P. Bruthiaux, T. Boswood and B. Bertha (eds), *Explorations in English for professional communication* (pp.1–19). Hong Kong: City University of Hong Kong.

Bhatia, V. K. (1997) Genre-mixing in academic introductions, *English for Specific Purposes, 16*, 181–96.

Bhatia, V. K. (1998) Generic conflicts in academic discourse. In F. Inmaculado, J.C. Plamer, S. Posteguillo and J.F. Coll (eds), *Genre studies in English for academic purposes* (pp.15–28). Bancaixa, Fundacio Caixa Castello.

Bhatia, V. K. (1999a) Disciplinary variation in business English. In M. Hewings and C. Nickerson (eds), *Business English: Research into practice* (pp.129–43). Harlow: Addison Wesley Longman.

Bhatia, V. K. (1999b) Integrating products, processes, purposes and participants in professional writing. In C. N. Candlin and K. Hyland (eds), *Writing: Texts, processes and practices* (pp.21–39). London: Longman.

Bhatia, V. K. (2000) Genres in conflict. In A. Trosborg (ed.), *Analysing professional genres* (pp.147–62). Amsterdam/Philadelphia: John Benjamins Publishing Company.

Bhatia, V. K. (2001) Genres in the world of reality. Paper presented at the American

Association of Applied Linguistics (AAAL) conference, 24–27 February 2001, St Louis, USA.

Bhatia, V. K. and Tay, M. (1987) *Teaching of English in meeting the needs of business and technology, Volumes 1 and 2*. Department of English Language and Literature, National University of Singapore.

Biber, D., Johansson, S., Leech, G., Conrad, S. and Finegan, E. (1999) *Longman grammar of spoken and written English*. Harlow: Longman.

Biesenbach-Lucas, S. and Weasenforth, D. (2001) E-mail and word processing in the ESL classroom: How the medium affects the message. *Language Learning & Technology, 5,* 135–65 <http://llt.msu.edu/vol5num1/weasenforth/default.html>.

Bijker, W., Hughes, T. and Pinch, T. (eds) (1987) *The social construction of technological systems*. Cambridge, MA: MIT.

Birkerts, S. (1994) *The Gutenberg elegies: The fate of reading in an electronic age*. Boston: Faber and Faber.

Bizzell, P. (1992) *Academic discourse and critical consciousness*. Pittsburgh: University of Pittsburgh Press.

Blair, D. C. and Maron, M. E. (1985) An evaluation of retrieval effectiveness for a full-text document-retrieval system. *Communications of the ACM, 28,* 289–99.

Bloch, J. (2001) Plagiarism and the ESL student: From printed to electronic texts. In D. Belcher and A. Hirvela (eds), *Linking literacies: Perspectives on L2 reading-writing connections* (pp.209–28). Ann Arbor, MI: University of Michigan Press.

Bloch, J. and Brutt-Griffler, J. (2001) Implementing CommonSpace in the ESL composition classroom. In D. Belcher and A. Hirvela (eds), *Linking literacies: Perspectives on L2 reading-writing connections* (pp.309–33). Ann Arbor, MI: University of Michigan Press.

Bloor, M. and Bloor, T. (1988) Predicting the future in modern English: A comparison of written genres. Unpublished paper presented to the inter-disciplinary conference on *Prophecy and the Nature of Prophetic Discourse*. University of Durham.

Bloor, M. and Bloor, T. (1993) How economists modify propositions. In W. Henderson, T. Dudley-Evans and R. Backhouse (eds), *Economics and language* (pp.153–72). London: Routledge.

Bloor, T. (1998) Conditional expressions: Meanings and realizations in two genres. In A. Sanchez-Macarro and R. Carter, *Linguistic choice across genres: Variation in spoken and written English* (pp.47–64). Amsterdam: John Benjamins.

Bloor, T. and Bloor, M. (1995) *The functional analysis of English. A Hallidayan approach*. London: Arnold.

Bloor, T. and Pindi, M. (1990) Schematic structure in economics forecasts. In T. Dudley-Evans and W. Henderson, *The language of economics: The analysis of economics discourse* (pp.55–66). London: Modern English Publications in Association with the British Council.

Bolter, J. D. (1991) *Writing space: The computer, hypertext, and the history of writing*. Hillsdale, NJ: Lawrence Erlbaum.

Bourdieu, P. (1984) *Distinction: A social critique of the judgement of taste*. Cambridge MA: Harvard University Press.

Bourdieu, P. (1990) *The logic of practice*. Stanford, CA: Stanford University Press.

Bowden D. (1999) *The mythology of voice*. Portsmouth, NH: Heinemann Boynton/Cook.

Bowker, G. C. and Star, S. L. (1999) *Sorting things out*. Cambridge, MA: MIT.

Braine, G. (1997) Beyond word processing: Networked computers in ESL writing classes. *Computers and Composition, 14*, 45–58.

Bramki, D. and Williams, R. (1984) Lexical familiarisation in economics text and its pedagogical implications in reading comprehension. *Reading in a Foreign Language, 2*, 169–81.

Brett, P. (1994) A genre analysis of the results section of sociology articles. *English for Specific Purposes, 13*, 47–59.

Brodkey, L. (1996) *Writing in designated areas only*. Minneapolis: University of Minnesota Press.

Brown, V. (1993) Decanonizing discources: Textual analysis and the history of economic thought. In W. Henderson, T. Dudley-Evans and R. Backhouse (eds.), *Economics and Language* (pp. 44–84). London: Routledge.

Brown, V. (1994) *Adam Smith's discourse: Canonicity, commerce and conscience*. London: Routledge.

Brown, V. (1997) 'Mere Inventions of the Imagination': A survey of recent literature on Adam Smith. *Economics and Philosophy, 13*, 281–312.

Campbell, T. D. (1971) *Adam Smith's Science of Morals*. London: Allen & Unwin.

Canagarajah, S. (1996) 'Nondiscursive' requirements in academic publishing, material resources of periphery scholars, and the politics of knowledge production. *Written Communication, 13,* 435–72.

Canagarajah, S. (1997) Safe houses in the contact zone: Coping strategies of African American students in the academy. *College Composition and Communication, 48*, 173–96.

Candlin, C. N. and Hyland, K. (eds) (1999) *Writing: Texts, processes and practices*. London: Longman.

Candlin, C. N. and Plum, G. A. (1999) Engaging with challenges of interdiscursivity in academic writing: Researchers, students and tutors. In C. N. Candlin and K. Hyland (eds), *Writing: Texts, processes and practices* (pp.193–217). London: Longman.

Carson, J.G., Chase, N., Gibson, S. and Hargrove, M. (1992) Literacy demands of the undergraduate curriculum. *Reading Research and Instruction, 31*, 25–50.

Carson, R. (1962) *Silent Spring*. Boston: Houghton Mifflin.

Casanave, C. P. (1992) Cultural diversity and socialization: A case study of a Hispanic woman in a doctoral program in sociology. In D. E. Murray (ed.), *Diversity as resource: Redefining cultural literacy* (pp.202–32). Alexandria, VA: TESOL.

Channell, J. (1990) Precise and vague expressions in writing on economics. In W. Nash (ed.), *The writing scholar: Studies in academic discourse* (pp.95–117). Newbury Park, California: Sage Publications.

Channell, J. (1994) *Vague language.* Oxford: Oxford University Press.

Chapman, M. (1994) The emergence of genres: Some findings from an examination of first-grade writing. *Written Communication, 11,* 348–80.

Cheater, A. P. (1986) *Social Anthropology: An alternative introduction.* Gweru: Mambo Press.

Cheater, A. P. (1989) *Social Anthropology: An alternative introduction* (2nd edn). London: Routledge.

Chesterman, A. (2000) A causal model for translation studies. In M. Olohan (ed.), *Intercultural faultlines. Research models in translation studies I. Textual and cognitive aspects* (pp.15–28). Manchester: St. Jerome.

Chiseri-Strater, E. (1991) *Academic literacies.* Portsmouth, NH: Boynton/Cook.

Christie, F., Gray P., Martin, J., Macken, M., Gray, B. and Rothery, J. (1990) *Exploring reports.* Sydney: Harcourt, Brace, Jovanovich.

Christie, F., Gray, P., Martin, J., Macken, M., Gray, B. and Rothery, J. (1992) *Exploring explanations.* Sydney: Harcourt, Brace, Jovanovich.

Clifford, J. (1986) Introduction: Partial truths. In J. Clifford and G. Marcus (eds), *Writing culture: The poetics and politics of ethnography* (pp.1–26). Berkley & Los Angeles: University of California Press.

Coffin, C. (1997) Constructing and giving value to the past: An investigation into secondary school history. In F. Christie and J. R. Martin (eds), *Genre and institutions: Social processes in the workplace and school* (pp.196–230). London: Pinter.

Collins COBUILD English Grammar (1990). London: Collins.

Collins, R. (1979) *The credential society.* New York: Academic Press.

Commoner, B. (1966) *Science and survival.* New York: Viking..

Connor, U. and Mauranen, A. (1999) Linguistic analysis of grant proposals: European Union research grants. *English for Specific Purposes, 18,* 47–62.

Conrad, S. and Biber, D. (2001) Adverbial marking of stance in speech and writing. In S. Hunston and G. Thompson (eds), *Evaluation in text: Authorial stance and the construction of discourse* (pp.56–73). Oxford: Oxford University Press.

Cope, B. and Kalantzis, M. (1993) *The powers of literacy.* London: Falmer Press.

Cope, B. and Kalantzis, M. (2000) *Multiliteracies: Literacy learning and the design of social futures.* London: Routledge.

Crismore, A. and Farnsworth, R. (1990) Metadiscourse in popular and professional discourse. In W. Nash (ed.), *The Writing Scholar: Studies in academic discourse* (pp.118–36). Newbury Park, California: Sage Publications.

Crismore, A., Markkanen, R. and Steffensen, M. (1993) Metadiscourse in persuasive writing: A study of texts written in American and Finnish university students. *Written Communication, 10,* 39–71.

Disadvantaged Schools Program (1988) *Teaching factual writing: A genre based approach.* Sydney: Disadvantaged Schools Program.

Dizard, W. B. (1982) *The coming information age.* New York: Longman.

Drury, H. (1997) *How to write a laboratory report.* Learning Centre, The University of Sydney.

Dudley-Evans, T. (1985) *Writing laboratory reports.* Melbourne: Nelson Wadsworth.

Dudley-Evans, A. (1987) *Genre Analysis and ESP.* ELR Journal, 1, The University of Birmingham.

Dudley-Evans, T. (1993) The debate over Milton Friedman's theoretical framework: an applied linguist's view. In W. Henderson, T. Dudley-Evans and R. Backhouse (eds), *Economics and language* (pp.132–52). London: Routledge.

Dudley-Evans, T. (1994) Genre analysis: An approach to text analysis for ESP. In M. Coulthard (ed.), *Advances in written text analysis* (pp.219–28). London: Routledge.

Dudley-Evans, T. (2001) Foreword. In S. Benesch, *Critical English for academic purposes: Theory, politics, and practice* (pp.ix–xv). Mahwah, NJ: Lawrence Erlbaum.

Dudley-Evans, T. (2002) The teaching of a problematic genre: The academic essay. In A. M. Johns (ed.), *Genre in the classroom: Multiple perspectives.* Mahwah, NJ: Lawrence Erlbaum.

Dudley-Evans, A. and Swales, J. (1980) Study modes and students from the Middle East. *ELT Documents 109,* 91–103.

Dudley-Evans, T. and St John, M. J. (1998) *Developments in English for specific purposes.* Cambridge: Cambridge University Press.

Duszak, A. (ed.) (1997) *Culture and styles of academic discourses.* Berlin: Mouton de Gruyter.

Elbow, P. (1973) *Writing without teachers.* New York: Oxford University Press.

Endres, A. M. (1991) Adam Smith's rhetoric of economics: An illustration using 'Smithian' compositional rules. *Scottish Journal of Political Economy, 38,* 76–95.

Endres, A. M. (1992) Adam Smith's treatment of historical evidence as illustrated from the theory of investment priorities. *Journal of European Economic History, 21,* 217–49.

Endres, A. M. (1995) Adam Smith's advisory style as illustrated by his trade policy prescriptions. *Journal of the History of Economic Thought, 17,* 86–105.

Even-Zohar, I. (1990) Polysystem studies. *Poetics Today, 11.*

Faigley, L. (1992) *Fragments of rationality: Postmodernity and the subject of composition.* Pittsburgh: University of Pittsburgh Press.

Faigley, L. (1997) Literacy after the revolution. *College Composition and Communication, 48,* 30–43.

Fairclough, N. (1989) *Language and power.* London: Longman.

Fairclough, N. (1992a) *Discourse and social change.* Cambridge: Polity Press.

Fairclough, N. (1992b) Discourse and text: Linguistic and intertextual analysis within discourse analysis. *Discourse and Society, 3,* 193–217.

Fairclough, N. (1993) Critical discourse analysis and the marketization of public discourse: The universities. *Discourse and Society, 4,* 133–68.

Fairclough, N. (1995) *Critical discourse analysis.* London: Longman.

Fairclough, N. and Mauranen, A. (1997) The conversationalisation of political discourse: A comparative view. In J. Blommaert and C. Bulcaen (eds), *Political Linguistics. Belgian Journal of Linguistics* 11 (pp.89–120). Antwerpen: John Benjamins.

Flower, L. and Hayes, J. (1981) Plans that guide the composing process. In C. Frederiksen and J. Dominic (eds), *Writing: The nature, development, and teaching of written communication* (pp.39–58). Hillsdale, NJ: Lawrence Erlbaum.

Fortune, R. (1989) Visual and verbal thinking: Drawing and word-processing software in writing instruction. In G. Hawisher and C. Selfe (eds), *Critical perspectives on computers and composition instruction* (pp.145–161). New York: Teachers College.

Foucault, M. (1970) *The order of things: An archaeology of the human sciences.* New York: Vintage Books.

Foucault, M. (1980) *Power/knowledge.* New York: Pantheon Books.

Francis, G. (1993) Corpus-driven grammar and its relevance to the learning of English in a cross-cultural situation. In A. Pakir (ed.), *English in education: Multicultural perspectives.* Singapore: Unipress.

Francis, G. (1994) Labelling discourse. In M. Coulthard (ed.), *Advances in written text analysis* (pp.83–101). London: Routledge.

Francis, G., Hunston, S. and Manning, E. (1996) *Collins COBUILD grammar patterns 1: Verbs.* London: HarperCollins.

Frawley, W. (1984) Prolegomenon to a theory of translation. In W. Frawley (ed.), *Translation: Literary, linguistic and philosophical perspectives* (pp.159–75). London and Toronto: Associated University Presses.

Freedman, A. (1993) Show and tell? The role of explicit teaching in the learning of new genres. *Research in the Teaching of English, 27,* 222–51.

Freedman, A., Adam, C., and Smart, G. (1994) Wearing suits to class: Simulating genres and genres as simulations. *Written Communication, 11,* 193–226.

Giddens, A. (1993) *Sociology* (2nd edn). Cambridge: Polity Press.

Gieryn, T. F. (1999) *Cultural boundaries of science: Credibility on the line.* Chicago: University of Chicago Press.

Gilbert, G. N. and Mulkay, M. (1984) *Opening Pandora's box: A sociological analysis of scientific discourse.* Cambridge: Cambridge University Press.

Gopen, G. D. and Swan, J. A. (1990) The science of scientific writing. *American Scientist, 78,* 550–58.

Graetz, N. (1985) Teaching EFL students to extract structural information from abstracts. In J. M. Ulijn and A. K. Pugh (eds), *Reading for professional purposes. Methods and materials in teaching languages* (pp.123–35). Leuven, Belgium: ACCO.

Gregory, J. and Miller, S. (1998) *Science in public.* Cambridge, MA: Perseus.

Griswold, C. L., Jr (1999) *Adam Smith and the virtues of enlightenment.* Cambridge: Cambridge University Press.

Groom, N. (2000) Attribution and averral revisited: Three perspectives on manifest intertextuality in academic writing. In P. Thompson (ed.), *Patterns and perspectives: insights into EAP writing practice.* Reading: Centre for Applied Language Studies, University of Reading.

Gumperz, J. (1982) *Discourse strategies.* Cambridge: Cambridge University Press.

Gunnarsson, B.-L. (1996) Text, discourse community and culture. A social constructive view of texts from different cultures. In T. Hickey and J. Williams (eds), *Language, education and society in a changing world* (pp.157–69). Dublin: IRAAL/Multilingual Matters.

Haas, C. (1996) *Writing technology: Studies on the materiality of literacy.* Mahwah, NJ: Lawrence Erlbaum.

Hall, M. B. (1984) *All scientists now.* Cambridge: Cambridge University Press.

Halliday, M. A. K. (1984) *An introduction to functional grammar.* London: Edward Arnold.

Halliday, M. A. K. (1994) *An introduction to functional grammar* (2nd edn). London: Edward Arnold.

Halliday, M. A. K. and Martin, J. R. (eds) (1993) *Writing science.* London: The Falmer Press.

Handa, C. (1990) Politics, ideology, and the strange, slow death of the isolated composer or why we need community in the writing classroom. In C. Handa (ed.), *Computers and community: Teaching composition in the twenty-first century* (pp.160–84). Portsmouth, NH: Heinemann Boynton/Cook.

Harklau, L., Losey, K. M. and Siegal, K. (eds) (1999) *Generation 1.5 meets college composition.* Mahwah, NJ: Lawrence Erlbaum.

Härmä, R.-L. (1994) Cultural differences in the rhetoric of American and Finnish self-help books. Involvement as a method of persuasion. Unpublished MA thesis, University of Joensuu, Savonlinna School of Translation Studies, Finland.

Hartley, J., Sydes, M. and Blurton, A. (1996) Obtaining information accurately and quickly: Are structured abstracts more efficient? *Journal of Information Science, 22,* 349–56.

Harrison, J. R. (1995) Imagination and aesthetics in Adam Smith's epistemology and moral philosophy. *Contributions to Political Economy, 14,* 91–112.

Harwood, J. (1995) Are there national styles in scientific thought? Genetics in Germany, 1900–1933. In P. Weingart (ed.), *Grenz berschreitungen in Wissenshaft* (pp.31–53). Baden-Baden: Nomos Verlagsgesellschaft.

Hawisher, G. E., and Sullivan, P. (1998) Women on the networks: Searching for e-spaces of their own. In S. Jarratt and L. Worsham (eds), *Feminism and composition studies: In other words* (pp.172–97). New York: Modern Language Association of America.

Heilbron, J. (1979) *Electricity in the 17th and 18th centuries: A study of early modern physics.* Berkeley: University of California Press.

Heim, M. (1987) *Electric language: A philosophical study of word processing.* New Haven, CT: Yale University Press.

Henderson, W., Dudley-Evans, A. and Backhouse, R. (eds) (1993) *Economics and Language.* London: Routledge.

Henderson, W. and Hewings, A. (1986) Entering the hypothetical world: 'assume', 'suppose', 'consider' and 'take' as signals in economics text. Unpublished paper, University of Birmingham.

Henderson, W. and Hewings, A. (1987) Economics terminology: The problem of vocabulary. *Economics, 24,* 123–7.

Henderson, W. and Hewings, A. (1990) A language of model building? In T. Dudley-Evans and W. Henderson (eds), *The language of economics: The analysis of economics discourse. ELT Documents 134* (pp.43–54). London: Modern English Publications/The British Council.

Herrington, A. and Curtis, M. (2000) *Persons in process.* Urbana, IL: National Council of Teachers of English.

Hewings, A. (1999) Disciplinary engagement in undergraduate writing: An investigation of clause-initial elements in geography essays. Unpublished PhD thesis, University of Birmingham.

Hewings, M. (1999) The academy meets the real world: Response to audience in academic business writing. In M. Hewings and C. Nickerson (eds), *Business English: Research into practice* (pp.144–56). English Language Teaching Review. Harlow: Addison Wesley Longman.

Hewings, M. and Dudley-Evans, A. (1997) *Course design and evaluation in ESP.* Hemel Hempstead: Prentice Hall Macmillan.

Hewings, M. and Hewings, A. (in press) 'It is interesting to note...': a comparative study of anticipatory 'it' in student and published writing. *English for Specific Purposes.*

Hinds, J. (1987) Reader versus writer responsibility: A new typology. In U. Connor and R. Kaplan (eds), *Writing across languages: Analysis of L2 text* (pp.141–52). Reading, MA: Addison-Wesley.

Holmes, R. (1997) Genre analysis and the social sciences: an investigation of the structure of research article discussion sections in three disciplines. *English for Specific Purposes, 16,* 321–37.

Holton, G. J. (1986) *The advancement of science, and its burdens.* New York: Cambridge University Press.

Hopkins, A. and Dudley-Evans, T. (1988) A genre-based investigation of the discussion sections in articles and dissertations. *English for Specific Purposes, 7*, 113–21.

Houghton, D. (1996) The importance of tenses and time perspective in learning through case study: Designing a course. In M. Hewings and T. Dudley-Evans (eds), *Evaluation and course design in EAP* (pp.142–50). London: Prentice Hall Macmillan in Association with the British Council.

Houtkoop-Steenstra, H. (2000) *Interaction and the standard survey interview*. Cambridge: Cambridge University Press.

Howard, M. C. (1989) *Contemporary cultural anthropology* (3rd edn). New York: HarperCollins.

Howard, R. M. (1999) *Standing in the shadow of giants: Plagiarists, authors, collaborators*. Stamford, CT: Ablex.

Huckin, T. (1997) Cultural aspects of genre knowledge. In A. Mauranen and K. Sajavaara (eds), *AILA Review 13* (pp.68–78).

Huddleston, R. (1971) *The sentence in written English*. Cambridge: Cambridge University Press.

Hurford, J. R. (1994) *Grammar: A student's guide*. Cambridge: Cambridge University Press.

Hutchby, I. (1996) *Confrontation talk*. Hillsdale, NJ: Lawrence Erlbaum.

Hyland, K. (1994) Hedging in academic writing and EAP textbooks. *English for Specific Purposes, 13*, 239–454.

Hyland, K. (1996) Writing without conviction? Hedging in science research articles. *Applied Linguistics, 17*, 433–54.

Hyland, K. (1997) Scientific claims and community values: Articulating an academic culture. *Language and Communication, 16*, 19–32.

Hyland, K. (1998a) *Hedging in scientific research articles*. Amsterdam: John Benjamins.

Hyland, K. (1998b) Persuasion and context: The pragmatics of academic metadiscourse. *Journal of Pragmatics, 30*, 437–55.

Hyland, K. (1999a) Talking to students: Metadiscourse in introductory coursebooks. *English for Specific Purposes, 18,* 3–26.

Hyland, K. (1999b) Disciplinary discourses: Writer stance in research articles. In C. Candlin and K. Hyland (eds), *Writing: Texts, processes and practices* (pp.99–121). Harlow: Addison Wesley Longman.

Hyland, K. (2000) *Disciplinary discourses: Social interactions in academic writing*. Harlow: Longman.

Ingberg, M. (1987) Argumentative style in Finland-Swedish student compositions. Paper presented at the 10th Scandinavian Conference of Linguistics, Bergen, Norway, 11–13 June 1987.

Isaksson-Wikberg, M. (1999) *Negotiated and committed argumentation. A cross-cultural study of American and Finland-Swedish student writing*. Åbo Akademi University Press.

Ivanic, R., Clark, R. and Rimmershaw, R. (2000) What am I supposed to make of this?

The messages conveyed to students by tutors' written comments. In M. R. Lea and B. Stierer (ed.), *Student writing in higher education: New contexts* (pp.47–65). Buckingham: Open University Press.

Jacob, M. C. (1988) *The cultural meaning of the scientific revolution.* Philadelphia: Temple University Press.

Johns, A. M. (1997) *Text, role, and context: Developing academic literacies.* New York: Cambridge University Press.

Johns, A. M. (2000) An interdisciplinary, interinstitutional learning communities program: student involvement and student success. In I. Leki (ed.), *Academic writing programs* (Case studies in TESOL practice series) (pp.61–72). Alexandria, VA: TESOL.

Johns, A. M. (2002) Destabilizing novice students' genre theories. In A. M. Johns (ed.), *Genre and pedagogy: Multiple perspectives* (pp.237–48). Mahwah, NJ: Lawrence Erlbaum.

Johns, A. M. and Dudley-Evans, A. (1993) English for specific purposes: International in scope, specific in purpose. *TESOL Quarterly, 25,* 297–314.

Johns, T. F. and Dudley-Evans, A. (1980/1988) An experiment in the team-teaching of overseas postgraduate students in transportation and plant biology. *Team teaching in ESP. ELT Documents 106* (pp.6–23). London: The British Council. (Reprinted in J. Swales (ed.) (1988) *Episodes in ESP* (pp.140–53). London: Prentice Hall.)

Johnson-Eilola, J. (1997) *Nostalgic angels: Rearticulating hypertext writing.* Norwood, NJ: Ablex.

Jonassen, D. H. (1991) Designing hypertext for learning. In E. Scanlon and T. O'Shea (eds), *New directions in educational technology* (pp.123–30). Berlin: Springer-Verlag.

Jordan, R. R. (1980) *Academic writing course.* London and Glasgow: Collins.

Kantor, R., Anderson, T. and Armbruster, B. (1983) How inconsiderate are children's textbooks? *Journal of Curriculum Studies, 15,* 61–72.

Kaplan, R. B. (1966) Cultural thought patterns in intercultural education. *Language Learning 16,* 1–20. (Reprinted in Croft, K. (ed.) (1972) *Readings on English as a second language for teachers and teacher trainees.* Cambridge, MA: Winthrop.)

Kintsch, W. and Van Dijk, T. A. (1978) Toward a model of text comprehension and production. *Psychological Review, 85,* 363–94.

Kojima, S. and Kojima, K. (1978) S (inanimate subject) + V + O: A syntactical problem in EST writing for Japanese. In L. Trimble, M. Trimble and K. Drobnic (eds), *English for specific purposes: Science and technology* (pp.198–226). Oregon: Oregon State University.

Kramsch, C., A'Ness, F. and Lam, W. S. E. (2000) Authenticity and authorship in the computer-mediated acquisition of L2 literacy. *Language Learning & Technology, 4,* 78–104 <http://llt.msu.edu/vol4num2/kramsch/default.html>.

Kress, G. (1995) *Writing the future: English and the making of a culture of innovation.* Urbana, IL: National Council of Teachers of English (NCTE).

Kuhn, T. S. (1962) *The structure of scientific revolutions.* Chicago and London: University of Chicago Press.

Lakoff, G. (1972) Hedges: A study in meaning criteria and the logic of fuzzy concepts. *Chicago Linguistic Society Paper, 8,* 183-228.

Landow, G. P. (1997) *Hypertext 2.0.* Baltimore, MD: Johns Hopkins University Press.

Lanham, R. (1993) *The electronic word: Democracy, technology, and the arts.* Chicago, IL: University of Chicago Press.

Larsen, R. L. (1982) The 'research paper' in the writing course: A non-form of writing. *College English, 44,* 811–16.

Latour, B. (1987) *Science in action.* Cambridge, MA: Harvard University Press.

Latour, B. and Woolgar, S. (1979*) Laboratory life.* Beverly Hills: Sage.

Lave, J. and Wenger, E. (1991) *Situated learning: Legitimate peripheral participation.* Cambridge: Cambridge University Press.

Layton, E. T. (1986) *The revolt of the engineers: Social responsibility and the American engineering.* Baltimore, MD: Johns Hopkins University Press.

Leech, G. and Svartvik, J. (1994) *A communicative grammar of English* (2nd edn). London: Longman.

Lemke, J. (1987) The topology of genre: Text structures and text types. Unpublished manuscript, Brooklyn College School of Education, City University of New York.

Lindeberg, A-C. (1988). Coherence, cohesion and coherence patterns in expository and argumentative student essays in EFL: An exploratory study. Mimeo. Åbo Akademi.

Lodge. D. (1988) *Nice Work*, London: Secker and Warburg.

Love, A. (1991) Process and product in geology: An investigation of some discourse features of two introductory textbooks. *English for Specific Purposes, 10,* 89–109.

Love, A. (1993) Lexico-grammatical features of geology textbooks: Process and product revisited. *English for Specific Purposes, 12,* 197–218.

Love, A. (1999) Coming to terms with diversity. In *Proceedings of the 1st International Conference on Knowledge and Discourse,* Hong Kong, 17–21 June 1996.

Lyotard, J. (1979) *The postmodern condition: A report on knowledge.* Minneapolis, MN: University of Minnesota Press.

Maeda, T. (1981) An approach toward functional text structure analysis of scientific and technical documents. *Information Processing and Management, 17,* 329–39.

MacDonald, S. P. (1994) *Professional academic writing in the humanities and social sciences.* Carbondale: Southern Illinois University Press.

Martin, J. R. (1985) *Factual writing: Exploring and challenging the experiential world.* Geelong, Victoria: Deakin University Press.

Martin, J. R. (1992) *English text: System and structure.* Amsterdam: Benjamins.

Martin, J. R. (1993a) Literacy in science: Learning to handle text as technology. In M.

A. K. Halliday and J. R. Martin (eds), *Writing science* (pp.166–202). London: The Falmer Press.

Martin, J. R. (1993) Technicality and abstraction: language for the creation of specialized texts. In M. A. K. Halliday and J. R. Martin (eds), *Writing science* (pp.203–20). London: The Falmer Press.

Martin, J. R. (1994) Mentoring somogenesis: Genre-based literacy pedogogy. In F. Christie (ed.), *Pedagogy and the shaping of consiousness* (pp, 123–55), London: Casssell.

Martin, J. R. (1994) Macro-genres: The ecology of the page. *Network 21*, 29–52.

Martin, J. R. and Matthiessen, C. M. (1991) Systemic typology and topology. In F. Christie (ed.), *Literacy in social processes* (pp.345–83). Papers from the Inaugural Australian Systemics Linguistics Conference, Darwin. Centre for Studies in Language in Education, Northern Territory University.

Martin, J. R., Matthiessen, C. M. and Painter, C. (1997) *Working with functional grammar*. London: Arnold.

Martin, J. R. and Peters P. (1985) On the analysis of exposition. In R. Hasan (ed.), *Discourse on discourse* (pp.61–92). Applied Linguistics Association of Australia, Occasional Papers 7.

Martin, J. R. and Veel, R. (eds) (1998) *Reading science. Critical and functional perspectives on discourses of science*. London: Routledge.

Martineau, H. (1832) *Life in the wilds: A tale*. London: Charles Fox.

Master, P. (1991) Active verbs with inanimate subjects in scientific prose. *English for Specific Purposes, 10*, 15–33.

Master, P. (in press) *English grammar and technical writing*. Washington, DC: US State Department.

Mauranen, A. (1993) *Cultural differences in academic rhetoric. A textlinguistic study*. Frankfurt: Peter Lang.

Mauranen, A. (1994) Two discourse worlds: Study genres in Britain and Finland. In A. Mauranen and R. Markkanen (eds), *Students abroad. Aspects of exchange students' language*. Finlance Vol XIII 1994, 1–40.

McCabe, A. M. (1999) Theme and thematic patterns in Spanish and English History texts. Unpublished PhD thesis, University of Aston, Birmingham.

McCloskey, D. (1994) How to do a rhetorical analysis and why. In R. Backhouse (ed.), *New directions in economic methodology* (pp.319–42). London: Routledge.

Mead, R. and Henderson, W. (1983) Conditional form and meaning in economics text. *ESP Journal, 2*, 139–60.

Melander, B. (1996) Culture or genre? Issues in the interpretation of cross-cultural differences. Paper presented at the AILA 96 Congress, Jyväskylä, Finland, 4–9 August 1996.

Merton, R. K. (1973) *The sociology of science*. Chicago: University of Chicago Press.

Miller, C. R. (1984) Genre as social action. *Quarterly Journal of Speech, 70*, 157–78.

Morrell, J. and Thackray, A. (1981) *Gentlemen of science.* Oxford: Clarendon Press.

Myers, G. (1989) The pragmatics of politeness in scientific articles. *Applied Linguistics,* *10,* 1–35.

Myers, G. (1990) *Writing biology: Texts in the social construction of scientific knowledge.* Madison: University of Wisconsin Press.

Myers, G. (1991) 'In this paper we report...'. Speech acts and scientific facts. *Journal of Pragmatics, 17,* 295–313.

Myers, G. (1992) Textbooks and the sociology of scientific knowledge. *English for Specific Purposes, 11,* 3–18.

Myers, G. (1998) Displaying opinions: Topics and disagreement in focus groups. *Language in Society, 27,* 85–111.

Nash, W. (1990) Introduction: The stuff these people write. In W. Nash (ed.), *The writing scholar: Studies in academic discourse* (pp.8–30). Newbury Park, California: Sage.

Nelkin, D. (ed.) (1979) *Controversy: Politics of technical decisions.* Beverly Hills, CA: Sage.

Nelkin, D. (1987) *Selling science: How the press covers science and technology.* New York: W. H. Freeman.

Paasikivi, M.-L. (1995) On the communicative effectiveness of cosmetics sales promotion texts. Unpublished MA thesis, University of Tampere, Finland, Department of Translation Studies.

Pagnucci, G. S. and Mauriello, N. (1999) The masquerade: Gender, identity, and writing for the Web. *Computers and Composition, 16,* 141–51.

Palmer, F. R. (1974) *The English verb* (2nd edn). London: Longman.

Palmer, F. R. (1979) *Modality and the English modals.* London: Longman.

Panferov, S. (2000, March) Email peer reviews: Are they helpful? Paper presented at the 34th Annual TESOL Convention, Vancouver, BC, Canada.

Paulson, W. (1988) *The noise of culture: Literary texts in a world of information.* Ithaca, NY: Cornell University Press.

Peng, J. (1987) Organisational features in chemical engineering research articles. In T. Dudley-Evans (ed.), *Genre analysis and ESP* (pp.79–116). ELR Journal, 1. The University of Birmingham.

Pennycook, A. (1996) Borrowing others' words: Text, ownership, memory and plagiarism. *TESOL Quarterly, 30,* 201–30.

Pindi, M. (1988) *Schematic structure and the modulation of propositions in economic forecasting text.* Unpublished PhD thesis, University of Aston, Birmingham.

Pindi, M. and Bloor, T. (1987) Playing safe with predictions: Hedging, attribution and conditions in economics forecasting. In T. Bloor and J. Norrish (eds), *Written language* (pp.55–69). British Studies in Applied Linguistics 2. London: CILT.

Porter, T. (1995) *Trust in numbers.* Princeton, NJ: Princeton University Press.

Prior, P. (1998) *Writing/disciplinarity: A sociohistoric account of literate activity in the academy.* Mahwah, NJ: Lawrence Erlbaum.

Purves, A. C. (ed.) (1988) *Writing across languages and cultures. Issues in contrastive rhetoric.* Newbury Park: Sage.

Quirk, R., Greenbaum, S., Leech, G. and Svartvik, J. (1985) *A comprehensive grammar of the English language.* London: Longman.

Rawlins, J. (1980) What's so wrong with 'In my opinion'? *College Composition and Communication, 41,* 670–74.

Rea, A. and White, D. (1999) The changing nature of writing: Prose or code in the classroom. *Computers and Composition, 16,* 421–36.

Richards, C. (2000) Hypermedia, Internet communication, and the challenge of redefining literacy in the electronic age. *Language Learning and Technology, 4,* 59–77 <http://llt.msu.edu/vol4num2/richards/default.html>.

Robbins, L. (1981) Economics and political economy. *American Economic Review, Papers and Proceedings, 71,* 1–10.

Roberts, D. (1997) *The student's guide to writing essays.* London: Kogan Page.

Robertson, R. (1995) Glocalization: time-space and homogeneity-heterogeneity. In M. Featherstone, S. Lash and R. Robertson (eds), *Global modernities* (pp.25–44). London: Sage.

Rodrigues, D. and Tuman, M. (1996) *Writing essentials.* New York: Norton.

Rodriguez, R. (1981) *Hunger of memory.* Boston, MA: D. R. Godine.

Rose, D. (1997) Science, technology and technical literacies. In F. Christie and J. R. Martin (eds), *Genre and institutions: Social processes in the workplace and school* (pp.40–72). London: Pinter.

Ross, I. S. (1995) *The life of Adam Smith.* Oxford: Clarendon Press.

Rudwick, M. J. S. (1985) *The great Devonian controversy: The shaping of scientific knowledge among gentlemanly specialists.* Chicago: University of Chicago Press.

Sacks, H. (1992) *Lectures on conversation.* Oxford: Blackwell.

Salager-Meyer, F. (1994) Hedges and textual communicative function in medical English written discourse. *English for Specific Purposes, 13,* 149–70.

Sarangi, S. and Candlin, C. N. (2001) 'Motivational relevancies': Some methodological reflections on social theoretical and sociolinguistic practice. In N. Coupland, S. Sarangi and C. N. Candlin (eds), *Sociolinguistics and social theory* (pp.350–88). Harlow: Pearson.

Schwegler, R. and Shamoon, L. (1991) Meaning attribution in ambiguous texts. In C. Bazerman and J. Paradis (eds), *Textual dynamics of the professions* (pp.216–34). Madison: University of Wisconsin Press.

Sclove, R. (1995) *Democracy and technology.* New York: Guilford Press.

Scollon, R. (1997) Contrastive rhetoric, contrastive poetics, or perhaps something else? *TESOL Quarterly, 31,* 352–8.

Scollon, R. (1998) *Mediated discourse as social interaction: A study of news discourse.* London: Longman.

Shapin, S. (1982) History of science and its sociological reconstructions. *History of Science, 20*, 157–211.

Shapin, S. (1994) *A social history of truth: Civility and science in seventeenth-century England.* Chicago: University of Chicago Press.

Shapin, S. and Schaffer, S. (1985) *Leviathan and the air-pump.* Princeton: Princeton University Press.

Skelton, J. (1988) Comments in academic articles. In P. Grunwell (ed.), *Applied Linguistics in Society* (pp.98–108). London: CILT/BAAL.

Skelton, J. (1989) The care and maintenance of hedges. *English Language Teaching Journal, 42*, 37–44.

Skinner, A. S. (1972) Adam Smith: Philosophy and science. *Scottish Journal of Political Economy, 19*, 307–19.

Skinner, A. S. (1983) Adam Smith, rhetoric and the communication of ideas. In A.W. Coats (ed.), *Methodological controversy in economics: Essays in honour of T.W. Hutchison* (pp.71–88). London: JAI.

Smith, A. [1759] (1976) *Adam Smith: The Theory of Moral Sentiments.* D. D. Raphael and A. L. Macfie (eds). Oxford: Clarendon Press.

Smith, A. [1776] (1952) *An inquiry into the nature and causes of the wealth of nations.* Chicago: Encyclopaedia Britannica.

Still, J. (1997) *Feminine economics: Thinking against the market in the Enlightenment and the late twentieth century.* Manchester: Manchester University Press.

Suchman, L. and Jordan, B. (1990) Interactional troubles in face-to-face survey interviews. *Journal of the American Statistical Association, 85*, 232–41.

Swales, J. (1971) *Writing scientific English.* London: Thomas Nelson.

Swales, J. (1981) *Aspects of article introductions.* Aston ESP Research Report No. 1, Language Studies Unit, University of Aston, Birmingham, UK.

Swales, J. (1985) *Episodes in English for specific purposes.* Oxford: Pergamon.

Swales, J. (1990) *Genre analysis.* Cambridge: Cambridge University Press.

Swales, J. (1996) Toward a textography of an academic site. Paper presented at the AILA 96 Congress, Jyväskylä, Finland, 4–9August 1996.

Swales, J. (1998) *Other floors, other voices. A textography of a small university building.* Mahwah, N.J: Lawrence Erlbaum.

Swales, J. M. and Feak, C. B. (1994) *Academic writing for graduate students.* Ann Arbor: The University of Michigan Press.

Swales, J. M. and Feak, C. B. (2000) *English in today's research world: A writing guide.* Ann Arbor: The University of Michigan Press.

Taddio, A., Pain, T., Fasoss, F. F. *et al.* (1994) Quality of nonstructured and structured abstracts of original research articles in the *British Medical Journal,* the *Canadian Medical Association Journal* and the *Journal of the American Medical Association. Canadian Medical Association Journal, 150*, 1611–15.

Tadros, A. (1985) *Prediction in text*. Discourse Analysis Monograph 10. University of Birmingham: English Language Research.

Tannen, D. (1998) *The argument culture: Moving from debate to dialogue*. New York: Random House.

Tarone, E., Dwyer, S., Gillette, S. and Icke, V. (1981) On the use of the passive in two astrophysics journal papers. *The ESP Journal, 1*, 123–40.

Tarone, E., Dwyer, S., Gillette, S. and Icke, V. (1998) On the use of the passive and active voice in astrophysics journal papers: With extensions to other languages and other fields. *English for Specific Purposes, 17*, 113–32.

Thomas, J. (1983) Cross-cultural pragmatic failure. *Applied Linguistics, 4*, 91–112.

Thompson, G. (1994) *Collins COBUILD English Guides 5: Reporting*. London: HarperCollins.

Thoreau, H. D. (1980) *The natural history essays*. Salt Lake City: Peregrine Smith.

Tirkkonen-Condit, S. (1996) Explicitness vs. implicitness of argumentation: An intercultural comparison. *Multilingua, 15*, 253–73.

Toury, G. (1995) *Descriptive translation studies and beyond*. Amsterdam: John Benjamins.

Trosborg, A. (1996) Analysing hybrid political texts. Paper presented at the AILA 96 Congress, Jyväskylä, Finland, 4–9 August 1996.

Tuman, M. (1992) *Word perfect: Literacy in the computer age*. Pittsburgh, PA: University of Pittsburgh Press.

Unsworth, L. (1996) Explanation genres in school science books: Issues of typology, topology and delicacy in descriptions of schematic structure. Paper presented to the ISFC23 International Functional Linguistics Congress, University of Technology, Sydney.

Van Nostrand, A. D. (1997) *Fundable knowledge*. Mahwah, NJ: Lawrence Erlbaum.

Vande Kopple, W. J. (1985) Some exploratory discourse on metadiscourse. *College Composition and Communication, 36*, 82–93.

Veel, R. (1997) Learning how to mean scientifically speaking: Apprenticeship into scientific discourse in secondary school. In F. Christie and J.R. Martin (eds), *Genre and institutions: Social processes in the workplace and school* (pp.161–95). London: Pinter.

Veel, R. (1998) The greening of school science: Ecogenesis in secondary classrooms. In J. R. Martin and R. Veel (eds.), *Reading science: Critical and functional perspectives on discourses of science* (pp.114–51). London: Routledge.

Ventola, E. and Mauranen, A. (eds) (1996) *Academic writing. Intercultural and textual issues*. Amsterdam: John Benjamins.

Vygotsky, L. (1991) The genesis of higher mental functions. In P. Light, S. Sheldon and B. Woodhead (eds), *Learning to think* (pp.32–41). London: Routledge. (Originally published in Leontyev, A., Luria, A. and Smirnoff, A. (eds) (1966) *Psychological Research in the USSR, Vol. 1*. Moscow: Progress Publishers.)

Walvoord, B. E. (1997) *In the long run*. Urbana, IL: National Council of Teachers of English.

Walvoord, B. E. and McCarthy, L. (1990) *Thinking and writing in college*. Urbana, IL: National Council of Teachers of English.

Warschauer, M. (1999) *Electronic literacies: Language, culture, and power in online education*. Mahwah, NJ: Lawrence Erlbaum.

Weissburg, R. and Buker, S. (1990) *Writing up research*. New Jersey: Prentice-Hall.

Wingard, P. (1981) Some verb forms and functions in six medical texts. In L. Selinker, E. Tarone and V. Hanzeli (eds), *English for academic and technical purposes: Studies in honour of Louis Trimble* (pp.53–64). Rowley, Mass: Newbury House.

Winner, L. (1977) *Autonomous technology: Technics-out-of-control as a theme in political thought*. Cambridge MA: MIT.

Winsor, D. A. (1996) *Writing like an engineer*. Mahwah, NJ: Lawrence Erlbaum.

Yates, J. and Van Maanen, J. (eds) (2001) *IT and organizational transformation*. Thousand Oaks CA: Sage.

Young, D. J. (1980) *The structure of English clauses*. London: Hutchinson.

Zak, H. and Dudley-Evans, T. (1986) Features of word omission and abbreviation in telexes. *English for Specific Purposes, 5*, 59–70.

Zamel, V. and Spack, J. (eds) (1998) *Negotiating academic literacies: Teaching and learning across languages and cultures*. Mahwah, NJ: Lawrence Erlbaum.

Zuck, J. G. and Zuck, L. V. (1984) Scripts: An example from newspaper texts. *Reading in a Foreign Language, 2*, 1–6.

Index